Foss   Iowa

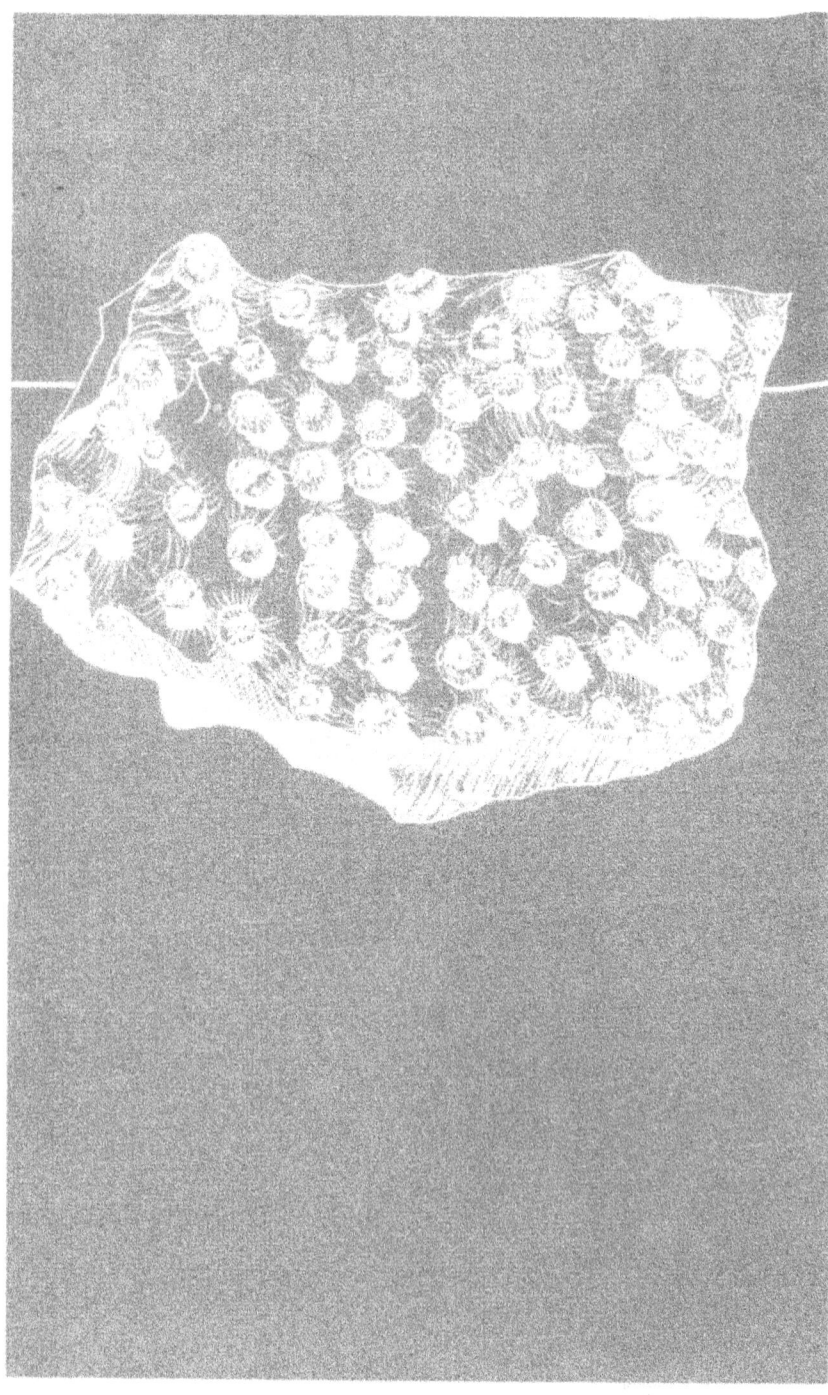

Fossils of Iowa
FIELD GUIDE TO PALEOZOIC DEPOSITS

Robert Charles Wolf

ILLUSTRATED BY Carol Ann Ratcliff

All rights reserved, including without limitation the right to reproduce this book or any portion thereof in any form or by any means, whether electronic or mechanical, now known or hereinafter invented, without the express written permission of the publisher.

Originally published by Iowa State University Press.

Copyright © 1983, 2006 by Robert Charles Wolf

ISBN: 978-1-5040-3291-9

Distributed in 2016 by Open Road Distribution
180 Maiden Lane
New York, NY 10038
www.openroadmedia.com

CONTENTS

List of Plates vii

Preface ix

1 Introduction 3

2 Precambrian and Cambrian Periods 9

3 Ordovician Period 13

4 Silurian Period 29

5 Devonian Period 37

6 Mississippian Period 54

7 Pennsylvanian Period: Desmoinesian and Morrowan Series 72

8 Pennsylvanian Period: Missourian Series 83

9 Pennsylvanian Period: Virgilian Series 106

10 Permian Period 119

Plates	125
Glossary	187
References	189
Index	195
About the Author	197

PLATES

1	Orthid brachiopods	126
2	Orthid and strophomenid brachiopods	128
3	Strophomenid brachiopods	130
4	Strophomenid and terebratulid brachiopods	132
5	Pentamerid and spiriferid brachiopods	134
6	Spiriferid brachiopods	136
7	Spiriferid brachiopods	138
8	Spiriferid brachiopods	140
9	Spiriferid brachiopods	142
10	Rhynchonellid brachiopods	144
11	Chonetid and productid brachiopods	146
12	Productid brachiopods	148
13	Productid brachiopods	150
14	Solitary corals	152
15	Trilobites	154
16	Stromatoporoid	156
17	Colonial corals and stromatoporoids	158
18	Miscellaneous fossils and bryozoans	160

		PLATES
19	Miscellaneous fossils	162
20	Gastropods	164
21	Gastropods and nautiloids	166
22	Nautiloid	168
23	Echinoderms	170
24	Echinoderms	172
25	Pelecypods	174
26	Pelecypods	176
27	Plant fossils	178
28	Plant fossils	180
29	Plant fossils	182
30	Plant fossils	184

PREFACE

THIS BOOK is a geological field guide written primarily for amateurs and students involved with paleontology. One hundred and fifty-eight sites are described throughout Iowa and adjacent parts of Nebraska and Minnesota, one hundred and fifty of which were examined in person. Two hundred geological deposits are included, to this collector's knowledge offering the most complete single coverage of Paleozoic deposits in the state.

This book incorporates several field guides published by three state geological surveys as well as other publications. In addition it shares firsthand knowledge gathered through six years of intense field work and ten additional years of amateur collecting. Most of the common and some of the rarer fossils available in the state are shown in two hundred and thirty illustrations. For the convenience of the reader, a glossary of terms used is given in the back of the book.

Those who wish to view the results of the author's collecting should visit the Sanford Museum and Planetarium in Cherokee, to which four hundred different fossil species, both fauna and flora, have been donated.

Many people do not know how much they have helped with this book. Geologists at the three state universities of Iowa, the University of Nebraska, the Minnesota Geological Survey, and the Iowa Geological Survey provided essential information and help. The Minnesota Geological Survey permitted the following illustrations to be sketched from the *Guide to Fossil Collecting in Minnesota* by Hogberg, Sloan, and Tufford (1967): Plate 2-7B, Plate 14-1, Plate 15-1, Plate 20-5, Plate 25-1. The Conservation and Survey Division of the University of Nebraska permitted the following illustrations to be sketched from *Record in Rock* by Pabian (1970): Plate 10-8; Plate 26-1, 2, 3, 4, 5, 6, 7; and from *Brachiopoda of the Pennsylvanian System in Nebraska* by Dunbar and Condra (1932): Plate 9-8B. The Iowa Geological Survey permitted the following illustrations to be sketched from *Fossils and Rocks of Eastern Iowa* by Rose (1967): Plate I-4, 5, 6B; Plate 2-7A, 8; Plate 5-4; Plate 8-5; Plate 9-3, 4; Plate 14-8; Plate 17-1A, 1B, 3, 4, 6, 10; Plate 18-4, 6A; Plate 20-9; Plate 23-1, 3, 4, 5, 6, 7; and Plate 24-1.

Thanks are owed to the following geologists, who aided me in gathering valuable field information: Phillip Heckel (University of Iowa) led a field trip to Pennsylvanian cyclothems in Madison County; Brian Witzke

(Iowa Geological Survey) led a field trip to Silurian deposits in Linn and Jones counties; and Daniel Burggraf, Howard White, Robert Palmquist, and John Lemish (all of Iowa State University) led a field trip to Cherokee sandstones in Webster County.

Various civic officials, earth science teachers, fellow amateurs, and others were helpful in locating owners of several sites. Farmers and quarry owners deserve thanks for allowing collecting on private property.

The author is also grateful to those who offered moral support: friends, family members, and especially Gilbert Copper and Barbara Hartsock. People who offered help in the form of criticism or skepticism were also essential. Special thanks go to my two "coauthors": Linda Dornath for the excellent typing and Carol Ratcliff for the excellent illustrations. Finally, the author thanks the Iowa State University Press for help, understanding, and perseverance.

Fossils of Iowa

FIELD GUIDE TO
PALEOZOIC DEPOSITS

1

Introduction

FOR OVER 3 billion years life has inhabited the earth, but it was very primitive for most of this history. Dramatically, during the Cambrian Period, which began about 600 million years ago, more advanced life forms began to flourish. Three hundred million years later, thick forests and swamps covered parts of the continents, reptiles and amphibians roamed the forests, and insects filled the air. The Cambrian Period marked the beginning of the Paleozoic Era, which includes the Ordovician, Silurian, Devonian, Mississippian, and Pennsylvanian periods. The Paleozoic ended with the close of the Permian Period around 225 million years ago (a span of 375 million years).

Cambrian fossils from Iowa include burrows, trilobite fragments, and brachiopods. Burrows are very common and occur in several formations. Trilobite fragments are not very abundant and are usually only small pieces. Most of the brachiopods are inarticulates, but early orthids have been found. Cambrian fossils are more common in Minnesota and Wisconsin.

Fossils from the Ordovician Period in Iowa include a wide variety of marine organisms. Most orders of brachiopods can be found, but orthids and strophomenids are the most common. Other common fossils include echinoderm debris, nautiloids, gastropods, trilobites, corals, graptolites, pelecypods, and several others.

Iowa Silurian fossils include several types of brachiopods, the most conspicuous being the pentamerids. Stromatoporoids, a wide variety of corals, nautiloids, echinoderm debris, and other fossils can also be found.

The Devonian fossils from Iowa include many types of marine organisms. Spiriferid brachiopods, corals, echinoderms, stromatoporoids, and other fossils, including fish teeth, can be found. Some collecting sites exposing Devonian formations are quite famous for their well-preserved fossils.

Fossils from the Mississippian Period in Iowa include abundant brachiopods (of which the spiriferids are the most common), bryozoans, corals, pelecypods, fish teeth, gastropods, and echinoderm debris; several other forms can also be found. Iowa is famous for well-preserved Mississippian crinoid crowns. These occur mostly in the Hampton, Gilmore City, and Burlington formations.

Pennsylvanian fossils from Iowa include both flora and fauna. Abundant plant fossils occur in the Caseyville Formation and the Cherokee Group. Marine fossils are abundant mainly in the southwestern part of the state and include several types of brachiopods (mostly strophomenids, including productids and chonetids), pelecypods, gastropods, echinoderm debris, corals, bryozoans, fusulinids, nautiloids, trilobites, and several others.

During the latter half of the Paleozoic Era, beginning in the Devonian Period, North America, Europe, and parts of Africa and South America were joined into one continental mass. Seas frequently invaded the inner regions of the continent, and Iowa was flooded many times. In the Pennsylvanian and Permian periods, the rising and falling water levels of the seas were markedly rhythmic, forming cyclic deposits of alternating shales and limestones.

The Permian Period saw the rise of early, large reptiles that were the ancestors of mammals, and further advancements of marine and plant life occurred. However, by the start of the Mesozoic Era many life forms had become extinct, including several types of brachiopods, trilobites, eurypterids, blastoids, many types of crinoids and gastropods, and others. Most of the plants composing the Paleozoic forests soon became extinct also. There are no known Permian deposits in Iowa, but the system is well represented in some neighboring states, and the Permian System of Nebraska is briefly touched upon in this book.

This book is a field guide written for amateur fossil collectors and geology enthusiasts. Most of the Paleozoic deposits in Iowa are examined, beginning with the Cambrian Wonewoc Formation and ending with the Pennsylvanian Wabaunsee Group. Most of the sites listed are in Iowa and were examined firsthand unless otherwise noted. For collectors wishing information on additional exposures of the Paleozoic Era, the addresses of seven state geological surveys in the Midwest are given in the references. Several publications listing additional sites are also listed.

This book is not intended to be an introduction to fossil collecting. There are several excellent books serving that purpose. However, the need for personal safety equipment cannot be repeated enough. Some working quarries require such equipment for any visitor. The requirements include eye protection, hard hat, and steel-toed shoes. A sturdy pair of gloves is also recommended, and a compass not only will get you back to the main highway but will also direct you to your vehicle when hiking. A snakebite kit as well as boots are good precautions. Venomous snakes were encountered on a few field trips; one cannot be certain when or where they will be found, so always be prepared. Some sites in Nebraska are infested with scorpions, but none were encountered at any of the road cuts examined for this study. If stung by a scorpion, seek medical help promptly.

Suggestions on collecting are given throughout the text. The best time to visit a particular working quarry, where to obtain permission, special precautions, and other important points are included. When being permit-

INTRODUCTION

ted access to private property, try to make sure you do nothing to cause future collectors to be denied this privilege. Also, listen to the owners. They know the hazards of the area and can provide helpful hints as to where the best and safest exposures can be found. You may be required to sign a release form. An attempt to contact owners of the quarries described in this book was made, and replies are mentioned throughout the text.

In addition to being a field guide, this book is a faunal survey. In most cases when a fossil fauna is described, such terms as "few" or "abundant" are either substantiated or replaced with percentages. For example, the spiriferid brachiopod *Spinocyrtia iowensis* represents 63 percent of the fauna of the Solon Member of the Cedar Valley Formation at Vinton. However, since techniques vary, this collector will explain how these figures were derived.

1. Personal studies of the Mississippian and Pennsylvanian faunas in the Fort Dodge area have shown that at least one hour of collecting will provide a fairly accurate representation of the most abundant fossils. This was the time spent at most of the fossiliferous deposits examined for this book. Any specimens found through additional collecting were not considered when figuring the percentages. This one-hour survey varied slightly from highly fossiliferous shale to poorly fossiliferous limestone. If a deposit yielded no fossils after 15 to 30 minutes of searching, no further time was spent and the deposit was labeled nonfossiliferous. This does not necessarily mean that such a deposit is totally lacking in fossils, just that the casual collector is not likely to find many specimens with the unaided eye.
2. Loose specimens and fossiliferous slabs were collected for later identification and tabulation. When the rock was so dense that too much time would be spent in freeing specimens, those seen in the field were recorded and then extracted after the one-hour survey was completed. The deposits that warranted such an approach were few. The best example of this situation occurs in the Wise Lake Member of the Galena Formation at Millville.
3. Educated guesses were made when dealing with numerous fossil fragments such as crinoid columns, bryozoans, and graptolites. In such cases only specimens over a certain size were counted; this size factor varied from fauna to fauna. In faunas made up of numerous small fragments, this collector used his own judgment in deciding what fraction should be used. Burrows represented a similar problem and were counted in the same manner. When burrows or fragmented fossils were few in number, each specimen was counted. Fusulinids and other small, unfragmented fossils presented a different problem. To remedy this situation, fossiliferous slabs were collected, and each specimen was counted later.
4. Every effort was made to examine all accessible parts of an exposure, trying not to concentrate merely on the most fossiliferous areas when making a faunal survey, unless there was a marked change in lithology.
5. Bulk samples were taken from some shales. These varied from 25 to 100

pounds. A bulk sample of at least 25 pounds should prove enlightening if the deposit is fossiliferous. Such a sample provides data on certain aspects of a fauna that are usually missed in the field, such as fragmentation of fossils; mortality rates based on numbers of immature forms; the smaller elements of a fauna, some of which can be extremely abundant; and specimens that are inconspicuous in the field. When collecting a bulk sample, small amounts of shale were taken from different areas of the same deposit at the same exposure, forming a composite. At home, the shale was rinsed with water through a sieve (mesh size 2 mm). The material remaining was removed and left to dry before the fossils were sorted by hand.
6. The faunal surveys included in the text are the findings of a typical amateur collector. They are included as an aid in identification for other collectors but do not necessarily reflect actual abundances. The references used most often in identifying fossils are given with each faunal list. When conflicts arose among references, Morre (1965) took precedence for brachiopods, Shimer and Shrock (1972) for others.

The localities of most sites are given as sections of townships. Iowa county maps and those issued by other states list townships and sections. Iowa maps are available for a nominal charge from the Iowa Department of Transportation, Office Supplies, Ames Storeroom, Ames, IA 50010.

Each township usually has 36 sections. Each section is 1 square mile (640 acres). An example of a site location is C/N½/SW¼/SE¼ sec. 10, T99N, R3W. This translates to the center of the northern half of the southwest quarter of the southeast quarter of section 10 in township 99 north, range 3 west. This particular township lies in the ninety-ninth tier north of a particular base line or latitude line and is the third township west of a particular principal meridian or longitude line. These figures appear on the margins of county maps.

Section 10 lies in the north-central area of a township. The section is subdivided by the example in this manner: the southeast quarter of section 10, the southwest quarter of that quarter, and the central part of the northern half of that quarter.

Most sites mentioned in this book include references given with the stratigraphic column listed for the site. These direct the reader to the original data sources. Very little information could be found for some sites, and in these cases the author had to measure and identify the exposures to the best of his ability. A description of the divisions of a stratigraphic column is given below.

Era—The largest division of a column. There were five such eras: the Archeozoic (the earliest time span extending back to the very creation of the earth), Proterozoic, Paleozoic (the subject of this book), Mesozoic, and Cenozoic (which includes the last 70 million years of geological history).

Period—Eras are divided into major systems of deposits called periods. At one time each period was thought to have ended rather abruptly, leaving a gap in the stratigraphic column before the next period began.

INTRODUCTION

Although in geological history major breaks or gaps are common, in which no new deposits were laid down for a considerable time and older deposits were eroded, they do not necessarily occur at the end of each period. The English River Formation of Iowa, for example, appears to be transitional, being deposited near the end of the Devonian Period and toward the beginning of the Mississippian.

Series—Periods are divided into series roughly corresponding to their lower (early), middle (mid), and upper (late) portions.

Group—Series are frequently split into associations of similar rock units (groups).

Formation—Groups in turn are usually composed of several formations, which are the primary units of a stratigraphic column. They are defined by lithology and stratigraphic position.

Member—Some formations are split into members based primarily on variations in lithology.

Iowa has abundantly fossiliferous deposits from the Ordovician, Silurian, Devonian, Mississippian, and Pennsylvanian periods. Faunas of the Cambrian and Permian periods can be found just outside Iowa's borders. This book, with its strong emphasis on prehistoric life, is intended to help the reader to better understand Paleozoic deposits in the state, assist in planning field trips, and aid in dating many exposures in this area that are not covered here.

As this book goes to print, geologists are actively revising and more precisely defining the stratigraphic column of Iowa. Some of the current work concerning the Paleozoic Era includes:

1. Revision of the Desmoinesian Series of the Pennsylvanian Period.
2. Research by Dr. Gilbert Klapper of the University of Iowa and Dr. James Barrick of Texas Tech University on a newly recognized Devonian Formation.
3. Preliminary reinterpretation of the Lower Mississippian in north-central Iowa (Glenister and Sixt 1982):
   a. The Gilmore City Formation exposed at Gilmore City is now believed to be the equivalent of the Chapin Member of the Hampton Formation at Le Grand. The Chapin Member is laterally equivalent to the Starrs Cave Formation of southeastern Iowa, but the Chapin may actually be slightly older.
   b. The limestone exposed in the Humboldt area is no longer considered to be part of the Gilmore City Formation, but is called the "Humboldt Oolite." It is equivalent to the Eagle City and Iowa Falls members of the Hampton Formation. Therefore, it is slightly younger than the Gilmore City Formation. The Humboldt Oolite is well exposed in the P & M Hodges Quarry north of Dakota City in Humboldt County (N½ sec. 32, T92N, R28W). The lower levels of the quarry carry an abundant and diverse gastropod-coral fauna, including the tabulate

coral *Syringopora*. Permission and safety equipment are required. Contact Weaver Construction Company, Iowa Falls, IA 50126. Exposures of the Humboldt Oolite also occur along the Des Moines River in Humboldt.

c. The poorly fossiliferous limestone quarried in the Alden area in Hardin County is probably equivalent to the Humboldt Oolite.

4. The Wise Lake and Dunleith, once thought to be members of the Galena Formation, are now considered as separate formations. The Galena is no longer used as a formation name.

5. A recently discovered site: E½NW¼ sec. 22, T100N, R4W. Allamakee County. To reach the site take Highway 26 north from Lansing for about 9 miles to the bridge over the Upper Iowa River. Just south of the bridge turn left (west) onto a gravel road. Continue west and south for a fraction of a mile to two quarries on the east side. The Lodi Siltstone Member of the Saint Lawrence Formation, Cambrian Period, is exposed here. Fossils are particularly abundant in the southern quarry. Thin beds of burrows are common throughout the exposure, and the lower levels contain fairly abundant trilobite fragments between the burrow beds. Carefully split the rock as thinly as possible into one layer at a time, paying close attention to the layers immediately below the burrows. Cranidia, spines, thorax segments, and pygidia of the trilobite *Dikelocephalus* were found during three hours of collecting. Also found with the trilobite fragments were a dozen small inarticulate brachiopods believed to be *Dicellomus*, a few small specimens of the gastropod *Proplina*, and a small cranidium fragment probably of the trilobite *Brassicephalus*.

Two dense, tan colored, sandy dolomite rocks found on the floor of the southern quarry contained abundant brachiopods. They probably originated from the middle of the face but this could not be positively determined. Both contained a total of sixty specimens of the orthid brachiopod *Finkelnburgia* and a few possible specimens of the inarticulate brachiopod *Lingulepis*. However, the rock must be thoroughly broken up to find the specimens.

2
Precambrian and Cambrian Periods

Site 1. Location: sec. 11, T100N, R49W. Red quartzite (Sioux Quartzite) of the Precambrian Period crops out along the Big Sioux River in the extreme northwest corner of Iowa in the vicinity of the Gitchie Manitou State Preserve in Lyon County. This is the oldest exposed bedrock in the state. Collecting inside the preserve is not permitted. The age of this rock has been estimated to be about 1.5 billion years old.

The Cambrian System of Iowa includes various sandstones, siltstones, and dolomites of the St. Croixan Series (Upper Cambrian). Cambrian exposures occur in Allamakee and Clayton counties. The earliest abundant fossils occur in the Cambrian and specimens can be found in Iowa, although they are more common in Minnesota and Wisconsin. The Cambrian Period began around 600 million years ago and lasted for 100 million years. The stratigraphic column for the Cambrian System in northeast Iowa is given below:

SERIES	GROUP	FORMATION	MEMBER	DESCRIPTION
St. Croixan	Trempealeau	Jordan	Coon Valley	sandy dolomite
			Waukon	sandstone
			Van Oser	sandstone
			Norwalk	sandstone
		St. Lawrence	Lodi	dolomitic siltstone
			Black Earth	glauconitic dolomite
	Tunnel City	Lone Rock	Reno	glauconitic sandstone
			Tomah	sandstone
			Birkmose	sandstone
	Elk Mound	Wonewoc	Ironton	sandstone
			Galesville	sandstone
		Eau Claire		sandstone
		Mt. Simon		sandstone

Site 2. Location: W½/NE¼ sec. 12, T99N, R4W. Just under 4 miles north of Lansing on Highway 26 in Allamakee County is an exposure of the Ironton Member of the Wonewoc Formation. Brown coarse-grained sandstone is exposed along a stream on the north side of a bridge. The Ironton is the oldest exposed Paleozoic deposit in the state.

Site 3. Location: NW¼/SE¼ sec. 1, T99N, R4W. The Ironton Member of the Wonewoc Formation is exposed in a road cut along Highway 26 a little over 4 miles north of Lansing in Allamakee County.

Site 4. Location: C/SE¼/NW¼ sec. 21, T100N, R4W. To reach the site, turn west on county road A-26 (paved) from Highway 26 about 10 miles north of Lansing in Allamakee County. Continue west for about 2 miles and turn north (right) on a gravel road. The Ironton Member of the Wonewoc Formation is well exposed here on the east side of the road, but it is partially overgrown. Burrows are common in places, and brachiopods and trilobite fragments have been reported to be fairly common; however, this collector found only burrows.

Site 5. Location: SE¼/NE¼ sec. 29, T99N, R4W. Along Highway 26 just north of the intersection with Highway 9 in Lansing in Allamakee County is an exposure of sandstone and glauconitic (green) sandstone of the Reno Member of the Lone Rock Formation. Burrows are common.

Site 6. Location: NE¼ sec. 29 and sec. 20, T99N, R3W. Just north of Lansing in Allamakee County along the west side of Highway 26, the Reno Member of the Lone Rock Formation is exposed in road cuts and is composed of glauconitic sandstone. At the northern end of the sequence (about 0.5 mile), brown siltstone of the Lodi Member of the St. Lawrence Formation overlies the Reno Sandstone. Burrows occur in both units.

Site 7. Across the border into Minnesota, the Franconia Formation (Lone Rock Formation in Iowa and Wisconsin) is well exposed in a high bluff on the west side of Highway 26 at Reno, Houston County. Glauconitic sandstone predominates here. Trilobite fragments are fairly numerous, but most are difficult to identify. Burrows are very common in certain zones at this site. This burrow-trilobite fauna is typical of most Cambrian faunas around the world. A total of 215 fossils was found here, including the following:

IDENTIFICATION	PERCENT
Brachiopods?, inarticulate	2.32
Burrows	93.02
Trilobites	
Ptychaspis sp.	0.46
Pygidia	3.76
Unidentified fossils	0.46

Source: Hogberg et al. 1967.

The inarticulate brachiopods found here were so poorly preserved that their identification was doubtful. Trilobite fragments are more abundant than this list indicates because only pygidia (tails) were counted.

Site 8. Location: C/SW¼/NW¼ sec. 31, T100N, R4W. Along county road A-26 (paved) about 6 miles west of Highway 26 near Lansing in Allamakee County is a quarry exposing the Reno Member of the Lone Rock Formation. The glauconitic sandstones here carry abundant burrows. Road cuts also expose the Reno Member and the St. Lawrence Formation. These cuts and the quarry are on the north side of the road. The stratigraphic column for this site is described below (Anderson et al. 1979):

I. St. Croixan Series
  A. Trempealeau Group
    1. Jordan Formation: exposed high on the slope
    2. St. Lawrence Formation
      a. Upper Lodi Member: covered
      b. Black Earth Member: glauconitic dolomite, partially covered
      c. Lower Lodi Member: 16 feet of siltsone, covered
    3. Lone Rock Formation
      a. Reno Member: over 30 feet of glauconitic sandstone exposed in the main part of the quarry

Site 9. Location: C/W½/SE/SW sec. 32, T100N, R5W. The site is a quarry on the north side of county road A-26 (paved) about 3.5 miles east of Highway 76 in northwestern Allamakee County. Exposed here is mostly brown dolomitic siltstone of the upper part of the Lodi Member of the St. Lawrence Formation. Burrows are common. The Norwalk Member of the Jordan Formation is exposed on the slope above the quarry.

Site 10. Location: C/NW¼ sec. 6, T99N, R5W. To reach the site, take county road A-26 east from Highway 76 in northwestern Allamakee County for 2 miles. There are two road cuts. The eastern cut exposes the Jordan Formation. The western cut exposes the St. Lawrence-Jordan contact. The composite stratigraphic column for both cuts is described below (Anderson et al. 1979):

I. St. Croixan Series
  A. Trempealeau Group
    1. Jordan Formation
      a. Coon Valley Member: 17 feet of brown sandy dolomite and some sandstone
      b. Upper Van Oser Member: 29 feet of sandstone with burrows; similar to the lower Van Oser
      c. Waukon Member: 19 feet of brown fine-grained sandstone; some burrows
      d. Lower Van Oser Member: 29 feet of brown sandstone with

ledges that are more resistant to weathering than the rest of the unit; burrows common
   e. Norwalk Member: 18 feet of brown sandstone, generally finer grained than the Van Oser; some burrows
2. St. Lawrence Formation
   a. Lodi Member: 19 feet of brown dolomitic siltstone and silty dolomite exposed at the western end of the sequence; burrows

Site 11. Exposures of sandstone from the Jordan Formation, probably the Norwalk Member, occur along Highway 18 between Marquette and McGregor, Clayton County. No fossils were seen.

Site 12. Location: W½/NW¼/NW¼ sec. 12, T99N, R6W. A series of road cuts occur along the western side of Highway 76 just south of the bridge over the Upper Iowa River in Allamakee County. Proceed for about 0.5 mile south to the southern end of the sequence. The Ordovician-Cambrian contact is exposed at this site. The stratigraphic column for this section is described below (Anderson et al. 1979):

I. Ordovician Period, Canadian Series
   A. Prairie du Chien Group
      1. Oneota Formation: at least a few feet of dolomite are exposed at the top of the cut. Gastropods and burrows reportedly occur near the base of the unit, but none were seen by the author.
II. Cambrian Period, St. Croixan Series
   A. Trempealeau Group
      1. Jordan Formation
         a. Coon Valley Member: estimated 17 feet of brown sandy dolomite and dolomitic sandstone with soft, coarse sandstone at the top and base
         b. Van Oser Member: at least a few feet of coarse sandstone exposed at the base of the cut

Site 13. Location: S½ sec. 27, T99N, R4W. The Ordovician-Cambrian contact was examined about 4 miles west of Lansing in Allamakee County on the north side of Highway 9. The Coon Valley Member of the Jordan Formation is composed of sandstone and sandy dolomite. It is overlain by dolomite of the Oneota Formation (Ordovician), which also includes a thin zone of conglomerate at the base. Other exposures of the Coon Valley and Van Oser members occur to the east in road cuts. Cuts to the west expose several Ordovician formations from the Oneota through the Galena. These are discussed in Chapter 3 (see Site 15).

Collectors interested in other exposures of the Cambrian Period along the upper Mississippi River should find Hogberg et al. (1967) interesting. The Wisconsin Geological and Natural History Survey also offers information on the Cambrian Period in this vicinity.

3
Ordovician Period

THE ORDOVICIAN PERIOD began 500 million years ago and ended 425 million years ago. Iowa's oldest well-preserved fossils occur in the Ordovician System. There are excellent exposures along the Mississippi River, in quarries, along small rivers and streams, and in road cuts in northeastern Iowa and southeastern Minnesota. The stratigraphic column for the Ordovician System in Iowa is described below:

SERIES	GROUP	FORMATION	MEMBER	DESCRIPTION
Cincinnatian (Upper Ordovician)		Maquoketa	Neda	shale
			Brainard	shale
			Fort Atkinson	cherty limestone
			Clermont	shale
			Elgin	shale and limestone
	Galena	Dubuque		dolomitic limestone
		Galena?	Wise Lake	dolomite
			Dunleith	dolomitic limestone
Champlainian (Middle Ordovician)	Galena?	Decorah	Ion	shale and limestone
			Guttenberg	limestone
			Spechts Ferry	shale
		Platteville	Quimbys Mill	shale
			McGregor	limestone
			Pecatonica	dolomitic limestone
	Ancell	Glenwood	Harmony Hill	shale
			Starved Rock	sandstone
			Harmony Hill	shale
		St. Peter	Tonti	sandstone
			Readstown	shale
Canadian (Lower Ordovician)	Prairie du Chien	Shakopee	Willow River	dolomite
			New Richmond	sandstone
		Oneota		dolomite

Site 14. In Winona and Houston counties of Minnesota, along the Mississippi River, exposures of the Oneota Formation occur in bluffs along

Highway 61. Poorly preserved gastropods and burrows can be found in the lower part of the formation in this area. Excellently preserved gastropods reportedly have been found in chert nodules of the Oneota here, but none were seen by this collector at one bluff.

Site 15. Location: N½ sec. 32, SE¼ sec. 29, S½ sec. 28, S½ sec. 27, all in T99N, R4W. A series of road cuts between Churchtown and Lansing in Allamakee County expose Ordovician and Cambrian formations. The stratigraphic column for the series of cuts is described below (modified from Rose 1967):

I. Ordovician Period, Champlainian Series
   A. Galena Group
      1. Galena? Formation
         a. Dunleith Member: lower part present, several feet of weathered, brown, fossiliferous dolomitic limestone
      2. Decorah Formation
         a. Ion Member: 18 feet of brownish shale with limestone zones and fossils
         b. Guttenberg Member: 16 feet of fossiliferous limestone
         c. Spechts Ferry Member: 8 feet of gray shale with fossils
   B. (no group name)
      1. Platteville Formation
         a. McGregor-Pecatonica members: limestone with some fossils, combined thickness 35 feet
   C. Ancell Group
      1. Glenwood Formation
         a. Harmony Hill Member: 5 feet of green shale
      2. St. Peter Formation
         a. Tonti Member: 47 feet of sandstone
II. Canadian Series
   A. Prairie du Chien Group
      1. Shakopee Formation
         a. Willow River Member: 25 feet of dolomite
         b. New Richmond Member: 24 feet of sandstone
      2. Oneota Formation: at least 150 feet of dolomite
III. Cambrian Period, St. Croixan Series
   A. Trempealeau Group
      1. Jordan Formation
         a. Coon Valley Member: at least 15 feet of sandy dolomite and sandstone
         b. Van Oser Member: not measured; sandstone

The western end of the sequence occurs in Churchtown, where a talus slope on the northern side of Highway 9 exposes brown dolomitic limestone of the Dunleith Member of the Galena? Formation. The next exposure can be seen on both sides of the highway on the eastern edge of Churchtown. The Dunleith Member occurs at the top of the northern cut and contains

ORDOVICIAN PERIOD

some fossils. The Ion Member of the Decorah Formation is quite fossiliferous here and appears on both sides of the road. The upper part of the Guttenberg Limestone can be found at the base of this cut as well as on both sides of the highway. It is also fossiliferous.

An excellent starting point for this series of road cuts is at the exposure of the St. Peter Sandstone at the northern end of the base of the cut just east of the Dunleith-Guttenberg cut on the north side of the highway (SE¼/SE¼/SE¼/SE¼ sec. 29, T99N, R4W). The Glenwood and Platteville formations are exposed in the same cut west of the St. Peter Formation. The Spechts Ferry Member of the Decorah Formation can be found at the top of the western end of this cut.

Several road cuts to the east of the St. Peter Sandstone expose the Shakopee and Oneota formations. The base of the Oneota Dolomite and the contact with the Coon Valley Member of the Jordan Formation (Cambrian Period) are exposed on the north side of Highway 9 about 4 miles west of Lansing in Allamakee County (S½ sec. 9, T99N, R4W). The sequence of cuts continues east for some distance and exposes the Coon Valley and Van Oser members of the Jordan Formation. The Ordovician-Cambrian contact was also examined in western Allamakee County (see Site 12).

An excellent fauna was collected from the Ion Shale on the south side of the cut just east of Churchtown in Allamakee County. This is one of the best collecting sites for Ordovician fossils that was examined for this guide. Brachiopods, bryozoans (including the mound-shaped genus *Prasopora*), pelecypods, crinoid columnals, and other fossils can be found in abundance. Other exposures of the Ion Shale, which were examined and are covered later in this chapter, do not seem to be as richly fossiliferous as this one. One hour of collecting provided 735 fossils, including the following:

IDENTIFICATION	PERCENT
Brachiopods	
Platystrophia trentonensis (orthid)	2.31
Campylorthis sp. (orthid)	0.40
Mimella sp. (orthid)	2.04
Hesperorthis tricenaria (orthid)	0.68
Hebertella frankfortensis (orthid)	1.22
Paucicrura rogata (orthid)	17.82
Rhynchotrema increbescens (rhynchonellid)	1.36
Sowerbyella curdsvillensis (strophomenid)	13.87
Rafinesquina alternata (strophomenid)	0.81
Strophomena sp. (strophomenid)	0.68
Unidentified fragments	0.27
Bryozoans	
Prasopora insularis	10.74
Branching (several types)	30.34
Encrusting	0.18
Coral	
Streptelasma corniculum	1.22
Echinoderm debris (mostly crinoid columnals)	13.86
Gastropods	
Raphistomina sp.	0.27

IDENTIFICATION	PERCENT
Pelecypods	
Orthodesma sp.	0.13
Ctenodonta sp.	0.40
Shells, burrowed	0.13
Trilobite pygidia	0.40

Source: Hogberg et al. 1967, Moore 1965, Rose 1967, Shimer and Shrock 1972.

The largest brachiopods in this fauna are usually broken and disarticulated. Most of the pelecypods are also damaged, but they are still articulated. Brachiopods tend to be most common in the lower half of the Ion Shale, whereas the bryozoans are most common in the upper half. The brachiopod *Sowerbyella* appears to be the most common fossil in the Guttenberg Limestone, but no examination of that fauna was made.

A 25-pound bulk sample of the Ion Shale at this site yielded 1,568 fossils, 80 percent of which were bryozoans. Occasional examples of bryozoans encrusting *Platystrophia* and *Streptelasma* were found in the sample. The bryozoan *Prasopora,* in its very early stages of growth, occasionally encrusted *Paucicrura* and *Campylorthis.*

Site 16. Location: N½ sec. 28, T95N, R3W. A sequence of exposures similar to those described in Site 15 occurs near McGregor in Clayton County on the north side of Highway 18 west of town. The first exposure on the western edge of McGregor belongs to the St. Peter Sandstone Formation. Farther west along the highway the Pecatonica and McGregor Members of the Platteville Formation are well exposed. The Glenwood Member was not seen here but is probably covered by boulders from these two overlying members, The Spechts Ferry Shale Member of the Decorah Formation is reportedly exposed here but was not seen by this collector. Gastropods are reportedly common in the McGregor Limestone here. A brief survey yielded 31 specimens, which included orthid and strophomenid brachiopods, pelecypods, bryozoans, corals, and pygidia of the trilobite *Illaenus americanus.* The McGregor Member comprises bedded limestone with thin shale zones. The Pecatonica Member comprises massive dolomitic limestone.

The western end of this sequence of cuts along Highway 18 contains limestone of the Guttenberg Member and limestone with a considerable amount of interbedded shale of the Ion Member; both are in the Decorah Formation. These two members are not as fossiliferous as the exposures at Churchtown, but the Ion Shale here still provides good fossil collecting. A 25-pound bulk sample was taken, and the results were very similar to those of the Churchtown sample. However, the bryozoans at this site seemed to be much less numerous, representing barely 40 percent of the 465 fossils found. *Sowerbyella curdsvillensis* and *Paucicrura rogata* were the two most common brachiopods found, with percentages very close to those of the same species found at Churchtown. Other brachiopods, corals, echinoderm debris, trilobite pygidia, and a few other fossils were also found here.

Site 17. Location: C sec. 34, T95N, R3W. Another exposure of the beds at Site 16 occurs along Highway 340 between McGregor and Pikes Peak State Park in Clayton County. North of the cut is a small quarry opened up in the Tonti Sandstone of the St. Peter Formation. There may be an exposure of dolomite of the Willow River Member of the Shakopee Formation below the Tonti Sandstone, but no close examination of the quarry was made. Collecting from the quarry is not allowed. The St. Peter Formation is also exposed at the base of the northern end of the cut. Above this sandstone and continuing south along the base of the cut is a total of 15 feet of dolomitic limestone of the Pecatonica Member of the Platteville Formation. A few brachiopod and pelecypod casts were found in the Pecatonica at this site. The green shale of the Glenwood Member is present in the cut but is covered by debris from the Pecatonica. Around 20 feet of thin-bedded and shaly limestone of the McGregor Member overlie the Pecatonica, varying from gray to brown and fossiliferous in places. This unit is best reached at the middle of the cut where it slopes to road level. At the south end of the cut, at least 8 feet of fossiliferous gray shale of the Spechts Ferry Member of the Decorah Formation is exposed along with a few feet of brown limestone of the Guttenberg Member. An old quarry southwest of the cut, not visible from the road, exposes the Dunleith Member of the Galena? Formation, but collecting from the quarry is not allowed.

The fauna of the McGregor Member at this site is composed mostly of fragmented or disarticulated fossils, and some forms are commonly found in clusters. Fossils appear to be more common in the Spechts Ferry Shale and more evenly distributed than in the McGregor Limestone at this site. Most specimens are generally better preserved. The earliest abundant epifauna (organisms attached to other organisms) described in this guide comes from the Spechts Ferry Member. Bryozoans encrusting the orthid brachiopods *Paucicrura* and *Doleroides gibbosus* were found. The faunas of the McGregor and Spechts Ferry Members at this site included the following:

IDENTIFICATION	McGREGOR	SPECHTS FERRY
	(%)	(%)
Brachiopods		
Mimella sp. (orthid)	4.39	...
Doleroides gibbosus (orthid)	...	7.76
Paucicrura rogata (orthid)	14.86	20.51
Plaesiomys (*Dinorthis*) *pectinella* (orthid)	6.08	2.40
Glyptorthis sp. (orthid)	...	1.66
Platystrophia sp. (orthid)	...	0.36
Pionodema subaequata (orthid)	0.33	5.91
Hesperorthis tricenaria (orthid)	1.68	...
Campylorthis sp. (orthid)	21.62	...
Rostricellula sp. (rhynchonellid)	...	0.36
Rhynchotrema incribescens (rhynchonellid)	2.36	...
Sowerbyella sp. (strophomenid)	20.60	46.02
Rafinesquina sp. (strophomenid)	4.05	2.77
Strophomena sp. (strophomenid)	2.70	2.40
Unidentified	...	0.36

IDENTIFICATION	McGREGOR	SPECHTS FERRY
	(%)	(%)
Bryozoans		
Branching	5.74	4.43
Encrusting	...	0.55
Prasopora sp.	...	0.36
Burrows		
Chondrites sp.	6.75	2.21
Coral		
Streptelasma corniculum	1.35	1.29
Echinoderm debris (mostly crinoid columnals)	3.37	0.54
Gastropods	0.33	...
Ostracods		
Eoleperditia fabulites	0.33	...
Pelecypods	0.33	...
Stromatoporoids	2.02	...
Trilobite pygidia	1.01	...

Source: Hogberg et al. 1967, Moore 1965, Rose 1967, Shimer and Shrock 1972.

A total of 296 fossils was collected from the McGregor Member and 541 from the Spechts Ferry Member. Note the presence of an ostracod in the McGregor. Ostracods are numerous in several Paleozoic deposits in Iowa, but most are small. No examinations were made of the microscopic elements of any fauna. The ostracod species *Eoleperditia fabulites* is among the largest known and occurs in the McGregor Member. It can be very abundant at several localities, but this collector failed to find a large quantity of the fossil.

Site 18. Location: SE¼/SE¼/NW¼ sec. 27, T95N, R4W. Another exposure of the Spechts Ferry Member of the Decorah Formation was examined near Spook Cave. To reach the site, take Highway 18 west out of McGregor in Clayton County for about 7 miles to the town of Giard, then turn north for 2 miles to the cave. The cave opens in the Platteville Formation, and fossils can be seen in the ceiling. The Spechts Ferry Member is exposed in a road cut along the same gravel road just north of the cave and across a small stream. Brachiopods and other fossils are fairly numerous in the grayish shale. Rather large but poorly preserved nautiloids are present but are few in number. Along the stream more resistant material of the Spechts Ferry Shale can sometimes be found and is packed with brachiopods and a few trilobite pygidia. A 25-pound bulk sample yielded 273 fossils. Echinoderm debris (mostly crinoid columnals) represented 41 percent of the fauna; bryozoans, 26 percent; *Sowerbyella*, 14 percent; and *Paucicrura rogata*, 10 percent. Small nautiloids, gastropods, trilobite pygidia, and strophomenid and orthid brachiopods made up the rest of the fauna found.

The Dunleith Member of the Galena? Formation is well exposed in a quarry north of this cut and on the east side of the same gravel road. It offers some excellent fossils and is discussed more fully under Site 21.

Site 19. Location: sec. 31, T98N, R5W. Just south of Waukon in Allamakee County on Highway 9 is an operating quarry on the west side of the road. Exposed here are an estimated 20 feet of grayish white limestone of the Platteville Formation. The face is probably a combination of the Pecatonica and McGregor members. Stop at the quarry office for permission to collect. The best time to visit is on Saturday mornings. In all operating quarries, even abandoned ones, a hard hat, steel-toed shoes, and eye protection are strongly suggested even if not required.

Two rather distinct faunas were seen in the eastern part of the quarry. One was collected from the talus at the base of the face and the other from the talus slope opposite the face. Few similarities exist between these two faunas despite the fact that they came from the same quarry. It is possible that the fauna found in the slope is slightly younger than that found at the face. The trilobite *Illaensis americanus* serves as an index fossil for the McGregor Member.

Only 81 fossils were found at the face after one hour of collecting, but 366 were found in the slope in the same time. These faunas included:

IDENTIFICATION	FACE	SLOPE
	(%)	(%)
Brachiopods		
Paucicrura rogata (orthid)	3.70	28.68
Plaesiomys (*Dinorthis*) sp. (orthid)	1.23	1.91
Glyptorthis sp. (orthid)	...	0.81
Platystrophia sp. (orthid)	...	0.54
Rostricellula sp. (rhynchonellid)	4.93	...
Sowerbyella curdsvillensis (strophomenid)	71.60	57.10
Rafinesquina sp. (strophomenid)	1.23	...
Bryozoans, branching	4.93	1.09
Burrows		
Chondrites sp.	...	5.46
Crinoid columnals	2.46	...
Corals		
Colonial?	3.70	...
Solitary, unidentified	...	1.09
Gastropods		
Raphistomina sp.	...	0.27
Unidentified	4.93	...
Unidentified (different species)	...	0.27
Pelecypods, unidentified	...	0.27
Trilobites		
?*Thaleops* sp. (fragment)	1.23	...
Illaensis americanus (pygidia)	...	2.45

Source: Hogberg et al. 1967, Moore 1965, Rose 1967, Shimer and Shrock 1972.

Site 20. The Platteville and Decorah formations were also examined near Chatfield in Olmsted County, Minnesota. The exposures occur along Highway 30, beginning just east of the town and continuing east for some distance. The western end of the sequence was examined. It exposes shale of the Decorah Formation with limestone of the McGregor Member of the Platteville Formation at the base of the cut. Toward the eastern end of the sequence, dolomite of the Galena? Formation is exposed. No examination of the Galena? Formation was made, but in a brief stop a few bryozoans were found in the Decorah Shale and a few specimens of the trilobite *Illaensis americanus* were found in the McGregor Limestone.

Site 21. Location: SW¼ sec. 22, T95N, R4W. The Dunleith Member of the Galena? Formation was examined in a quarry north of Spook Cave in Clayton County. To reach the quarry, take Highway 18 west out of McGregor for about 7 miles to the town of Giard; then turn north on a gravel road. The cave is located 2 miles to the north. Pass the cave and an exposure of Spechts Ferry Shale (Site 18) and continue to the quarry located on the east side of the road. Exposed here are cherty dolomitic limestone and limestone that varies from brown to dark gray. The most numerous and best preserved fossils occur in the tan dolomitic zones. *Chondrites* burrows are very numerous in parts of the limestone but do not seem to occur very often with other fossils.

Ischadites iowensis, believed to be a calcareous green algae (plant), is an index fossil for the Dunleith Member and occurs in clusters of three or four in this quarry. Although some of the specimens are fragmented, most are excellently preserved and seem to occur only in the dolomite near the base of the face. This unit appears to be the most fossiliferous of the quarry, but collection was not limited to it. The fauna found at this quarry included:

IDENTIFICATION	PERCENT
Algae	
Ischadites iowensis	2.87
Brachiopods	
Platystrophia sp. (orthid)	0.63
Paucicrura rogata (orthid)	0.95
Glyptorthis sp. (orthid)	0.31
Rostricellula sp. (rhynchonellid)	1.91
Rafinesquina sp. (strophomenid)	21.08
Sowerbyella sp. (strophomenid)	17.89
Bryozoans, branching	1.27
Burrows	
Chondrites sp.	31.94
Corals	
?*Halysites* sp. (colonial)	0.31
Streptalasma sp.	1.27
Gastropods	
?*Hormotoma* sp.	0.31
Loxoplocus (Donaldiella) bowdeni	1.27
?*Raphistomina* sp.	0.95
High-spired, unidentified	6.38
Low-spired, unidentified	6.33
Nautiloids, unidentified	1.27
Pelecypods, unidentified	2.23
Trilobites	
Isotelus sp. (fragments)	0.63

Source: Hogberg et al. 1967, Moore 1965, Rose 1967, Shimer and Shrock 1972.

ORDOVICIAN PERIOD

Gastropods are fairly common in this quarry and many types are present, but most are represented as incomplete casts or molds. One hour of collecting yielded a total of 313 fossils.

Site 22. Location: NW¼/NW¼/SW¼ sec. 15, T91N, R2W. There are many exposures in the vicinity of Millville, Clayton County. These range from the Galena? Formation to the Silurian Hopkinton Formation. One site was examined along Highway 52 south of Millville and 0.3 mile south of the bridge over the Turkey River. The Silurian Hopkinton, Blanding, and Tête des Morts formations are exposed in a high bluff. These are discussed in more detail in Chapter 4 (see Site 33). A creekbed exposure to the south of the bluff is part of the Wise Lake Member of the Galena? Formation. The poor exposures and talus in the deep ravine north of the bluff and on the west side of the highway are part of the Dunleith Member. Boulders of dense brown dolomite can be found in abundance in the ditches on both sides of the road south of the bluff. These belong to the Wise Lake Member, but a few grayish white, very dense dolomite boulders of the Hopkinton Formation (Silurian Period) are also present. The fauna of the Wise Lake Dolomite here is similar to that of the Dunleith Member found at Site 21. The density of the rock and the poor preservation of most fossils at this site hampered identification of the Wise Lake fauna. However, gastropods appear to be the most common fossils here; they are considerably more numerous than in the Dunleith fauna. The calcareous green algae of the Wise Lake fauna, *Receptaculites oweni*, reaches its greatest abundance in this member but does not occur in younger Ordovician deposits in Iowa. This genus is similar to *Ischadites* but is much larger and generally not as well preserved. Its large size makes extraction from the rock difficult. Sixty-four fossils were seen in the field during one hour of searching in the Wise Lake Member. These included the following:

IDENTIFICATION	PERCENT
Algae	
Receptaculites oweni	25.00
Brachiopods, unidentified	12.50
Bryozoans, branching	10.93
Corals, solitary	3.12
Crinoid columnals	1.56
Gastropods	
Low-spired	35.93
High-spired	6.25
Nautiloids	4.68

Source: Rose 1967.

A similar, more complete exposure of these beds occurs about 0.5 mile south of this site (NE¼/NE¼/NE¼ sec. 21, T91N, R2W). The stratigraphic column for this exposure is described below by the author.

The author has attempted to modify the Silurian part of the sequence described by Rose (1967) to comply with current terminology, but discrepancies occur between the description of this site and the similar one 0.5 mile north.

I. Silurian Period, Llandoverian Series
   A. Hopkinton Formation: at least 20 feet of fossiliferous dolomite exposed at the top of the cut
   B. Blanding Formation: 13 feet of cherty dolomite
   C. Tête des Morts Formation: estimated 20 feet of dolomite with some chert
   D. Mosalem Formation: estimated 40 feet of dolomite, lower half covered. Blocks of this and the Tête des Morts Formation can be seen sliding down the upper part of the Maquoketa shales on the west side of Highway 52.
II. Ordovician Period, Cincinnatian Series
   A. Maquoketa Formation: about 250 feet of badly eroded and partially covered shales
   B. Galena Group, Dubuque Formation: around 20 feet of dolomite with fossils and shaly partings
   C. Galena Group, Galena? Formation
      1. Wise Lake Member: 46 feet of dolomite with fossils
III. Ordovician Period, Champlainian Series
   A. Galena Group, Galena? Formation
      1. Dunleith Member: at least 130 feet of dolomite and dolomitic limestone, partially covered with shaly partings and fossils; exposed above the Little Turkey River

Site 23. Location: SE¼/NE¼ sec. 20, T92N, R2W. There are several road cut exposures of the Galena?, Decorah, and Platteville formations in the vicinity of Guttenberg in Clayton County. One occurs in the southern part of town on the west side of Highway 52 north of the intersection with county road C-7X. The exposed beds are described below (Rose 1967):

I. Champlainian Series
   A. Galena Group, Galena? Formation
      1. Dunleith Member: at least 50 feet of dolomitic limestone exposed at the top of the cut; more of the Dunleith Member exposed elsewhere in the area
   B. Galena Group, Decorah Formation
      1. Ion Member: 15 feet of fossiliferous shale and limestone
      2. Guttenberg Member: 15 feet of fossiliferous limestone
      3. Spechts Ferry Member: 8 feet of fossiliferous gray shale
   C. Platteville Formation
      1. McGregor Member: 30 feet of thin-bedded limestone with fossils
      2. Pecatonica Member: a maximum of 10 feet of dolomitic limestone exposed at the base of the cut

Collecting is virtually impossible in all but the lowest levels of this particular cut because of the steep slope.

Site 24. An exposure of the Dubuque Formation with the basal part of the Elgin Member of the Maquoketa Formation was examined in Dubuque,

Dubuque County. The site is located below the Leath furniture store parking lot at the corner of Devon Drive and Dodge Street (Highway 20). This is about 2 miles west of the junction of Highways 20 and 52. The best exposure occurs just west of the parking lot along a northbound gravel road. Dolomite of the Dubuque Formation is exposed and contains a few fossils. The Elgin Member of the Maquoketa Formation is mostly covered above the Dubuque Dolomite, but abundant fossils can be found in the residue resting on the dolomite. A brief sampling of the Elgin fossils revealed an abundance of pelecypods, small nautiloids, crinoid columnals, small bryozoans, gastropods, brachiopods, and other fossils.

Site 25. Location: SW¼/SW¼ sec. 16, T89N, R1E. Northeast of Graf in Dubuque County on the north side of a gravel road is an abandoned quarry. The face exposes around 5 feet of dolomite of the Wise Lake Member of the Galena? Formation, overlain by dolomite of the Dubuque Formation. A few feet of shaly limestone of the Maquoketa Formation (Elgin Member) are present at the top of the quarry face. Fossils are not common here (Rose 1967).

Site 26. The Dubuque and Maquoketa formations were also examined west of Granger in Fillmore County, Minnesota, which is just north of the Iowa border. The first cut on the south side of the gravel road at the eastern end of the sequence exposes around 20 feet of fossiliferous, gray to tan shaly limestone believed to be of the Dubuque Formation. The next cut to the west and on the north side of the road exposes fossiliferous, gray to tan limestone of the Elgin Member of the Maquoketa Formation. The third cut, at the western end of the sequence, exposes grayish shaly limestone that is also of the Elgin Member, but fossils do not seem to be abundant in this cut. Most of the Maquoketa Formation in Minnesota has been correlated with the Elgin Member of the Maquoketa Formation in Iowa.

Most of the fossils of the Dubuque and Elgin faunas are either fragmented or disarticulated, with the exception of several brachiopods. The graptolites of the Elgin Member at this site are generally uncrushed and 1 to 2 inches long, which makes them the best of such specimens mentioned in this guide. A total of 1,314 fossils were found in the Dubuque Formation, and 411 fossils in the Elgin Member at the middle cut. These included:

IDENTIFICATION	DUBUQUE	ELGIN
	(%)	(%)
Brachiopods		
?*Schizocrania* sp. (inarticulate)	0.07	0.72
Diceromyonia tersa (orthid)	25.24	12.65
Paucicrura sp. (orthid)	2.30	7.29
Platystrophia sp. (orthid)	0.07	...
Plaesiomys subquadrata (orthid)	0.07	1.45
Lepidocyclus laddi (rhynchonellid)	...	0.24
Sowerbyella sp. (strophomenid)	65.15	20.19
Strophomena sp. (strophomenid)	0.61	1.94
Rafinesquina sp. (strophomenid)	0.38	1.94
Bryozoans, unidentified branching	...	0.48

IDENTIFICATION	DUBUQUE	ELGIN
	(%)	(%)
Burrows		
Chondrites sp.	0.23	...
Conularids		
Conularia trentonensis	0.30	0.97
Coral, unidentified solitary	...	0.24
Crinoid columnals	0.07	...
Fossils, unidentified	0.07	...
Gastropods		
Ophiletina sublaxa	...	0.24
Hormotoma sp.	0.07	...
Bellerophon sp.	...	0.24
Crytolites orantus	...	0.24
Graptolites		
Diplograptus sp.	1.07	11.19
Nautiloids		
Isorthoceras sp.	0.07	0.24
Pelecypods		
Orthodesma subnasutum	0.69	5.35
Vanuxemia hayniana	0.38	9.24
Modiolopsis sp.	0.23	...
Ctenodonta sp.	1.68	16.30
Trilobites		
Flexicalymene meeki (cranidia)	...	0.48
Isotelus gigas (pygidia)	1.15	7.54
Illaensis sp. (pygidia)	...	0.24
Pygidia, unidentified	...	0.48

Source: Hogberg et al. 1967, Moore 1965, Rose 1967, Shimer and Shrock 1972.

The two faunas collected here are among the most varied and abundant examined in this study. These exposures provide the best fossil collecting of the Ordovician System that this collector has seen. Many forms in these faunas occur in clusters, such as the brachiopods *Sowerbyella* and *Diceromyonia,* the pelecypods *Ctenodonta* and *Vanuxemia,* and a few other fossils. Only complete cranidia of the trilobite *Flexicalymene* were found here, which is unusual because complete pygidia usually are more common.

Site 27. Location: NE¼/SW¼ sec. 29, T89N, R1E. The Maquoketa Formation offers some of the most unique fossil collecting in Iowa. Two of these faunas were discussed under Sites 24 and 26. Five members of the Maquoketa are recognized in the state: the Neda, Brainard, Fort Atkinson, Clermont, and Elgin. All are fossiliferous; only the Neda Shale was not examined.

On a gravel road, a fraction of a mile southwest of Graf in Dubuque County is one of the state's most famous collecting sites. The cut occurs on the east side of the road. There is a deep ravine on the west side and no shoulder. A generalized stratigraphic column for the site is described below:

I. Maquoketa Formation
   A. Elgin Member:

1. Estimated 10 feet of shaly phosphatic dolomite with some fossils. A unit near the base is very fossiliferous, bearing many nautiloids and some small, diminutive fossils
2. Estimated 3 feet of gray to brown, thin-bedded shale with graptolites in places, mostly crushed and badly fragmented
3. Estimated 6 feet of brown, phosphatic dolomite and shale containing many small fossils; lower portion covered by talus

These beds are a portion of the lower part of the Elgin Member and among the most fossiliferous of those mentioned in this guide. After one hour of collecting, 1,711 fossils were found at level three. These included the following:

IDENTIFICATION	PERCENT
Brachiopods	6.83
Bryozoans	0.05
Echinoderm debris (mostly crinoidal)	0.53
Gastropods	
High-spired	10.75
Low-spired	2.63
Nautiloids	
Large (fragmented)	1.75
Small	76.09
Pelecypods	1.28

Source: Rose 1967.

This fauna is composed of small fossils and fragments of larger fossils and is called a depauperate or, more correctly, diminutive fauna. Similar diminutive faunas can be found in the upper levels of this cut, but the miniature nautiloids of level three were not seen above the graptolite level, which contains a fair abundance of *Diplograptus* (*Orthograptus*) *peosta*, but no other fossils were seen there. Above the graptolite level is one of rather large nautiloids. Although specimens are very abundant, many are broken. The other elements of this fauna are small and not damaged. The nautiloids seem to be fairly evenly scattered throughout the lower portion of level one, and many face an east-west direction. A total of 523 fossils were found after one hour of collecting at this level. The specimens included:

IDENTIFICATION	PERCENT
Brachiopods	
Diceromyonia tersa (orthid)	0.38
Gastropods	
High-spired	9.03
Low-spired	0.76
Nautiloids	
Isorthoceras sociale	95.60
Pelecypods	0.19
Trilobite pygidia	0.19

Source: Anderson 1978, Moore 1965, Rose 1967.

Site 28. Location: NW¼/SW¼ sec. 35, T95N, R7W. Just east of Clermont in Fayette County the lower part of the Elgin Member of the Maquoketa Formation is exposed in another popular collecting site. The exposures occur in a road cut and a dry creek bed under a bridge on county road B-60. Two faunas were collected, one from the exposure under the bridge and the other from the exposure in the road cut to the west.

The trilobite *Isotelus gigas* is abundant in both faunas here, but the only parts generally found intact are the pygidia (tails). These occur in abundance with a wide variety of sizes, but several were found broken or chipped. Pygidia are generally the most numerous and best preserved parts of the exoskeleton in any fauna where trilobite fossils are common. However, at this locality glabellae, isolated from the rest of the cranidia (heads), are also numerous. Cheek fragments are also common, but few thorax segments were found. Like most higher crustaceans, trilobites probably did not select certain areas for moulting (Schafer 1972). Their moulted exoskeletons were probably transported here by currents, representing an in situ accumulation.

Although the middle Elgin fauna is quite restricted in number of species at this site, it seems to be fairly evenly spread among the three major elements: the trilobite *I. gigas*, *Chondrites* burrows, and graptolite bits. Also present but much rarer are conularids (believed to be jellyfishlike coelenterata) and another species of *Isotelus*, *I. iowensis*. This species is difficult to distinguish from the much more numerous *I. gigas* unless entire specimens are found. In *I. iowensis* the cheeks are much longer, extending along the thorax part of the exoskeleton. This does not occur in *I. gigas*.

The majority of the fossils in the upper part of the Elgin, as with the middle fauna, are disarticulated or broken, with some forms occurring in clusters. The upper Elgin at this site carries abundant nautiloids of several types. Fragments measuring up to several inches in width and up to a foot long were found in the western cut during one hour of searching. These were of poor quality, however. More extensive collecting would probably yield some large, better quality nautiloids. The fauna at this cut included:

IDENTIFICATION	PERCENT
Burrows	
Chondrites sp.	15.15
Crinoid columnals	0.75
Fossils, unidentified	1.51
Gastropods	
Hormotoma sp.	1.51
Sinuites sp.	4.54
Graptolites	0.75
Nautiloids	
Endoceras fulgar	3.78
Actinoceras sp.	1.51
Dawsonoceras sp.	0.75
Isorthoceras sp.	40.15
Unidentified coiled	1.51
Trilobites	
Isotelus gigas (pygidia)	26.51
Unidentified pygidia	1.51

Source: Hogberg et al. 1967, Rose 1967, Shimer and Shrock 1972.

One hour of collecting provided 132 fossils from the upper Elgin Member. Although the graptolites at this level are few in number, they tend to be uncrushed and better preserved than those of the middle Elgin. Additional collecting yielded four specimens of the conularid *Conularia trentonensis*.

Site 29. Location: NW¼/NW¼/NE¼ sec. 10, T94N, R7W. There are many other exposures of fossiliferous limestone of the Elgin Member of the Maquoketa Formation in the vicinity of Clermont and Elgin in Fayette County. These occur in road and stream cuts. One of these occurs along the Turkey River between the two towns. Fossiliferous limestone of the Elgin Member can be found along the banks of the river under and near the Highway 172 bridge. Trilobite fragments are common here.

Site 30. Location: W½ sec. 18, T95N, R8W. The Clermont Member of the Maquoketa Formation consists of shales that are quickly eroded and grassed over. Exposures are few. A partial exposure, with the overlying Fort Atkinson Member, was examined along Highway 150 southwest of Eldorado in Fayette County. There is a high limestone bluff at this site (20 feet thick, estimated vertical measurement). This is part of the Fort Atkinson Member. The upper half of the bluff consists of brown cherty limestone with some fossils. The lower half consists of grayish cherty limestone, shaly near the base, and is rather fossiliferous. Fossils found near the base of the Fort Atkinson Member here include: trilobite fragments, brachiopods, crinoid columns, gastropods, nautiloids, and others. Many of the fossils are damaged, however. The contact between the Fort Atkinson and Clermont members is difficult to determine at most exposures because of the abundance of shale in the lower part of the Fort Atkinson Limestone. The Clermont Shale is best exposed just northeast of the face (Calvin Levorson, personal communication). The Clermont Member reportedly contains abundant brachiopod fauna, but no fossils were found at this site in a brief search. An exposure of dolomite occurs just south of this site and is believed to represent the Silurian Mosalem Formation.

Site 31. Location: NW¼ sec. 7, T88N, R2E. The Brainard Member of the Maquoketa Formation is composed of blue gray shale with brown dolomitic limestone interbeds, which can be very fossiliferous. An exposure was examined along Highway 20 just west of the Dubuque city limits in Dubuque County. The thick shale deposits here are not very fossiliferous. An interbed of dolomitic limestone occurs near the top of the slope and offers abundant fossils. Road cuts to the west expose Silurian formations.

The most abundant fossils here appear to be the bryozoans, the greatest concentration found by this author. The majority of fossils appear to be broken and/or disarticulated, with some forms more numerous in clusters. From what was seen, this type of preservation seems to be dominant in the Maquoketa faunas despite variations in lithology and fossils. A total of 503 fossils was found in the upper interbed of the Brainard Shale on the south slope of this site. This fauna included:

IDENTIFICATION	PERCENT
Brachiopods	
Diceromyonia tersa (orthid)	6.75
Platystrophia sp. (orthid)	4.17
Plaesiomys sp. (orthid)	3.37
Lepidocyclus laddi (rhynchonellid)	10.93
Strophomena sp. (strophomenid)	3.37
Bryozoans	
aff. *Prasopora* sp.	1.19
Branching, unidentified	43.73
Coral	
Streptelasma sp.	0.39
Crinoid columnals	19.88
Gastropods, unidentified	1.59
Mollusks	
Cornulites sp.	2.78
Nautiloids, unidentified	0.39
Trilobite pygidia, unidentified	0.19

Source: Anderson 1978, Hogberg et al. 1967, Moore 1965, Rose 1967, Shimer and Shrock 1972.

The mollusk *"Cornulites"* is an index fossil for the Brainard Member in Iowa. Although some of the largest Ordovician brachiopods can be found in the Brainard Shale at this site, particularly *Platystrophia*, most are not only disarticulated but fragmented as well. The Brainard fauna also has the greatest variety of crinoid columnals found in this study.

Site 32. Location: SW¼/SW¼/SW¼/SW¼ sec. 26, T88N, R3E. Another site exposing the Brainard Shale was located south of King in Dubuque County. This is to the south of a long road cut exposing several Silurian formations and is discussed in Chapter 4 (see Site 34). Actually, the Brainard Member is exposed at two locations here. One is on the eastern end of a trailer court, and the other is a lesser exposure on the western end.

4

Silurian Period

THE SILURIAN PERIOD began around 425 million years ago and ended 405 million years ago. Six formations make up the Silurian System in Iowa. These are primarily dolomites, and they are exposed in the east-central part of the state. The stratigraphic column for the Silurian System in Iowa is described below:

SERIES	FORMATION	MEMBER	DESCRIPTION
Wenlockian	Gower		dolomite
(middle)	Scotch Grove		dolomite, some chert
Llandoverian	Hopkinton	Unit C	dolomite
(lower)		Unit B	dolomite
		Unit A	dolomite and chert
	Blanding		cherty dolomite
	Tête des Morts		dolomite, some chert
	Mosalem		dolomite, some chert

Site 33. Location: NW¼/NW¼/SW¼ sec. 15, T91N, R2W. About 0.3 mile south of the Highway 52 bridge over the Turkey River at Millville in Clayton County, a bluff exposes three Silurian formations. The stratigraphic column for the cut is described below (Brian Witzke, personal communication, and the author):

I. Silurian Llandoverian Series
   A. Hopkinton Formation
      1. Unit A: equivalent to the Sweeney Formation in Illinois; represented by a single knob of massive, grayish white dolomite at the very top of the cut
   B. Blanding Formation
      1. "Chert Beds": vertical estimate of 35 feet of cherty tan dolomite
      2. "Lower Quarry Beds": vertical estimate of 10 feet of grayish dolomite with some chert
   C. Tête des Morts Formation: estimated 10 feet of grayish to tan dolomite at the base of the cut

A creekbed exposure to the south of the bluff is part of the Wise Lake Member of the Galena? Formation; the Dunleith Member of the Galena? is exposed in the deep ravine north of the bluff. These Ordovician deposits are discussed in Chapter 3 (Site 22).

All three Silurian formations exposed in the bluff are known to be fossiliferous at some outcrops; however, fossils are most common in the Hopkinton, and silicified corals and stromatoporoids occur in that formation at this site. These can be found in the talus along the creek on both sides of the highway just to the south of the bluff. A few dense boulders of the Hopkinton can also be found in the talus, and these contain large molds of *Pentamerus* and a few other brachiopods. Do not confuse these few dolomite boulders with the more common tan dolomite boulders of the Wise Lake Member of the Galena? Formation.

A similar, more complete exposure of these beds occurs about 0.5 mile south of this site (NE¼/NE¼/NE¼ sec. 21, T91N, R2W). The Silurian Hopkinton, Blanding, Tête des Morts, and Mosalem formations, along with the Ordovician Maquoketa, Dubuque, and Galena? formations, are exposed here and are described in Chapter 3 (see Site 22).

Site 34. Location: SE¼ sec. 27, T88N, R3W. South of King in Dubuque County along Highway 52 just north of the Jackson County line is a series of road cuts exposing four Silurian formations. The stratigraphic column for the sequence is described below (modified from Rose 1967):

I. Silurian Llandoverian Series
  A. Hopkinton Formation
    1. Unit A: equivalent to the Sweeney Formation in Illinois; a maximum of 15 feet of red brown dolomite exposed at the northern end of the sequence just south of the town; a few corals seen
  B. Blanding Formation:
    1. "Chert Beds": estimated 40 feet of dense cherty dolomite
    2. "Lower Quarry Beds": 10 feet of dolomite
  C. Tête des Morts Formation: estimated 20 feet of massive dolomite with some chert
  D. Mosalem Formation: estimated 50 feet of thin-bedded argillaceous dolomite

The first cut at the western end of the sequence exposes both the Hopkinton and Blanding formations. The second cut exposes the Blanding, Tête des Morts, and Mosalem formations. The third and final cut at the eastern end of the sequence exposes the Tête des Morts and Mosalem formations and is the longest of the three. The entire sequence spans 0.5 mile. Just south of the series of road cuts, the Brainard Member of the Maquoketa Formation (Ordovician) is exposed and is described in Chapter 3 (Site 32).

Site 35. Location: N½ sec. 1, T90N, R4W. This site is an abandoned quarry located 3 miles west of Colesburg in Delaware County on the north side of Highway 3. Fossiliferous, somewhat cherty dolomite (tan, weathering to gray) believed to be of "unit A" Hopkinton Formation (Brian Witzke, personal communication) is exposed here. The best preserved and most abundant fossils seem to occur in the quarry floor. A few poor quality brachiopods were the only fossils found in the face. Ninety-five fossils were found after one hour of searching and included brachiopods, stromatoporoids, and some excellent corals. The specimens found are listed below:

IDENTIFICATION	PERCENT
Brachiopods	
Platystrophia sp. (orthid)	6.31
Resserella sp. (orthid)	1.05
Rhynchotreta sp. (rhynchonellid)	4.21
Unidentified	23.15
Bryozoans, unidentified branching	5.26
Corals	
Favosites sp. (colonial)	5.26
Unidentified solitary	15.78
Echinoderm debris (mostly crinoidal)	16.83
Nautiloids, unidentified	1.05
Stromatoporoids	21.05

Source: Moore 1965, Rose 1967, Shimer and Shrock 1972.

Site 36. Location: NW¼ sec. 18, T84N, R2E. A quarry exposing unit A of the Hopkinton Formation was examined north of Maquoketa in Jackson County. This is the Schnoor Brothers' Quarry located 1 mile north of town and east of Highway 61 on a gravel road. Stop at the quarry office for permission to collect. The best time to visit the quarry is probably on Saturday morning. The rock exposed here is a tan dolomite with some chert. Three separate faunas were noticed by this collector. The first was found near the top of the face. At this level, fossils were found in small, dense clusters; only rarely were they found outside these clusters. The predominant fossil at this level is the large pentamerid brachiopod *Pentamerus oblongus,* sometimes reaching lengths of over 6 inches. The fauna at this level included the following:

IDENTIFICATION	PERCENT
Brachiopods	
Pentamerus oblongus (pentamerid)	95.90
Leptaena rhomboidalis (strophomenid)	0.58
Coral, unidentified solitary	2.92
Gastropods, unidentified	0.58

Source: Rose 1967.

A total of 177 fossils were found after one hour of collecting. Very large specimens of the brachiopod *Pentamerus oblongus* represented around 16 percent of the fossils found. A similar large pentamerid, *Pentameroides,* occurs in parts of the Scotch Grove Formation.

The second fauna covers most of the quarry face above the water level and below the *Pentamerus* fauna. It is apparently made up mostly of colonial corals. Although some excellent specimens of *Halysites, Favosites,* and *Syringopora,* among others, can be found, these are not overly abundant.

Part of the quarry face is submerged, but a level only 5 feet above the water level was reached. The area examined was small, but the fauna suggests conditions different from the other two communities examined here. This level is composed of greenish gray dolomite and contains a fair amount of complete fossils. It appears quite similar to the quarry exposure west of Colesburg (Site 35). Only 17 fossils were found, the most common being the orthid brachiopod *Hesperorthis,* the colonial coral *Favosites,* and solitary corals. Stromatoporoids, other colonial corals, branching bryozoans, and other brachiopods were also found.

Site 37. Location: C sec. 26, T89N, R6W. To reach the site, begin in the town of Manchester, Delaware County. Proceed west on old Highway 20 (not Freeway 20) for about 2 miles from the city limits. The main road curves south here, but instead turn north on a gravel road. A series of road cuts will be seen extending for almost 1 mile. Exposed here is gray brown to greenish cherty limestone of the La Porte City Formation. Until fairly recently the La Porte City was considered to be a Lower Devonian formation with no known outcrops. These road cuts are now known to expose the La Porte City, and the fossils are clearly Silurian in age. Currently, the La Porte City is considered to be a limestone facies equivalent to the upper part of the Hopkinton, and the Scotch Grove formations. These particular cuts are laterally equivalent to the Hopkinton Formation "unit C" and the basal Scotch Grove Formation, which in turn is equivalent to the "Racine" Formation in northwest Illinois.

One hour of collecting here yielded a total of 200 fossils, of which the most common were crinoid columnals (most quite small), corals, and brachiopods. The fossils found are listed below:

IDENTIFICATION	PERCENT
Algae, green (*Ischadites*-like)	3.00
Brachiopods	
Resserella sp. (orthid)	1.00
Plicostricklandia sp. (pentamerid)	0.50
?*Microcardinalia* sp. (pentamerid)	1.00
Eospirifer sp. (spiriferid)	1.00
?*Cyrtia* sp. (spiriferid)	2.00
Strophonella sp. (strophomenid)	2.00
Unidentified	1.50
Burrows	1.50
Corals	
Halysites sp. (colonial)	5.50
Heliolites megastoma (colonial)	7.50
Syringopora sp. (colonial)	0.50
Favosites sp. (colonial)	5.00
Small solitary	13.00
Large solitary	10.00

SILURIAN PERIOD

IDENTIFICATION	PERCENT
Crinoid columnals	25.99
Nautiloids, unidentified small	5.00
Pelecypods, unidentified	2.00
Stromatoporoids	13.00

Source: Johnson 1975, Moore 1965, Rose 1967, Shimer and Shrock 1972.

Most fossils found at this site are undamaged and articulated; however, a few of the brachiopods are broken. Some excellent coral specimens can be found here, including some solitary corals in the chert that is so prevalent in the La Porte City Facies.

Site 38. Location: C sec. 7, T85N, R2W. An abandoned quarry and adjacent road cut exposing the base of the Scotch Grove Formation were examined north of Scotch Grove in Jones County. The quarry is located on the west side of Highway 38. The lower part of the Scotch Grove Formation, Buck Creek Quarry Facies, is considered to be late Llandoverian-Lower Silurian in age; the rest of the Scotch Grove Formation is Wenlockian-Middle Silurian (Witzke 1981). At some localities the lower Scotch Grove is reported to be quite fossiliferous (Witzke 1981), but at this site the author found only a few brachiopods and colonial corals.

Site 39. Location: W½ sec. 10, T84N, R4W. The upper part of the Buck Creek Quarry, Waubeek, Fawn Creek, and Palisades-Kepler Mound facies all occur in the upper Scotch Grove Formation and are laterally equivalent (Witzke 1981). An exposure of the Buck Creek Quarry Facies occurs in a small, abandoned quarry behind the Eden Golf Carts building in the southwestern part of Anamosa, Jones County, west of the Anamosa city park. Exposed here is fossiliferous, dense, cherty dolomite. Fossils commonly found in the Buck Creek Quarry Facies include brachiopods; nautiloids; gastropods; colonial corals, including *Halysites* and *Favosites;* solitary corals, including the "button coral" *Porpites;* and others. Collecting at this site is not permitted.

Site 40. Location: SE¼/NE¼ sec. 10, T84N, R4W. The Palisades-Kepler Mound Facies of the upper part of the Scotch Grove Formation is exposed in an abandoned quarry in a city park in the southwestern part of Anamosa, Jones County. This is east of Site 39. Brown dolomite is exposed here; some fossils can be found, including brachiopods, crinoid columns, and nautiloids, some of which can be quite large.

Site 41. Location: S½/NE¼ sec. 17, T85N, R5W. Exposed in a road cut near Waubeek in Linn County are at least 40 feet of brown dolomite of the Waubeek Facies of the Scotch Grove Formation. One way to reach the site is to begin at the bridge over the Wapsipinicon River in the northeastern part of the town. Take county road E-28 (gravel) in a northeastern direction for about 2.5 miles to the road cut on the north side of the road. Some fossils can usually be found here by breaking the rock. Crinoid columnals and small brachiopods were seen by this collector.

Site 42. Location: C sec. 10, T88N, R£W. Several exposures previously assigned to the Le Claire Facies of the Gower Formation are now assigned to the Palisades-Kepler Mound Facies of the Scotch Grove Formation. One of these is the Hunt Quarry. The name "Le Claire Facies" is still used but is restricted to outcrops in Scott County (Witzke 1981).

The Hunt Quarry is located north of Cedar Bluff in Cedar County. To reach the site, begin at the town of Cedar Bluff. On the east side of the Cedar River, turn north on a gravel road. Continue north for about 2 miles. The road curves east and back north again. At a T intersection turn west. After a fraction of a mile, this road curves north also. Continue north for just under 2 miles to the quarry entrance. Next to a farm you should see an east-bearing lane posted with a small rusted sign saying "no trespassing without permission from the owner." This lane leads to the Hunt Quarry. It is advisable to visit on a weekday.

Exposed here is a bioherm (reef) that rose from the sea floor to at least near the surface of the water of the Palisades-Kepler Mound Facies. The rock in the core, the center of which composes the hill at the beginning of quarry, is made up of massive, generally unbedded, grayish to tan dolomite. Although fossils can be found in the core, they are apparently more abundant and better preserved in the face opposite the hill.

The majority of fossils found here are empty molds, and the rock is quite dense. As many fossils as possible were removed for the survey, and the rest were recorded in the field. Some large, excellent stromatoporoids and colonial corals were found, some of which were too large to remove. Because of the difficulties in collecting, more time (about a half hour more) was spent compiling a faunal list here than for most other sites examined. Most fossils were found to occur in clusters, especially the brachiopod *Stegerhynchus,* of which around 200 specimens were found in one small, tightly packed cluster. Very long crinoid columns and groups of three or four calyces can be found. All the crinoid debris was attributed to the genus *Eucalyptocrinites,* with identification based on the calyces. Although most of the columns are very similar in appearance, there could have been several crinoid genera present whose calyces were not preserved. The fauna found at this site included:

IDENTIFICATION	PERCENT
Brachiopods	
Platystrophia sp. (orthid)	0.58
?*Rhipidomella* sp. (orthid)	0.29
Pliostricklandia sp. (pentamerid)	0.58
Stegerhynchus sp. (rhynchonellid)	58.65
Atrypa sp. (spiriferid)	0.87
Leptaena sp. (strophomenid)	0.87
Bryozoans	
Unidentified branching	0.58
Unidentified lacy	0.29
Corals	
Favosites sp. (colonial)	9.38
Unidentified solitary	1.75
Crinoids	
Eucalyptocrinites sp.	21.99

SILURIAN PERIOD   35

IDENTIFICATION	PERCENT
Gastropods, unidentified	3.22
Nautiloids, unidentified	0.29
Stromatoporoids	0.58

Source: Anderson 1978, Hinman 1968, Moore 1965, Rose 1967, Shimer and Shrock 1972.

A total of 341 fossils was found in the Palisades-Kepler Mound Facies in the Hunt Quarry. The rhynchonellid brachiopod *Stegerhynchus* would have been much less numerous if a dense cluster of specimens had not been found. On the other hand, more such clusters must exist here, and the collector cannot disregard them.

Site 43. Location: NW¼ sec. 6, T84N, R4W. The Weber Stone Company Quarry is just north of Stone City in Jones County. There are several quarries in this area. This one is located at the Weber office. Collectors are asked to obtain permission (Weber Stone Co., Inc., R.R. #1, Anamosa, IA 52205) and sign a release form at the office. Full safety equipment is required. Exposed in the quarry are the Scotch Grove and Gower formations. The Weber mine is located 0.5 mile east of this site and is opened up in the Gower Formation. The stratigraphic column for the quarry is described below (Witzke 1981):

I. Gower Formation
   A. Anamosa Facies
      1. "Upper unit": at least 20 feet of laminated porous dolomite exposed in the uppermost part of the third-level face
      2. "White unit": 40 feet of brown dolomite, laminated to thin-bedded with some chert; no fossils seen; exposed in the third-level face
      3. "Bad Ledge": 4 feet of grayish dolomite exposed at the base of the third-level face; no fossils seen
      4. "Gray unit": estimated 18 feet of brown laminated dolomite; no fossils seen; exposed in the second level of the quarry at the top of the lower face
II. Scotch Grove Formation
   A. Waubeek Facies: at least 30 feet of gray to brown dolomite with some fossils; exposed in the lower level of the quarry and on the quarry floor

This is the type locality for the Anamosa Facies.

Site 44. Location: NE¼ sec. 32, T85N, R4W. To reach the site, turn northwest on Iowa Street in Anamosa, Jones County, and continue northwest out of town on the paved road. Exposures of dolomite bearing characteristics of both the Waubeek and Fawn Creek facies occur along the road between the town and the old State Penitentiary Quarry located about 2 miles northwest of Anamosa along Buffalo Creek. The pavement ends here. Also note a road cut exposure just northwest of the quarry. The

Waubeek and Anamosa facies are exposed here. Continue northwest for about 1 mile from the quarry to another cut on the east side of the road, with Buffalo Creek to the west. The stratigraphic column for this cut is described below (Witzke 1981):

I. Gower Formation
   A. Anamosa Facies: at least 15 feet of dolomite, laminated at the base and 5 feet from the top, exposed in the cut; more of the Anamosa exposed in the slope above the cut
II. Scotch Grove Formation
   A. Waubeek Facies: around 8 feet of brown dolomite exposed in the lower part of the cut; a few crinoid columns and brachiopods seen

At this site the contact between the Waubeek and Anamosa facies is not clearly shown because of interbedding between the two, suggesting that the uppermost part of the Waubeek and the lowermost part of the Anamosa may be laterally equivalent (Witzke 1981).

Site 45. Location: NW¼/SE¼ sec. 14, T80N, R3W. The Brady Facies of the Gower Formation is laterally equivalent to the Anamosa Facies. In several quarries the brown, very fossiliferous, unbedded to steep-bedded dolomite of the Brady Facies contrasts sharply with the poorly fossiliferous, flat-bedded dolomites of the Anamosa Facies. Fossils in the Brady generally include a great abundance of rhynchonellid brachiopods, other brachiopods, corals, nautiloids, and others. Both facies are well exposed at the McGuire Quarry located southwest of Tipton in Cedar County (Brian Witzke 1981 and personal communication). To reach the quarry, take county road F-36 (paved) southwest out of Tipton for about 3 miles from the city limits. Then turn southeast on a gravel road and continue for about 1.5 miles to a T intersection. Turn east and continue for a fraction of a mile to another T intersection. Turn north and follow the road as it curves east and continue about 1 mile to the quarry on the south side of the road. This is the type locality for the Brady Facies.

A few other exposures of the Gower Formation are discussed in Chapter 5 in connection with Devonian deposits (Sites 48 and 49). These are not very fossiliferous.

5

Devonian Period

THE DEVONIAN PERIOD began 405 million years ago and ended 345 million years ago. The Devonian System of Iowa consists mostly of limestones, shales, and dolomitic limestones. At least two Devonian formations in the state are very famous for their abundant and well-preserved fossils—the Cedar Valley and Lime Creek formations. The stratigraphic column for the Devonian System in Iowa is listed below:

SERIES	FORMATION	MEMBER	DESCRIPTION
Upper Devonian	English River		siltstone
	Maple Mill		shale
	Aplington		dolomitic limestone
	Sheffield		shale
	Lime Creek	Owen	dolomite, limestone
		Cerro Gordo	shale, shaly limestone
		Juniper Hill	shale
	Shell Rock	Nora	limestone, shale
		Rock Grove	limestone, shale, dolomite
		Mason City	limestone
	State Quarry		limestone
Middle Devonian	Cedar Valley	Coralville	limestone
		Rapid	limestone
		Solon	limestone
	Wapsipinicon	Davenport	dolomitic limestone
		Spring Grove	dolomitic limestone
		Kenwood	shale
		Otis	limestone
		Coggon	dolomitic limestone
	Bertram		dolomite

The Sheffield, Aplington, Maple Hill, and English River formations make up the Yellow Spring Group, which is the only Devonian group recognized in Iowa.

Site 46. Location: S¼ sec. 29, T84N, R5W. On the western edge of Springville on Highway 151 in Linn County is an exposure of dolomite, which occurs on the north side of the highway east of a bridge and is described below:

1. Dolomite, at least 3 feet exposed at the top of the cut; brown; some chert
2. A covered interval of a few feet
3. Dolomite, at least 5 feet exposed at the base of the cut; gray and dense

There is a quarry located north and east of this cut; it reportedly exposes the Bertram Formation and the Palisades-Kepler Mound Facies of the Scotch Grove Formation (formerly the Le Claire Facies of the Gower Formation) (Anderson 1978). For this reason, this road cut has been identified as being part of the Bertram Formation. Visits to the quarry are not allowed.

Site 47. Location: SE¼/NE¼/NE¼ sec. 9, T82N, R6W. At the northeast corner of the junction of Highways 13 and 30 east of Cedar Rapids in Linn County is a road cut exposing the Otis Member of the Wapsipinicon Formation. Brachiopods are reportedly found here (Witzke 1981), but no collecting was done by the author.

Site 48. Location: SE¼ sec. 28, T86N, R6W. An excellent exposure of the Wapsipinicon Formation was examined near Central City in Linn County. A fraction of a mile north of the Wapsipinicon River bridge on Highway 13 at Central City, turn west on an unpaved road. Continue west for about 1 mile, passing a riverside park. A road cut will first come into view on the right side of the road. A quarry is located at the northern end of the cut and to the east. The stratigraphic column for the site is described below (modified from Rose 1967):

I. Devonian Wapsipinicon Formation
   A. Davenport Member: limestone, brecciated in places; a few feet reportedly present at the top of the quarry face but this not seen by the author; a few fragments believed to be of the Davenport found scattered about on the quarry floor
   B. Spring Grove Member: estimated 10 feet of yellowish to tan dolomitic limestone exposed at the top of the quarry face
   C. Kenwood Member: 15.5 feet of grayish shale and grayish dolomitic limestone
   D. Otis Member: 15 feet of light tan dolomitic limestone with a thin shale deposit near the base; the lower part of this member also present at the top of the road cut
   E. Coggon Member: 5.5 feet of brown dolomitic limestone; 1 foot exposed at the base of the quarry face; also forms the quarry floor; the entire member present in the road cut
II. Silurian Gower Formation: estimated 5 feet of dolomite exposed at the base of the road cut

Site 49. Location: SE¼/NW¼ sec. 8, T78N, R2W. The large operating quarry near Moscow in Muscatine County exposes a complicated sequence. To reach the site, go west on Highway 6 from the Moscow corner. Cross the bridge over the Cedar River and take the first road north on the western end of the bridge. The road is paved. Continue north, passing a gravel pit on the right. The quarry will appear on the left. Stop at the quarry office for permission to collect. This is a very busy site, and collectors are asked to visit on Saturday mornings. The sequence exposed is described below (Fred Dorheim, formerly of the Iowa Geological Survey, personal communication):

I. Devonian Cedar Valley Formation
   A. Rapid and Solon members: represented by a thick grayish white limestone in the upper face
II. Devonian Wapsipinicon Formation
   A. Spring Grove Member: 18 feet of brown dolomitic limestone and limestone
III. Silurian Gower Formation: around 10 feet of brown dolomite exposed in the lower part of the quarry

Fossils are apparently rare in this quarry. The few exceptions occur in the Solon Member. Twenty-four brachiopods were found in one isolated cluster, and most were badly fragmented. The specimens found are listed below:

IDENTIFICATION	PERCENT
Brachiopods	
Schizophoria sp. (orthid)	8.33
Orbiculoidea sp. (inarticulate)	4.16
Atrypa sp. (spiriferid)	66.66
Tenticospirifer sp. (spiriferid)	8.33
Cranaena sp. (terebratulid)	8.33
Burrows	4.16

Source: Moore 1965, Rose 1967.

Site 50. Location: SW¼/SE¼/SW¼ sec. 10, T85N, R10N. Quarry at Vinton in Benton County.

Site 51. Location: C/NW¼ sec. 2, T88N, R9W. Quarry at Independence in Buchanan County.

The Cedar Valley Formation of Iowa provides some excellently preserved prehistoric communities. The Solon Member is abundantly fossiliferous in places, one of which is the "Judge Nichols" Quarry north of Vinton. To reach the site, take Highway 101 north out of Vinton and cross the Cedar River twice. Then take the first gravel road east to the quarry. Stop at the quarry office for permission to collect. As with all operating quarries, it is a good idea to check back at the office when you leave. This quarry exposes the Solon Member, with part of the Rapid Member occurring at the top of the quarry face. Few fossils can be found in the Rapid here, and the member is difficult to distinguish from the Solon.

The Solon Member is also exposed in a quarry on the south side of old Highway 20 (not Freeway 20) on the eastern edge of Independence. The Davenport Member of the Wapsipinicon Formation reportedly occurs in the deepest part of this quarry (Rose 1967) but was not seen by this collector.

At both these quarries, the Solon Member is represented by gray to tan fossiliferous limestone. Preservation at both quarries is very similar, and environmental conditions during deposition must have been similar as well. A total of 589 specimens were found at Vinton and 709 at Independence. The fossils found are listed below:

IDENTIFICATION	VINTON	INDEPENDENCE
	(%)	(%)
Brachiopods		
Schizophoria sp. (orthid)	5.77	5.21
Gypidula typicalis (pentamerid)	...	0.18
Productella sp. (productid)	2.03	0.70
Spinocyrtia iowensis (spiriferid)	62.64	4.51
Atrypa independensis (spiriferid)	5.77	47.39
Spinatrypa "bellula" (spiriferid)	2.88	2.11
Acutatheca propria (spiriferid)	7.64	1.83
Spinocyrtia macbridei (spiriferid)	1.69	...
Strophodonta sp. (strophomenid)	...	0.84
Cranaena sp. (terebratulid)	...	0.70
Bryozoans		
Encrusting	0.84	0.84
Branching (small)	...	5.92
Branching (large)	...	0.28
Lacy	...	1.41
Corals		
Aulopora sp. (colonial)	3.39	...
Favosites sp. (colonial)	...	1.12
Hexagonaria sp. (colonial)	...	0.14
Heliophyllum halli (solitary)	0.50	1.83
Cystiphyllum sp. (solitary)	...	5.92
Zaphrentis sp. (solitary)	...	0.56
Crinoid columnals	1.69	14.10
Gastropods		
Straparollus sp.	...	0.14
Nautiloids, unidentified	0.16	...
Pelecypods, unidentified	1.18	0.14
Stromatoporoids	1.86	3.52
Trilobites		
Greenops sp. (pygidia)	0.16	...
Worm tubes		
Spirorbis sp.	1.01	0.42
Vertebrate fragments	0.67	...

Source: Moore 1965, Rose 1967, Shimer and Shrock 1972.

Some species are found in dense clusters at both quarries. The spiriferid *Atrypa independensis* occurs in loosely defined clusters at Vinton and seems to be associated with solitary corals. The spiriferid *Spinocyrtia iowensis* is also found in dense clusters but, unlike *A. independensis*, is only rarely found as isolated individuals. Also found in the *S. iowensis* clusters, sometimes occurring as isolated individuals, are the spiriferids *S. macbridei* and *Acutatheca propria* and the orthid *Schizophoria*. The only colonial corals and bryozoans found at Vinton were commensals. (Note: Additional collecting at Vinton revealed a few small, branching bryozoans in an *Atrypa* cluster, but they are not included in the faunal list because they were not found in the first hour of collecting.) The encrusting bryozoans generally were found near the anterior margin of *S. iowensis*, but a few were also found encrusting pelecypods. The coral *Aulopora* and the *Spirorbis* worm tubes also were found on *S. iowensis* but not on any other species here.

The dominant species at Independence is the spiriferid *Atrypa independensis* (47 percent). At Vinton this species represents only 6 percent of the fauna. Furthermore, the dominant species at Vinton (*S. iowensis*, 63 percent) represents only 5 percent of the fauna at Independence. Like the Vinton fauna, these two species formed clusters at Independence. The spiriferids *S. macbridei* and *Acutatheca propria*, which commonly occurred in the *S. iowensis* clusters at Vinton, are much less numerous at Independence. The fifth spiriferid, *Spinatrypa*, occurs in equal abundance in both faunas. Also note that the *Atrypa independensis* clusters of Vinton were usually found in association with solitary corals and sometimes included branching bryozoans. All three forms are much more numerous at Independence.

The Independence fauna also has an epifauna, but no specimens of *Aulopora* were found. Unlike the Vinton epifauna, which favored *S. iowensis* as a host, the Independence epifauna favored *A. independensis*. However, since *S. iowensis* is much less numerous at Independence yet still served as host for several commensals, these organisms probably favored that brachiopod, but many were evidently forced to switch to *Atrypa* in this fauna. Bryozoans are much more numerous at Independence, and encrusting bryozoans on *S. iowensis* occur almost as frequently as at Vinton; but in the Independence fauna, bryozoans encrust *A. independensis* twice as often as *S. iowensis*. At Vinton no bryozoan encrustations of *A. independensis* were found. (Please note that these observations were made by the author and may not necessarily reflect scientific fact).

At Independence, the limestone is crinoidal in places. At Vinton, pygidia and other fragments of the trilobite *Greenops* were found, and entire specimens may also be present. Additional collecting at Vinton also revealed the presence of the pentamerid brachiopod *Gypidula typicalis*.

Site 52. Location: C sec. 34, T88N, R8W. Exposures of the Cedar Valley Formation, probably the Solon Member, occur along the Wapsipinicon River in the vicinity of Quasqueton in Buchanan County. One exposure was examined and is located under the Highway 282 bridge on the southern edge of town. Solitary corals were found in abundance, and a few brachiopods were also collected.

Site 53. Location: NE¼/NE¼ sec. 33, T84N, R11W. An exposure of the Cedar Valley Formation was also examined near Garrison in Benton County west of Vinton. There are two quarries here, located on both sides of county road E-22 (paved) south and east of Garrison. The southern quarry was examined. Collectors are advised to visit the quarry on Saturday mornings. The upper part exposes roughly 10 feet of tan to gray limestone, probably of the Rapid Member. A wide variety of stromatoporoids can be found at this level; some are replaced by pyrite, but they are generally not very abundant. A few large nautiloid fragments were also found. The most striking fossils found here, however, are a few white bryozoan colonies preserved in pockets of reddish orange limestone. The contrast in color is striking. Below this level is a zone of gray shale at least 1 foot thick, in which no fossils were seen. Below the shale zone is a zone of brown dolomitic limestone several feet thick. This level is also believed to be in the Rapid Member. An abundance of brachiopod casts occur here. One hour of collecting yielded 209 fossils. These are listed below:

IDENTIFICATION	PERCENT
Brachiopods	
Camarotoechia sp. (rhynchonellid)	5.03
Atrypa independensis (spiriferid)	89.92
Spinocyrtia iowensis (spiriferid)	0.71
Unidentified	2.15
Burrows	1.43
Nautiloids, unidentified	0.71

Source: Moore 1965, Rose 1967, Shimer and Shrock 1972.

Fossils occur in clusters in this level. Below the dolomitic limestone is limestone of considerable thickness. This is probably the rest of the Rapid Member and the Solon Member. However, this lower level of the quarry was not accessible because the road was flooded.

Site 54. Location: eastern boundary between sec. 16 and 21, T92N, R14W. An exposure of the Rapid Member of the Cedar Valley Formation was examined north of Waverly in Bremer County. To reach the road cut, take Highway 218 south out of Plainfield for 4.5 miles; then turn eastward on a paved county road (C-33), which is unmarked. Continue for just under 3 miles, crossing the Cedar River. The exposures are on both sides of the road, the best occurring just west of a small creek. Present here is gray to brown, bedded limestone. Chert and small quartz geodes were found, but no fossils were seen.

Site 55. Location: E½ sec. 16, T79W, R6W. Exposures of the Coralville Member of the Cedar Valley Formation occur in Iowa City, Johnson County, near the western bank of the Iowa River. Fossils can be found here, including brachiopods and corals, but no serious collecting was done.

DEVONIAN PERIOD

Site 56. Location: SW¼/SW¼/SW¼/SW¼ sec. 26, T81N, R7W. An excellent exposure of the Coralville Member occurs north of North Liberty in Johnson County. The quarry is abandoned and is located about 2 miles north of the town along Highway 218. This is the Mid-river Quarry, just north of the Marina 218, on the west shore of the Coralville Reservoir, and is the northern one of two public picnic sites in the area. Exposed here are gray to brown limestones that vary from thick-bedded to shaly. Most of the quarry exposes the Coralville Member, but part of the Rapid Member also occurs in the lower levels. Some brown, thin-bedded zones of the Coralville Member here contain burrows identical to those found in the Mississippian Gilmore City Formation at Gilmore City. The fauna collected from this quarry is one of the most highly varied examined for this book. The fossils found are listed below:

IDENTIFICATION	PERCENT
Brachiopods	
Schizophoria sp. (orthid)	3.32
Gypidula typicalis (pentamerid)	1.03
Atrypa independensis (spiriferid)	17.87
Atrypa waterlooensis (spiriferid)	1.03
Spinocyrtia iowensis (spiriferid)	12.68
Theodossia sp. (spiriferid)	0.20
Tenticospirifer sp. (spiriferid)	1.24
"*Spirifer*" *orestes* (spiriferid)	0.20
Strophodonta sp. (strophomenid)	0.20
Douvillina sp. (strophomenid)	0.83
Strophonelloides sp. (strophomenid)	0.41
Leptaena sp. (strophomenid)	0.20
Cranaena romingeri (terebratulid)	1.03
Cranaena iowensis (terebratulid)	1.03
Bryozoans	
Branching (large)	4.98
Branching (small)	2.07
Encrusting	0.20
Lacy	1.45
Burrows	10.39
Corals	
Hexagonaria parvula (colonial)	0.83
Favosites sp. (colonial)	2.49
Aulopora sp. (colonial)	0.41
Billingsastrea billingsi (colonial)	0.20
Heliophyllum halli (solitary)	2.28
Zaphrentis sp. (solitary)	0.83
Cystiphyllum sp. (solitary)	2.70
Crinoid columnals	20.79
Echinoid spines	0.20
Mollusks	
Tentaculites sp.	6.02
Stromatoporoids	1.45
Trilobites	
Proetus sp. (pygidiun)	0.20

Source: Moore 1965, Rose 1967, Shimer and Shrock 1972.

Spirifer is a Mississippian genus, but a few specimens of a very similar but unidentified genus were found in several Devonian formations in Iowa and are listed as *"Spirifer."*

A total of 481 fossils were found in this quarry. Thin zones of small fossils were observed and contained crinoid columnals, the spiriferid *Tenticospirifer*, the mollusk *Tentaculites*, and a pygidium of the trilobite *Proetus*, as well as other specimens.

Site 57. Location: near C sec. 5, T80N, R6W. An exposure of the State Quarry Formation was examined near North Liberty in Johnson County. To reach the site, begin at the junction of county roads W-66 (paved, bears northwest) and F-28 (paved, bears north and then east). The junction occurs in the northeastern part of town. Go east on county road F-28 for about 3 miles to the Mahaffey Bridge over the Coralville Reservoir. At the western end of the bridge, turn south into a parking area. (Note: If you approach Mahaffey Bridge from Solon, the road crosses a smaller bridge before the larger Mahaffey Bridge.) From the parking area proceed south on foot along the western shore of the reservoir for about 0.5 mile to the old State Quarry from which the formation got its name. Exposures of the State Quarry Formation can also be seen on the opposite shore of the reservoir. Limestone from this quarry was used in the construction of several buildings in Iowa City, including the old State Capitol Building.

The limestone here is grayish white and quite fossiliferous. A brief stop yielded an abundance of brachiopods, including *Atrypa* and *Douvillina*; a wide variety of crinoid columnals; branching bryozoans; and both solitary and colonial corals, including an excellent specimen of *Billingsastrea*.

The road cut at the eastern end of the Mahaffey Bridge exposes fossiliferous limestone of the Coralville Member of the Cedar Valley Formation, but the site is on a geological preserve and collecting is not permitted.

Site 58. At least 5 feet of brown and gray limestone is exposed in a road cut west of Osage in Mitchell County. The site is located just west of the Highway 9 bridge over the Cedar River. An abundance of stromatoporoids was found, but no other fossils were seen. This is probably part of the Cedar Valley Formation, Coralville? Member.

Site 59. Location: NE¼/NE¼/NE¼/NE¼ sec. 18, T96N, R18W. The Shell Rock Formation is well exposed in the Nora Springs area in Floyd County. The lower levels of the Mason City Member of the Shell Rock Formation and part of the Coralville Member of the Cedar Valley Formation are exposed in a low bluff on the eastern bank of the Shell Rock River just south of the Highway 18 bridge in Nora Springs. Fossils reportedly occur in both members, but no collecting was done. The Rock Grove and Nora members of the Shell Rock Formation also crop out along the river in this area (Koch 1970).

Site 60. Location: near C sec. 7, T96N, R18W. The rest of the Mason City Member and the lower part of the Rock Grove Member are exposed in

DEVONIAN PERIOD

Mill Dam Park and on the opposite bank of the Shell Rock River in Nora Springs. To reach the park, turn north from Highway 18 on the street leading to the city park east of the river. Continue north on this street, passing the city park. The road then curves west and follows the river to Mill Dam Park. Fragments of the Mason City and Shell Rock members can be found along the river here, and a few fossils are present. A stream cut near the parking area exposes the Mason City Member, but the Rock Grove is only poorly exposed. Fossils occur in the Mason City Member, but this exposure may not be very accessible when the water level is high. The best fossil collecting can be done in the bluffs across the river. To reach them, turn north on the first street west of the Highway 18 bridge over the Shell Rock River. Continue north on this street until it meets the river at the Mill Dam. Exposed here are at least 5 feet of grayish green limestone representing the Mason City Member of the Shell Rock Formation. The lower, thin-bedded units exposed just above the water level can be reached at only a few places here. This level contains a fair abundance of brachiopods, and the limestone is partially crinoidal. The top of the bluff is well exposed and offers the best of the preserved coral-stromatoporoid communities described in this book. Brachiopods and a few gastropods are also present at this level. This fauna will be labeled the "upper" Mason City fauna, and the fauna collected just above the water level will be labeled the "middle" Mason City fauna. Alternating thin beds of brown to gray shale and limestone of the overlying Rock Grove Member have been bricked over to slow erosion.

The faunas of the Mason City Member found at the Mill Dam included the following (a total of 157 fossils of the middle fauna and 306 fossils of the upper fauna were found):

IDENTIFICATION	MIDDLE	UPPER
	(%)	(%)
Brachiopods		
Schizophoria sp. (orthid)	...	0.65
Gypidula sp. (pentamerid)	...	1.63
Camarotoechia sp. (rhynchonellid)	...	5.22
Tenticospirifer sp. (spiriferid)	26.11	1.30
Spinatrypa sp. (spiriferid)	3.82	0.98
Atrypa sp. (spiriferid)	5.09	20.91
Cyrtospirifer sp. (spiriferid)	...	1.63
Douvillina sp. (strophomenid)	...	3.92
Cranaena sp. (terebratulid)	0.63	4.57
Corals		
Pachyphyllum woodmani (colonial)	...	6.86
Cystiphyllum sp. (solitary)	...	6.53
Zaphrentis sp. (solitary)	...	0.32
Homalophyllum sp. (solitary)	...	2.94
Crinoid columnals	63.39	0.98
Gastropods		
Straparollus sp.	...	0.65
Nautiloids, unidentified	0.63	...
Stromatoporoids	...	40.84

Source: Moore 1965, Rose 1967, Shimer and Shrock 1972.

Site 61. Location: NE/¼NE/¼/NE¼ sec. 17, T96N, R18W. The upper part of the Shell Rock Formation is exposed in an abandoned quarry near Nora Springs in Floyd County. On the eastern edge of town, take Rock Grove Drive south from Highway 18. The gravel road curves east. In a wooded area south of the road, near a small stream, is the old quarry. "No trespassing" signs are clearly visible, but collectors can obtain permission from the owner: Francis Sherman, Nora Springs, IA 50458. The exposure is described below (Rose 1967):

I. Shell Rock Formation
   A. Nora Member
      1. Dark gray limestone, a stromatoporoid biostrome; 5 feet exposed at the top of the face; abundance of stromatoporoids but no other fossils seen
      2. Five feet of yellowish shale; no fossils seen, not even in a 25-pound bulk sample
      3. Five feet of lighter gray limestone, the lower stromatoporoid biostrome of the Nora; stromatoporoids abundant, but a few corals and brachiopods also collected
   B. Rock Grove Member
      1. Nearly 5 feet of brown dolomite; brachiopod casts occur in clusters
      2. Around 7 feet of shale and thin limestone beds generally covered
      3. Six feet of brown dolomite, poorly exposed
      4. Thin shale and limestone beds poorly exposed along the stream. This is the level blocked over at the Mill Dam exposure (see Site 57).

Faunas were collected from the upper dolomite zone of the Rock Grove Member and from the lower biostrome of the Nora Member. One hour of collecting yielded 47 fossils from the Rock Grove, and these are listed below:

IDENTIFICATION	PERCENT
Brachiopods	
Gypidula sp. (pentamerid)	2.12
Cyrtospirifer sp. (spiriferid)	65.95
Spinocyrtia ulsterensis (spiriferid)	29.78
Atrypa sp. (spiriferid)	2.12

Source: Moore 1965, Rose 1967.

Site 62. Location: NW¼/SW¼ sec. 28, T96N, R18W. A nearly complete section of the Shell Rock Formation occurs at the Williams Quarry near Nora Springs in Floyd County. To reach the quarry, continue east from the previous exposure on Rock Grove Drive (Site 61). Within a short distance, a T intersection will come into view. To the north is Highway 18. Turn south on a gravel road. Continue south for a little less than 2 miles, following the Shell Rock River part of the way. Then turn west on the second gravel road bearing west. Follow this road to the quarry. The stratigraphic sequence exposed here is given below (Koch 1970):

I. Shell Rock Formation
   A. Nora Member: lower biostrome limestone, 5 feet exposed at the top of the face; grayish with abundant stromatoporoids, which can be found strewn about on the quarry floor
   B. Rock Grove Member
      1. Dolomite, 3 feet thick, yellowish orange, soft; no fossils seen
      2. Shale, yellowish, 3 feet thick; no fossils seen
      3. Limestone, gray, 10 feet thick; some pelecypods
   C. Mason City Member: maximum of 20 feet of various limestone beds; fossils occur in many

A fairly abundant fauna was collected in the Williams Quarry in a talus slope opposite the quarry face. Exposed in the slope is grayish white limestone of the Mason City Member. One hour of collecting yielded 220 fossils, which included:

IDENTIFICATION	PERCENT
Brachiopods	
Schizophoria sp. (orthid)	0.45
Productella sp. (productid)	0.90
Atrypa sp. (spiriferid)	17.72
Spinocyrtia sp. (spiriferid)	1.18
Spinatrypa sp. (spiriferid)	0.90
Tenticospirifer sp. (spiriferid)	0.90
Strophodonta sp. (strophomenid)	3.63
Cranaena sp. (terebratulid)	0.90
Bryozoans	
Branching	1.18
Encrusting	0.90
Burrows	2.27
Corals	
Heliophyllum halli (solitary)	0.90
Zaphrentis sp. (solitary)	0.90
Cystiphyllum sp. (solitary)	3.18
Crinoid columnals	45.45
Gastropods	
Straparollus sp.	0.45
Pelecypods, unidentified	0.45
Stromatoporoids	16.36

Source: Moore 1965, Rose 1967, Shimer and Shrock 1972.

The Mason City Limestone is crinoidal in places here, and most fossils are entire. In a zone about 6.5 feet above the quarry floor some cystoids were reported in the face (Koch and Strimple 1968).

Site 63. Location: near the center of the east line of sec. 11, T96N, R20W. An exposure of the Nora Member of the Shell Rock Formation and the Juniper Hill Member of the Lime Creek Formation reportedly occurs at the Highway 18 bridge over the Winnebago River in the eastern part of Mason City, Cerro Gordo County. The Juniper Hill Shale at this site reportedly contains an abundance of fish teeth (Koch 1970). This collector visited the site and found outcrops of Nora Limestone bearing abundant corals and stromatoporoids. The best exposure occurs on the south bank of the river near the bridge in Ashbury Park. Looking from this site, a minor exposure of shale was seen on the north bank of the river and to the east of the bridge. This is probably part of the Juniper Hill Shale but did not appear to be very accessible. Other exposures of the Juniper Hill Member, including the fish teeth unit as well as the Cedar Valley and Shell Rock Formations in this area, are described by Koch (1970).

Site 64. Location: NW¼ sec. 16, T95N, R18W. Rockford Brick and Tile Company pit in Floyd County.

Site 65. Location: SE¼ sec. 13, T95N, R19W. Bird Hill road cut in Cerro Gordo County.

The Lime Creek Formation is well exposed at these two popular collecting sites. The old Rockford Brick and Tile Company pit is located to the north of county road B-47 southeast of Rockford, adjacent to the Rockford Country Club. The pit is now owned by the Allied Construction Company, 1211 South Main, Charles City, IA 50616. The Bird Hill site is located 3.5 miles west of the Rockford pit along the same paved county road.

Exposed in the Rockford pit are shale of the Juniper Hill and shale and shaly limestone of the Cerro Gordo members of the Lime Creek Formation. However, the lower level of the pit may be flooded.

The Juniper Hill Shale is bluish gray, and no fossils were seen. Around 25 feet are exposed. The lower part of the Cerro Gordo Member here is composed of around 10 feet of blue gray claystone, and this collector could not define where the contact between these two members occurred in the face. This unit of the Cerro Gordo Shale is rather fossiliferous in places, and some dense clusters of the strophomenid brachiopod *Douvillina arcuata* can be found. This fauna is by far the most varied examined for this study. No species was found to represent more than 20 percent of the fauna, which may be one reason why this site is so popular. The rest of the Cerro Gordo Member is quite fossiliferous here also and is composed of brownish shale and thin, shaly limestone beds. The member is represented here by at least 30 feet.

To reach the area most productive for large brachiopods and gastropods, drive in the entrance at the western edge of the pit and park. Proceed on foot to the north, across a grassy field, to a large slope of gray talus from the Cerro Gordo Member.

The upper half of the Cerro Gordo Member (about 30 feet) and the lower part of the Owen Member of the Lime Creek Formation (about 3 feet) are exposed at Bird Hill. Fossil collecting is good here as well. The upper half of the Cerro Gordo Member at this site is quite similar to the lower half of the member at the Rockford pit. The grayish Owen Limestone exposed at the very top of the cut contains a zone rich in the stromatoporoid *Idiostroma* (stratigraphic sequence modified from Rose 1967). Four faunas were collected from these two sites. One (lower) was collected from the blue gray claystone at the base of the Cerro Gordo Member, and another (middle) fauna was collected from the rest of the lower half of the member, both at the Rockford pit. A third (upper) fauna was collected from the upper half of the Cerro Gordo Shale at Bird Hill; the fourth comes from the Owen Member at Bird Hill. The fossils found are listed below; the numbers at the top of each column refer to the number found:

IDENTIFICATION	(225) LOWER (%)	(288) MIDDLE (%)	(314) UPPER (%)	(627) OWEN (%)
Brachiopods, orthid				
Schizophoria iowensis	8.88	9.72	7.32	0.47
Brachiopods, productid				
Devonoproductus walcotti	3.11	5.90	20.06	0.47
Brachiopods, spiriferid				
"*Spirifer*" *orestes*	1.77	3.47	21.33	...
Cyrtospirifer whitneyi	4.44	5.55	0.95	1.43
Spinatrypa sp.	8.88	3.47	13.33	...
Atrypa devoniana	16.88	25.00	4.77	16.10
Theodossia hungerfordi	14.22	20.83	0.95	0.31
Spinocyrtia oweni	...	...	1.27	...
Cleiothyridina sp.	...	0.34	...	...
Tenticospirifer cyrtiniformis	...	...	...	0.15
Composita sp.	...	...	...	0.31
Brachiopods, strophomenid				
Nervostrophia rockfordensis	0.44	...	...	...
Nervostrophia sp.	...	...	7.64	...
Strophonelloides reversa	1.77	0.69	1.27	0.31
Douvillina (Douvillinella) variabilis	1.77	1.04	...	...
Douvillina arcuata	12.44	4.86	7.00	0.15
Strophodonta erratica	...	0.34	2.22	...
Brachiopods, terebratulid				
Cryptonella sp.	...	0.34	...	...
Bryozoans				
Encrusting	0.44	...	...	...
Branching (large)	12.88	1.38	...	...
Branching (small)	...	...	3.50	...
Lacy	1.33	...	...	...
Coral, colonial				
Pachyphyllum woodmani	0.44	0.34	...	...
Aulopora sp.	2.66	0.34	0.95	...
Coral, solitary				
Homalophyllum sp.	4.00	3.81	2.22	...
Heliophyllum sp.	...	0.69	...	...
Crinoid columnals	1.77	2.08	2.22	0.15
Gastropods				
Straparollus sp.	0.44	0.34	0.31	...
Holopea iowensis	0.44	1.38	0.31	...
Bucanella sp.	...	0.34	0.31	...
Floydia concentrica	...	0.69	...	...
Paracyclas sabini	...	1.38	1.27	...

IDENTIFICATION	(225) LOWER	(288) MIDDLE	(314) UPPER	(627) OWEN
	(%)	(%)	(%)	(%)
Pelecypods, unidentified	...	2.08	...	...
Stromatoporoids				
Idiostroma sp.	...	...	...	79.74
Unidentified	...	...	...	0.31
Worm tubes, annelid				
Spirorbis sp.	0.88	3.47	0.63	...

Source: Ager 1963, Moore 1965, Rose 1967, Shimer and Shrock 1972.

Bulk samples of 100 pounds were taken from the lower and middle zones of the Cerro Gordo Member at Rockford. These show how important bulk sampling can be. For example, the spiriferid brachiopod *Tenticospirifer cyrtiniformis* is fairly abundant in the lower half of the Cerro Gordo Shale, but because of its small size it is rarely found by hand collecting in the field. The mollusk *Tentaculites* also turns up more frequently in bulk samples than in the field. These two bulk samples also revealed an abundance of small bryozoans and immature brachiopods. Two hundred fossils were found in the bulk sample of the lower zone and 1,069 in the sample of the middle zone.

It is interesting to note that the two spiny brachiopods of the Lime Creek Formation, *Devonoproductus* and *Spinatrypa*, are more numerous in the upper half of the Cerro Gordo Member at Bird Hill than in the lower half of the same member at Rockford. At first this was thought to be an observational error by this collector, but Ager recorded similar results earlier (1963).

Site 66. Location: first two exposures, western line of sec. 15, T94N, R20W; third exposure NW¼ sec. 15, T94N, R20W. The rest of the Owen Member of the Lime Creek Formation is exposed on both sides of Highway 65 on the southern edge of a bridge just south of the Rockwell corner. The Owen Member is also exposed on the western side of the highway south of another bridge just south of the first one. A third exposure occurs to the east of the first bridge, along a stream through a golf course in the southern part of Rockwell in Cerro Gordo County. At all three sites the Owen Member is composed of brown dolomite and gray, dense limestone. Few fossils were seen.

Site 67. Location: along the boundary of sec. 1, T95N, R19W, and sec. 6, T95N, R19W. Three miles north of Bird Hill along paved county road S70, which lies on the boundary line between Cerro Gordo and Floyd counties, both the Cerro Gordo and Owen members of the Lime Creek Formation are exposed in the ditches on both sides of the road. Stromatoporoids are abundant, as are brachiopods and corals, including a few specimens of the colonial coral *Pachyphyllum*.

Site 68. Location: SW¼/SW¼/SW¼/SW¼ sec. 27, T93N, R20W. The Sheffield Formation is composed of bluish, poorly fossiliferous shale.

An exposure of this formation was examined east of Chapin in Franklin County. The exposure is a minor one and can be found in the eastern ditch of Highway 65 opposite the Chapin corner. Around 8 feet of the lower part of the Aplington Formation is well exposed here and is composed of yellow brown dolomitic limestone with some fossils. These fossils are white and occur in several outcrops of the formation. Among the fossils found was a very large spiriferid, ?*Cyrtospirifer,* which occurred as a dense cluster of four individuals, which were also white.

The Aplington Formation was also seen across the road at the northwestern corner of the intersection (SE¼/SE¼/SE¼/SE¼ sec. 28, T93N, R20W). This exposure is highly eroded and overgrown. Fossils are present, but most are represented as poorly preserved casts and are difficult to spot among the rest of the talus.

Site 69. Location: southern part of the boundary between sec. 10 and 9, T93N, R20W. A road cut exposing the Sheffield and Aplington formations was examined along both sides of Highway 65 south of the bridge over Bailey Creek just south of the town of Sheffield in Franklin County. The Aplington Formation is represented by highly weathered, brownish dolomitic limestone. The Sheffield Formation is a bluish green calcareous shale and is best exposed in the lower part of the eastside cut. A very similar exposure occurs along both sides of county road S-43 (paved). This is along the northern part of the boundary between sections 16 and 17, T93N, R20W. The road runs adjacent to the highway and connects Sheffield with Chapin. This cut also lies south of a bridge over a small creek on the southern edge of Sheffield. Some of the white brachiopods for which the Aplington Formation is noted occur in these two cuts, but most of the brachiopods are represented by poorly preserved casts that blend in with the rest of the talus.

Site 70. Location: near C/SW¼ sec. 20, T90N, R7W. The type section of the Aplington Formation is an old quarry located north of the town of Aplington in Butler County. To reach the site, turn north on a paved road off Highway 20 in town. Continue north for 0.5 mile until a grove appears to the west. Pull into a lane going west and park next to a mobile home; ask there for permission to collect. From here there is a trail leading into the abandoned quarry. The yellowish brown dolomitic limestone carries an abundance of white brachiopods. Their sharp color contrast with the rock aids in collecting. The fauna seems to be fairly evenly spread over certain layers, but fossil content varies from one layer to the next. A few brachiopods, particularly *Orbinaria,* appear to have been buried in life position. Most of the fossils were probably not transported very far before burial, since loose spines of *Orbinaria* are very numerous in places. The fauna was collected from the northeast part of the quarry. No examination of the western face was made.

One hour of collecting yielded 1,093 fossils, most of which were of the productid brachiopod *Orbinaria.* Although their white color makes them unusual, the surface features on many of the brachiopods were not preserved. This fauna included:

IDENTIFICATION	PERCENT
Brachiopods	
Rhipidomella sp. (orthid)	0.18
Schizophoria sp. (orthid)	0.54
Orbinaria sp. (productid)	63.31
Camarotoechia contracta (rhynchonellid)	5.76
Composita sp. (spiriferid)	23.69
Schellwienella sp. (spiriferid)	5.21
"*Spirifer*" *orestes* (spiriferid)	0.09
Cyrtospirifer sp. (spiriferid)	0.27
Corals	
Aulopora sp. (colonial)	0.82
Worms	
Spirorbis sp. (annelid)	0.09

Source: Moore 1965, Rose 1967, Shimer and Shrock 1972.

The species of ?*Cyrtospirifer* occurring in the lower Aplington Formation at Chapin can be found in the middle part of the Aplington here, but it is not quite as large. It occurs below the zone rich in *Orbinaria* and, as at Chapin, can be found in clusters of three or four. Few other fossils occur in this unit. The overlying *Orbinaria* zone also contains smaller, poorly defined zones of *Camarotoechia contracta* and *Composita*. The commensals *Spirorbis* and *Aulopora*, although not abundant here, were generally only found on the brachiopod *Orbinaria*. They were found on the pedicle valves, which is unusual because these were anchored to the sea floor during life. Evidently, these shells were worked free before becoming hosts for the commensals.

Site 71. Location: N½ sec. 16, T69N, R2W. The upper two formations of the Devonian System in Iowa, the Maple Mill and English River, are well exposed in the southeastern part of the state. The Maple Mill Formation is composed of grayish, poorly fossiliferous shale. The English River Formation is composed of bluish gray to light gray siltstone, with a localized zone of yellowish brown fossiliferous siltstone at the top. The English River Siltstone is considered to be borderline Devonian. In the Burlington area it seems to be Devonian, but in the Wellman area it seems to be Mississippian. Both the Maple Mill and the English River formations can be seen at the base of the exposure in Crapo Park in Burlington, Des Moines County. Because several Mississippian formations are also well exposed here, this site is discussed more fully in Chapter 6 (Site 75).

Site 72. Location: SE¼/SE¼/SE¼/SW¼ sec. 26, T71N, R2W. The Maple Mill Formation was seen in a road cut north of Burlington in Des Moines County. To reach the exposure, take Highway 99 north out of town for just under 7 miles. Then take a gravel road west to an eroded slope of gray shale. No fossils were seen.

Site 73. Location: NE¼/SW¼ sec. 35, T71N, R2W. An exposure of the English River Formation was examined south of the Maple Mill exposure discussed for Site 72. To reach the site, take Highway 99 north out of Burlington for about 6 miles. Note exposures of the Maple Mill and English River formations along the highway in northern Burlington. Turn west on a gravel road; continue a short distance until bluffs appear on both sides. These expose several Mississippian formations, i.e., McCraney, Starrs Cave (Site 77), Hampton, and Burlington. These will be discussed in Chapter 6 (Site 76).

The English River Formation is exposed at the base of the southern bluff here along a creek. It contains a bluish gray siltstone overlain by a yellowish brown siltstone. Fossils occur in both zones at this site, but they are most common in the upper yellowish brown zone. The dominant fossil in this zone is the chonetid brachiopod *Chonopectus fischeri*. Very young individuals occur right beside very old ones; however, few of the specimens are well preserved. The brachiopod is an index fossil for the formation. One hour of collecting provided 540 specimens, which included:

IDENTIFICATION	PERCENT
Brachiopods	
Chonopectus fischeri (chonetid)	83.14
Chonetes sp. (chonetid)	5.55
Camarotoechia sp. (rhynchonellid)	1.29
Paryphorhynchus sp. (rhynchonellid)	0.92
Theodossia sp. (spiriferid)	0.18
Mucrospirifer sp. (spiriferid)	1.11
Atrypa sp. (spiriferid)	0.18
Bryozoans	
Branching	0.18
Lacy	1.29
Crinoid columnals	2.96
Gastropods	
Straparollus sp.	0.55
Trepospira sp.	0.18
Pelecypods	
Pecten sp.	0.37
Edmondia sp.	0.18
Grammysia sp.	0.55
Clinopistha sp.	0.18
Nucula sp.	0.18
Allorisma sp.	0.92

Source: Moore 1965, Rose 1967, Shimer and Shrock 1972.

This fauna is quite different from the other Devonian faunas examined for this study, but this is also the only Devonian siltstone fauna examined. The fossils of the English River Formation are preserved as external and internal molds with some casts.

Site 74. Location: NW¼ sec. 19, T70N, R2W. The English River Siltstone is exposed at the base of the bluffs at Starrs Cave in the northern part of Burlington, Des Moines County. Since several Mississippian formations are exposed here, this site will be discussed more fully in Chapter 6 (Site 77).

6

Mississippian Period

THE MISSISSIPPIAN SYSTEM in Iowa is composed mostly of various limestones, several of which are fossiliferous, and some are well known for their fossils. The system is divided into four series: the Kinderhookian (Lower), Osagean (lower Middle), Meramecian (upper Middle), and Chesterian (Upper). The Mississippian Period began 345 million years ago and lasted 35 million years, ending 310 million years ago. The stratigraphic column for the Mississippian System in Iowa is given below:

SERIES	FORMATION	MEMBER	DESCRIPTION
Meramecian	Ste. Genevieve		shale, limestone
	St. Louis		limestone
	Spergen		limestone
Osagean	Warsaw		shale
	Keokuk		limestone
	Burlington	Cedar Fork Creek	limestone
		Haight Creek	limestone
		Dolbee Creek	dolomite
Kinderhookian	Gilmore City		limestone
	Hampton	(Iowa Falls)	dolomite
		Eagle City	limestone
		(Wassonville)	dolomite
		Maynes Creek	dolomite
	Starrs Cave		oolitic limestone
	(Chapin)		limestone
	Prospect Hill		siltstone
	McCraney		limestone

The McCraney, Prospect Hill, and Starrs Cave formations make up the North Hill Group. The Chapin Member of the Hampton Formation in central Iowa is the time equivalent of the Starrs Cave Formation in southeast

MISSISSIPPIAN PERIOD

Iowa. The Wassonville Formation in southeast Iowa is the time equivalent of the Maynes Creek Member of the Hampton Formation. Although the Iowa Falls Member can be seen overlying the Eagle City Member (both of the Hampton Formation) at some exposures, it is considered to be the time equivalent of the upper part of the Eagle City Member. The Chapin Member of the Hampton Formation and the Gilmore City Formation are also oolitic in places.

Site 75. Location: N½ sec. 16, T69N, R2W. The Kinderhookian Series is well exposed in Crapo Park in southern Burlington, Des Moines County. The bluff, not visible from the road, is located in the center of the park east of a historical building and near the Mississippi River. The bluff overlooks some railroad tracks. The following is exposed here (Rose 1967):

I. Mississippian Kinderhookian Series
   A. Hampton Formation
      1. Wassonville Member: at least 10 feet of brown cherty dolomite exposed at the top of the trail. The chert can be very fossiliferous.
   B. Starrs Cave Formation: 2 or 3 feet of white, fossiliferous, oolitic limestone exposed along the trail
   C. Prospect Hill Formation: 5 feet present but mostly covered by the trail. A thin zone of greenish siltstone can be seen underlying the Starrs Cave Formation along the base of the trail.
   D. McCraney Formation: around 10 feet of grassed-over, tan limestone exposed in the slope below the trail
II. (Upper) Devonian Period
   A. English River Formation: around 24 feet exposed; blue gray siltstone with a yellowish brown fossiliferous zone near the top
   B. Maple Mill Formation: around 5 feet of grayish shale exposed above the railroad tracks

Although collecting is not permitted in the park, several of these beds can be traced outside.

Site 76. Location: NE¼/SW¼ sec. 35, T71N, R2W. About 6 miles north of Burlington in Des Moines County are exposures similar to those at Crapo Park (Site 75). They occur in the form of high bluffs along both sides of a gravel road bearing west from Highway 99. The southern bluff exposes the following (Rose 1967):

I. Mississippian Kinderhookian Series
   A. Burlington Formation
      1. Dolbee Creek Member: brown dolomite with some chert; only a few feet exposed at the top of the eastern end of the bluff
   B. Hampton Formation
      1. Wassonville Member: a maximum of 8 feet of brown cherty dolomite with fossils

C. Starrs Cave Formation: 3.5 feet of gray to light tan, fossiliferous, oolitic limestone
D. McCraney Formation: 6 feet of brown dolomitic limestone with a thin zone of white oolitic limestone at the base

II. (Upper) Devonian Period
A. English River Formation: at least 6 feet of blue gray siltstone with a yellowish brown zone near the top; exposed along the creek at the base of the bluff

The northern bluff exposes cherty brown dolomite of the Dolbee Creek Member and possibly the Wassonville Member. Along the creek at the southern bluff, talus from the English River Formation to the Dolbee Creek Member can be found; fossils occur in all these deposits. The Wassonville Chert is usually highly fossiliferous, whereas the Dolbee Creek Chert is not so much so. The Prospect Hill Formation is absent from this bluff. Farther west along the same gravel road on the north side is an exposure of limestone believed to be of the Haight Creek Member of the Burlington Formation.

The white oolitic zone at the base of the McCraney Formation is quite similar in appearance to the Starrs Cave. The latter can be recognized by its larger oolites, which tend to be about twice the size of those of the McCraney Formation. The Starrs Cave Formation is difficult to reach here, but fragments from the deposit can be found among the talus at the base of the bluff. The formation contains an abundance of brachiopods, some of which are quite large, but no faunal list was compiled. The oolitic zone of the McCraney is the most fossiliferous level of that formation at this site. Brachiopods, pelecypods, trilobite pygidia, and solitary corals are the most prominent fossils in this zone. A total of 116 fossils was collected from this fauna and included:

IDENTIFICATION	PERCENT
Brachiopods	
Chonetes gregarious (chonetid)	33.62
Rhipidomella sp. (orthid)	20.68
Productellana bifaria (productid)	6.89
Composita sp. (spiriferid)	0.86
Spirifer sp. (spiriferid)	6.03
Bryozoans, unidentified branching	3.44
Corals, unidentified solitary	6.03
Crinoid columnals	8.62
Nautiloids, unidentified	0.86
Pelecypods	
Aviculopecten sp.	12.06
Trilobite pygidia, unidentified	0.86

Source: Moore 1965, Rose 1967, Shimer and Shrock 1972.

The fossils do not seem to be evenly scattered in this unit and some, especially the chonetid *Chonetes gregarious*, were found in clusters. The *Chonetes* clusters are generally quite small and contain many individuals, along with a few specimens of *Rhipidomella*. The pelecypod *Aviculopecten* is fairly abundant here and occurs in several similar limestones of the Kinderhookian in Iowa. This site is used frequently for target practice; collectors are urged to use caution.

Site 77. Location: NW¼ sec. 19, T70N, R2W. An exposure similar to Site 76 occurs at Starrs Cave Park, located on Irish Ridge Road on the northern edge of Burlington, Des Moines County. This is on the west side of county road X-60. Excellent exposures can be seen in the form of high bluffs on the shore of the Flint River opposite the park. These exposures are included in the park, which means that collecting is not permitted. To reach the bluffs, cross the river via the county road X-60 (paved) bridge and then proceed west on foot to the bluffs. The following sequence is exposed here (Rose 1967):

I. Mississippian Osagean Series
   A. Burlington Formation
      1. Haight Creek-Dolbee Creek members: 50 feet of limestone, dolomite, and dolomitic limestone; chert exposed high in the bluffs
II. Mississippian Kinderhookian Series
   A. Hampton Formation
      1. Wassonville Member: at least 11 feet of dolomite
   B. Starrs Cave Formation: at least 2.5 feet of oolitic limestone with fossils
   C. Prospect Hill Formation: at least 5 feet of gray siltstone
   D. McCraney Formation: 13 feet of dolomite and limestone, oolitic near the base
III. (Upper) Devonian Period
   A. English River Formation: 14 feet of siltstone; lower portion covered

Site 78. Dolomite is exposed along Highway 34 in western Burlington, Des Moines County. An examination of one exposure yielded fossiliferous chert of the Wassonville Member of the Hampton Formation. Bryozoans, small pelecypods, nautiloids, and one small blastoid were found in a brief stop.

Site 79. Location: SW¼/SW¼/SW¼/SW¼ sec. 7, T77N, R8W. North of Wellman in Washington County is an exposure of the Wassonville Member of the Hampton Formation. It occurs on the east side of county road W-38 south of the bridge crossing the English River. Brown dolomite of the upper Wassonville is exposed along the road. It contains several chert zones, as its lateral equivalent, the Maynes Creek Member, does. Unlike the Maynes Creek Chert, Wassonville Chert is very fossiliferous in spots. A quarry to the east better exposes the Wassonville Dolomite and the Burlington Formation, but trespassing is not permitted. Along the road, the Wassonville Dolomite also contains fossils, mostly an abundance of crinoid columnar molds. These also occur in the Maynes Creek Dolomite. The Wassonville Chert at this site contains one of the highest concentrations of fossils reported in this book. One hour of collecting yielded 3,069 fossils. Fossiliferous slabs of chert were collected for later examination. The fossils found are listed below:

IDENTIFICATION	PERCENT
Brachiopods	
Chonetes logani (chonetid)	45.45
Setigerites setigerites (productid)	0.06
Productellana bifaria (productid)	0.22
Rhynchopora sp. (rhynchonellid)	1.75
Cleiothyridina sp. (spiriferid)	0.19
Spirifer sp. (spiriferid)	1.46
Leptaena analoga (strophomenid)	2.57
Bryozoans	
Branching (average)	0.32
Branching (small)	1.43
Lacy	31.34
Crinoid columnals	9.77
Gastropods	
Naticopsis (Naticopsis) variata	0.06
Cerithioides sp.	0.03
Straparollus sp.	0.06
Bellerophon sp.	0.09
Nautiloids, unidentified	0.58
Pelecypods	
Aviculopecten sp.	0.52
Small (many varieties)	3.91
Trilobite pygidia, unidentified	0.09

Source: Moore 1965, Rose 1967, Shimer and Shrock 1972.

The crinoid columnals are probably more numerous here than this list indicates because they are more prominent in the most highly weathered slabs. Fossils are more common in certain chert zones, but no clusters of species were noted. Also, most of the fossils are small adults, immature individuals, or small fragments of larger specimens.

An unusual feature of the Wassonville Chert is its gastropods. Some very rare species have been found north of Wellman, and many of these are entirely new species (Rollins 1975). However, these do not seem to be very abundant, and the only specimens the casual collector is likely to find would be the more common species such as those in this faunal list. The abundance of lacy bryozoans in this fauna is also repeated in the Maynes Creek Dolomite.

Site 80. Location: SE¼/SE¼ sec. 13, T77N, R8W. A good exposure of the Wassonville Member occurs near Kalona in Washington County. To reach the site, take Highway 1 south out of town and cross the English River about 1 mile south of the junction of Highways 1 and 22. Then turn west on a gravel road. The Wassonville Dolomite is exposed along the south bank of the river for some distance, and fossiliferous chert is common. Exposures of older strata down to the English River Formation reportedly occur along the river in this vicinity, but only the Wassonville Member was seen.

Site 81. Location: NW¼ sec. 1, T83N, R17W. Some of Iowa's most famous Mississippian quarries are located near Le Grand in Marshall County. Many excellent crinoids have been found in this area. To reach the site, take county road T-37 (paved) north out of Le Grand. Some quarries do not expose the entire sequence. The following is a composite stratigraphic section of the beds exposed (Rose 1967):

I. Mississippian Kinderhookian Series
   A. Hampton Formation
      1. Eagle City Member: around 10 feet of brown, thin-bedded limestone exposed at the top of the face
      2. Maynes Creek Member: around 50 feet of limestone; various beds, mostly brown but some gray spots; a few burrows seen; grayish areas rich in brachiopods
      3. Chapin Member, Starrs Cave Formation equivalent: forms the floors in some quarries; around 18 feet of light oolitic limestone, more oolitic near the top; abundant fossils
II. (Upper) Devonian Period
   A. English River? Formation: a thin zone of conglomerate and some shale exposed in the deepest areas

The Le Grand crinoids occur in rare nests in the Maynes Creek Limestone here. They are rarely found as isolated individuals. The dark limestone areas of the Maynes Creek Member carry an abundant brachiopod fauna, mostly *Spirifer* and *Schuchertella lens.*

The best fossil collecting in the area can be done in the Chapin Limestone. The fossils seem to be fairly evenly distributed, particularly near the top of the unit, which is the most oolitic. Most of the larger brachiopods and all the pelecypods are disarticulated. Some large, well-preserved gastropods also occur at this level. A total of 210 fossils were found, including the following:

IDENTIFICATION	PERCENT
Brachiopods	
Chonetes sp. (chonetid)	9.52
Schizophoria sp. (orthid)	11.24
Marginicinctus sp. (productid)	2.85
Productellana sp. (productid)	0.47
Spirifer sp. (spiriferid)	8.09
Composita sp. (spiriferid)	1.42
Orthotetes sp. (strophomenid)	5.23
Cranaena sp. (terebratulid)	7.14
Unidentified	0.95
Bryozoans, unidentified lacy	0.47
Corals	
Lithostrotionella sp. (colonial)	0.47

IDENTIFICATION	PERCENT
Crinoid columnals	0.47
Gastropods	
Straparollus sp.	2.85
Mollusks, unidentified	0.47
Nautiloids, unidentified	0.47
Pelecypods	
Aviculopecten sp.	46.66
Trilobite pygidia, unidentified	0.47
Vertebrate fragments, unidentified	0.47

Source: Moore 1965, Rose 1967, Shimer and Shrock 1972.

The colonial coral *Lithostrotionella* is one of the few post-Devonian colonial corals found during this study. It was found in the lower, less oolitic part of the Chapin Member. The pelecypod *Aviculopecten* reaches large sizes here, but few specimens show any surface details.

Site 82. Location: SW¼/SW¼/SW¼/SW¼ sec. 29, and NE¼/NE¼/NE¼/NE¼ sec. 31, T93N, R20W. The type section for the Chapin Formation was a pair of abandoned quarries located west of Chapin in Franklin County. The Chapin Limestone was thought to be a separate formation at one time but is now considered to be a member of the Hampton Formation and the lateral equivalent of the Starrs Cave Formation of southeastern Iowa. To reach the quarries, turn west at the Chapin corner (county road C-23) on Highway 65. Continue west on the paved road through Chapin to an intersection with a gravel road 0.5 mile west of town. The quarries are located at the northeast and southwest corners of the intersection. The Chapin Limestone was not immediately visible in the southern quarry, but the Maynes Creek Member of the Hampton Formation is well exposed. Both members were examined in the northern quarry. When last visited (spring of 1980) the northern quarry was posted "no trespassing" and was flooded. The exposure in the northern quarry included around 5 feet of slightly oolitic, light gray, crinoidal, dense Chapin Limestone and around 8 feet of brown fossiliferous dolomite of the Maynes Creek Member. One hour of collecting in the Chapin Member provided 118 fossils, mostly crinoid debris. These included:

IDENTIFICATION	PERCENT
Brachiopods	
Chonetes sp. (chonetid)	1.69
Rhipidomella tenuicostata (orthid)	8.47
Spirifer sp. (spiriferid)	3.38
Corals	
Cyathaxonia arcuata (solitary)	1.69
Crinoid columnals	84.74

Source: Moore 1965, Rose 1967, Shimer and Shrock 1972.

Fossils in the Maynes Creek Dolomite are generally represented as casts, or molds in the case of the largest brachiopods; the solitary corals are usually represented by calyx imprints only. The majority of the fossils are articulated. One hour of collecting yielded 190 fossils, including the following:

IDENTIFICATION	PERCENT
Brachiopods	
Chonetes sp. (chonetid)	5.26
Rhipidomella sp. (orthid)	3.15
Productellana bifaria (productid)	3.15
Productina sp. (productid)	0.52
Rhynchopora sp. (rhynchonellid)	3.15
Paryphorhynchus sp. (rhynchonellid)	0.52
Eumetria sp. (spiriferid)	1.05
Spirifer sp. (spiriferid)	4.73
Cleiothyridina sp. (spiriferid)	4.21
Syringothyris sp. (spiriferid)	1.05
Spiriferid, unidentified	1.05
Dielasma sp. (terebratulid)	0.52
Unidentified	0.52
Bryozoans	
Branching, unidentified	3.68
Lacy, unidentified	11.57
Corals	
Cyathaxonia sp. (solitary)	2.10
Crinoid columnals	52.63
Mollusks, unidentified	2.10
Trilobite pygidia, unidentified	1.05

Source: Moore 1965, Rose 1967, Shimer and Shrock 1972.

The crinoid columnals of the Maynes Creek Dolomite, as with the Wassonville Dolomite, are represented by small molds. Additional collecting in the Maynes Creek Member here yielded a few excellent preserved green algae specimens.

Site 83. Location: near C/NW¼ sec. 18, T91N, R19W. The rest of the Maynes Creek Member of the Hampton Formation was examined west of Geneva in Franklin County. To reach the quarry, take Highway 134 west from Geneva and turn north on the first gravel road. Continue north for 1 mile. On the east side of the road is an operating quarry, formerly the Phillip's Quarry. Ask at the scale house for permission to collect. The best time to visit the quarry is probably on Saturday morning. The oldest pit near the quarry entrance exposes about 30 feet of reddish brown dolomite of the Maynes Creek Member. Chert is abundant but generally lacks fossils. The dolomite is quite fossiliferous and is very similar in appearance to the exposures west of Chapin. Also present in this pit are a few feet of the Eagle City Member of the Hampton Formation. Boulders of this member can be found on the quarry floor. The member was not seen in the face but must have been present at one time. At this site the Eagle City Member is composed of reddish, dense, crinoidal limestone. A few brachiopods were also found. Other parts of the quarry expose only the

Maynes Creek Dolomite. An abandoned quarry on the west side of the road reportedly exposes more of the Eagle City Limestone (Rose 1967).

Site 84. Location: E½ sec. 13, T89N, R20W. Both the Eagle City and Iowa Falls members of the Hampton Formation are exposed in Iowa Falls, Hardin County. At various sites along the Iowa River in this area are several exposures of the Iowa Falls Dolomite. The best exposures seen by the author occur along the river near Assembly Park in the northern part of town. This same sequence of bluffs occurs under the Highway 20 bridge over the river in Iowa Falls. The Iowa Falls Member is laterally equivalent to the upper part of the Eagle City Member and generally contains few fossils.

Site 85. Location: NE¼ sec. 19, T89N, R20W. The Eagle City and Iowa Falls members of the Hampton Formation are exposed at the Welden Brothers' Quarry in Iowa Falls. To reach the quarry, go south on Highway 65 in the southern part of town. Turn east immediately south of a railroad underpass. The road goes through a golf course before reaching the quarry. Part of the quarry is jointly owned by the Welden Brothers' Company and the Saint Regis Paper Company. Both have offices at the quarry, and it is advisable to get prior permission to collect here and then visit the quarry on a Sunday. The only part of the quarry seen by this collector appeared to be inactive. The face examined consisted of about 8 feet of yellow white embedded limestone of the Eagle City Member and a few feet of brown dolomite of the Iowa Falls Member. No fossils were found in the Iowa Falls Member but the Eagle City carries an abundant fauna in some places at this site. Brachiopods and some large, well-preserved gastropods were among the fossils found. One hour of collecting yielded 1,229 fossils, which included the following:

IDENTIFICATION	PERCENT
Brachiopods	
Allorhynchus heteropsis (rhynchonellid)	95.76
Spirifer sp. (spiriferid)	0.65
Corals, unidentified solitary	0.16
Crinoid columns	0.08
Gastropods	
Straparollus sp.	2.60
Pelecypods, unidentified	0.73

Source: Moore 1965, Rose 1967.

Over 1,000 specimens of the rhynchonellid *Allorhynchus heteropsis* were found here, making this one of the highest concentrations of a rhynchonellid brachiopod found in this study. The gastropod *Straparollus* occurs in clusters of four or five in this quarry. The pelecypods are represented only by poorly preserved casts.

Site 86. Location: SE¼ sec. 25, T92N, R31W. The Gilmore City Formation of the Kinderhookian Series is well exposed in several quarries north of Gilmore City in Pocahontas and Humboldt counties. To reach the quarry examined for this study take Highway 3 through Gilmore City and turn north on paved county road P-15 west of town near a cemetery. The quarry is the northernmost one along this road. Several other quarries, both abandoned and operating, are located to the east. Stop at the gatehouse on the west side of the road to ask for permission to collect and to check out when you leave the quarry. Collectors can usually visit any nonworking part of the quarry when it is in operation. Full safety equipment is needed (steel-toed shoes, eye protection, hard hat). The best collecting was done on the east side of the road. The strata at this particular site has been well worked and no large continuous face was seen. The lower part of the Gilmore City Formation is not exposed in these quarries. However, at least six separate units were seen, and these are listed below:

1. Dense, massive white limestone present in the lower part of this quarry; a few fossils found
2. Yellowish highly oolitic limestone, thickness not determined; abundant brachiopods in places, generally disarticulated
3. Dark gray limestone, sometimes argillaceous and usually bedded, at least 5 feet seen; abundant fossils in places, including a wide variety of burrows and a few crinoid crowns
4. Gray oolitic limestone varying to brown slightly dolomitic limestone; source of several crinoid crowns. Fossils are present but not very abundant. A few complete echinoids were found in this unit, but the casual collector is not likely to find any. Crinoids occur in "nests" and only rarely are found as individuals. Although crinoids are not abundant, this unit offers the best collecting in the state in the opinion of the author. The unit is about 5 feet thick.
5. Gray oolitic limestone varying in color to dark gray; contains a unit rich in concretions in the lower level, which also carries the most abundant fossils; oolitic in the lighter colored areas; 10 feet seen
6. Exposed in the upper levels; well exposed along the pit on the west side of the road north of the gatehouse; composed of gray to brown limestone with variable bedding and arenaceous in spots; 8 feet seen; an abundance of solitary corals near the top with a few other fossils present

The thicknesses of these units is not definite, because in most cases only partial exposures were seen. This is a composite section involving units found in different parts of the same quarry at different levels. One hour of collecting was spent in each of four units; the number at the top of each column refers to the number of fossils found. The faunas included the following specimens:

IDENTIFICATION	(166) UNIT 2 (%)	(327) UNIT 3 (%)	(75) UNIT 4 (%)	(325) UNIT 5 (%)
Brachiopods				
Chonetes sp. (chonetid)	1.80	...	...	...
Rhipidomella sp. (orthid)	...	...	2.64	...
Marginicinctus sp. (productid)	12.65	0.61	...	0.30
Linoproductus sp. (productid)	...	0.30	...	...
Productellana sp. (productid)	1.80	...	...	...
Rhynchopora cooperensis (rhynchonellid)	9.03	4.28	...	2.15
Spirifer sp. (spiriferid)	45.18	19.87	28.00	15.07
?*Tylothyris* sp. (spiriferid)	0.60	...	...	...
Eumetria verneuiliana (spiriferid)	5.42	1.22	...	0.92
Composita sp. (spiriferid)	2.40	...	...	0.30
Orthotetes sp. (strophomenid)	13.25	0.30	...	1.23
Schuchertella lens (strophomenid)	...	3.97	...	9.84
Cranaena sp. (terebratulid)	7.22	0.30	10.66	8.30
Bryozoans, unidentified branching	...	1.83	2.66	...
Burrows	...	30.58	8.00	...
Corals, unidentified solitary	0.60	...	...	0.30
Crinoid columns	...	30.58	40.00	30.76
Crinoid crowns	...	...	1.33	...
Echinoid spines	...	6.11	6.66	30.76

Source: Moore 1965, Rose 1967, Shimer and Shrock 1972.

No faunal list was made of unit 1; in unit 6 the solitary coral *Cyathophyllum* represented almost the entire fauna found, with a few specimens of the rhynchonellid brachiopod *Rhynchopora* composing the rest. The burrows of unit 3 are abundant and widely varied and would offer excellent study for anyone interested in this aspect.

Site 87. Location: sec. 17, T89N, R21W. The Gilmore City Formation is also extensively quarried in the Alden, Hardin County, area. The Weaver Construction Company quarries were examined. They occur on both sides of Highway 20 on the eastern edge of town. Stop at the quarry office for permission to collect. The Gilmore City limestone here varies from gray to tan and is oolitic with few fossils. This collector found only a few fragments of a lacy bryozoan.

Site 88. Location: E½ sec. 1, T71N, R4W. The Dolbee Creek and Haight Creek members of the Burlington Formation were mentioned earlier in relation to the lower Mississippian beds exposed in the Burlington area (see Sites 76, 77). The uppermost member of the Burlington Formation is the Cedar Fork Creek. The type section for the member is located at the Leonhard Quarry south of Roscoe in Des Moines County. The best way to reach the site is to go south on Highway 61 through Mediapolis. About 2 miles south of town, turn west on county road H-40 (gravel). Continue west for 4.5 miles to the quarry. Collecting is no longer permitted in the quarry itself, but natural exposures occur along Cedar Fork Creek next to it. The Cedar Fork Creek Limestone here is dense, gray to brown, and fossiliferous. The fauna found here is listed below:

MISSISSIPPIAN PERIOD

IDENTIFICATION	PERCENT
Brachiopods	
Chonetes sp. (chonetid)	1.79
Rhynchopora sp. (rhynchonellid)	0.59
Spirifer grimesi (spiriferid)	13.77
Athyris lamellosa (spiriferid)	16.16
Syringothyris carteni (spiriferid)	0.59
Unidentified	2.99
Crinoid columns	59.88
Coral, unidentified solitary	2.39
Vertebrate fragments	1.79

Source: Moore 1965, Rose 1967, Shimer and Shrock 1972.

A total of 167 fossils were found after one hour of collecting. Brachiopods seem to be more numerous in clusters, but many are poorly preserved. The Burlington Formation is noted for its well-preserved fauna, including large brachiopods and crinoid crowns at some sites, but this collector failed to find such specimens at this particular exposure.

Site 89. Location: NE¼ sec. 26, T72N, R2W. There are several quarries in southeastern Iowa belonging to the Raid Company. Some of these were examined for this study. To collect in any of these quarries, written permission is needed in advance and all personal safety equipment is required. Contact Raid Quarries, Division of Medusa Aggregates Company, P.O. Box 1085, Burlington, IA 52601.

At the Nelson Quarry, just west of the junction of county road H-38 (paved) and Highway 99 in Des Moines County (east of Mediapolis), the Haight Creek Member of the Burlington Formation is exposed. Natural exposures of all three members of the formation occur near the quarry (Harris and Parker 1964). The gray to brown limestone quarried here contains sporadic fossils. A brief stop yielded an abundance of crinoid columns and an excellent large specimen of the spiriferid brachiopod *Spirifer grimesi*. This appears to be the most fossiliferous of all the Raid quarries examined for this study.

Site 90. Location: SW¼/NE¼ sec. 25, T69N, R3W. The abandoned Raid Quarry southeast of Augusta in Lee County exposes the Burlington and Keokuk formations. To reach the quarry, go north on Highway 394 en route to Augusta. Turn east on the first gravel road just south of the Skunk River bridge. Follow the road to the quarry. The quarry was located, but no collecting was done because it was being used as a shooting range at the time. The stratigraphic sequence exposed here is described below (Rose 1967):

1. Mississippian Osagean Series
    A. Keokuk Formation
        1. Thirteen feet of thin-bedded dolomite and shale exposed at the top of the face.

2. Eight feet of limestone with chert
   3. Four and a half feet of thin-bedded dolomite with chert and a thin shale bed near the base
B. Burlington Formation
   1. Cedar Fork Creek Member
      a. Thirteen and a half feet of thick-bedded limestone with a few zones of fish teeth
      b. About 17 feet of dolomitic limestone and limestone with variable bedding and chert
   2. Haight Creek? Member: 5 feet of limestone cherty in the lower portion, exposed above a 7-foot covered slope

Fossils reportedly occur in this quarry, including some crinoid crowns of the Burlington Formation.

Site 91. Location: NE¼/NW¼ sec. 10, T68N, R6W. Limestone of the Burlington Formation is also quarried at the Hawkeye (Raid) Quarry west of West Point in Lee County. To reach the quarry, start at the junction of Highway 103 and county road X-23 in West Point. Take Highway 103 west for about 4 miles. Cross a bridge and take a south-bearing gravel road. After a fraction of a mile, turn west at an intersection. The quarry is 1 mile west and on the south side of the road along a creek. Fossils do not seem to be very abundant here.

Site 92. Location: NE¼ sec. 12, T70N, R9W. Another Raid quarry was visited northwest of Stockport in Van Buren County, the abandoned Cedar Quarry. It is difficult to find, and the face seemed to be completely submerged when this collector visited the site. The limestone quarried here is probably part of the Burlington Formation.

Site 93. Location: SW¼/SW¼/SW¼/SW¼ sec. 17, T66N, R6W. A semiabandoned Raid quarry is located south of Donnellson in Lee County. To reach the quarry, start at the junction of county roads W-68 and J-62, 3 miles south of town. Go south on W-68 (paved) for 4.5 miles through the town of Argyle and turn west on a gravel road. County road J-72 bears to the east at this intersection. The gravel road curves to the south and crosses some railroad tracks. Continue south for about a mile. A lane leading to the quarry bears west. This lane may be closed on weekends and holidays. The limestone quarried here contains a few fossils and is of the Burlington Formation.

Site 94. Location: SE¼ sec. 32, T67N, R8W. The Comanche (Raid) Quarry exposes grayish to brown limestone of the Burlington Formation, overlain by grayish interbedded limestone and shale of the Keokuk. A brief search of the Keokuk Shale yielded 56 pelecypods, mostly *Allorisma* and *Nucula*. To reach the quarry, take Highway 2 west out of Farmington, Van Buren County. Cross the Des Moines River. Just over 3 miles west of the bridge, turn south on a gravel road. This is the second south-bearing gravel road west of Farmington. Continue south for about 1 mile to the quarry.

Site 95. Location: western edge of the NE¼ sec. 8, T69N, R4W. The Keokuk, Warsaw, Spergen, and St. Louis formations are exposed in a road cut northwest of Augusta in Des Moines County. There are several exposures in this vicinity, but to reach the best exposure seen by the author, take Highway 394 north to Augusta, crossing the Skunk River. Turn westerly on the first gravel road north of the river. Continue in a northwest direction, following the Skunk River for about 3.5 miles. Then turn north on another gravel road; the cut appears on the west side. A few feet of limestone from the Keokuk Formation are exposed at the southern end of the cut. It is best seen along a stream on private property to the west and south of the cut. The formation is quite fossiliferous here. The upper part of the Keokuk Formation is composed of shale. Along the ditch a little farther north are at least 20 feet of partially covered bluish gray shale of the Warsaw Formation. Bryozoans are reportedly abundant in a brown dolomitic limestone zone of the Warsaw at this site (Rose 1967), but none were seen by this collector. Around 10 feet of reddish limestone of the Spergen Formation and at least 10 feet of sandy limestone of the St. Louis overlie the Warsaw Shale in the cut. No fossils were seen in these two formations, and they are not well exposed.

Two limestone units of the Keokuk Formation were observed at this site, and both are rather fossiliferous. The "upper" fauna was collected from a poorly exposed, grayish white limestone rich in brachiopods and bryozoans. The "middle upper" fauna was collected from a brown, thin-bedded limestone also rich in brachiopods, including some very large specimens of the strophomenid *Orthotetes keokuk*. A total of 252 fossils was found in the upper fauna, and 352 fossils were found in the middle upper fauna. These included the following:

IDENTIFICATION	UPPER	MIDDLE UPPER
	(%)	(%)
Brachiopods		
Productellana sp. (productid)	0.39	0.85
Marginicinctus sp. (productid)	0.39	6.25
Pugnoides sp. (rhynchonellid)	...	0.56
Spirifer keokuk (spiriferid)	44.84	3.40
Athyris lamellosa (spiriferid)	1.19	5.11
Athyris-Torynifer spp. (spiriferid)	1.98	17.89
Torynifer pseudolineata (spiriferid)	...	9.37
?*Tylothyris* sp. (spiriferid)	3.96	1.70
Eumetria sp. (spiriferid)	...	0.28
Composita sp. (spiriferid)	0.39	...
Orthotetes keokuk (strophomenid)	...	7.95
Unidentified	...	0.85
Bryozoans		
Branching	3.96	5.68
Lacy	0.39	4.82

IDENTIFICATION	UPPER (%)	MIDDLE UPPER (%)
Coral, unidentified solitary	...	3.12
Crinoid columnals	39.68	28.40
Pelecypods		
Allorisma sp.	1.98	...
Unidentified	0.79	...
Trilobite pygidia, unidentified	...	1.42
Vertebrate fragments	...	0.85

Source: Moore 1965, Rose 1967, Shimer and Shrock 1972.

The upper fauna of the Keokuk Limestone here is composed of generally fragmented or disarticulated fossils. Only a few brachiopods are still articulated. The pelecypods are all disarticulated, and all the bryozoans are fragmented. The fauna of the middle upper section is preserved in much the same manner. The spiriferid brachiopods *Athyris lamellosa* and *Torynifer pseudolineata* are similar in appearance, and precise identification could not be made on some specimens.

Site 96. Location: SW¼/SW¼/SW¼/SW¼ sec. 10, T69N, R4. Another Raid quarry exposing the Burlington Formation was examined near Site 95. To reach the Heinhold Quarry go south from the previous exposure to the intersection with the Skunk River road (gravel). Turn southeast and backtrack along this road for about 1.5 mile to another north-bearing gravel road, then turn north. Two abandoned quarries at this intersection (SE¼/SE¼/SE¼ sec. 9, T69N, R4W) reportedly expose rather fossiliferous limestone of the Keokuk Formation (Rose 1967). No examination of these quarries was made, and they occur on private property. The Heinhold Quarry occurs farther north and on the east side of the road, the best exposure occurs in the northern part. Advance permission is needed, and it is suggested that the quarry be visited when not in operation. Collectors are advised to use caution, for there are often explosives in the quarry. Few fossils were seen in a brief stop here.

Site 97. Location: Near C sec. 33, T71N, R7W. To reach the site, take county road W-55 (paved) south from Highway 34 just west of Mount Pleasant in Henry County. Continue south for a little over 5 miles, crossing the Skunk River. Then turn west on the third west-bearing gravel road south of the bridge. Continue west for 2.5 miles to the road cut on the south side of the road east of Big Cedar Creek. Exposed here is an estimated 10 feet of limestone of the St. Louis Formation, generally sandy in the lower part and with some shale in the upper. Poor quality brachiopods (mostly *Spirifer, Composita,* and *Chonetes*) and a few bryozoans can be found here, generally near the top of the cut. In the ditch west of the cut, pieces of chert can be found in fair abundance among the talus, and some quite colorful specimens are present. A large but poor quality specimen of the colonial coral *Lithostrotionella* was also found in a half-hour stop. The specimen was found by selecting small areas at random in the ditch talus and closely searching every limestone chunk about fist size or larger.

Site 98. Location: C sec. 27, T70N, R5W. A road cut exposing limestone believed to be from the St. Louis and Spergen formations was examined along Mud Creek east of Lowell in Henry County. To reach the site, take county road J-20 (gravel) east out of Lowell en route to Geode State Park. Continue east for a little over 1 mile and curve north; do not follow J-20 into the park. The exposure occurs on the west side of the road. The slope at the base of the bluff may cover the Warsaw Shale. Along Mud Creek, north of the exposure, geodes of the Warsaw Formation reportedly occur (Horick 1974).

Site 99. Location: EC sec. 24, T71N, R7W. The St. Louis Formation was also examined in a road cut along county road H-46 (paved) east of the town of Oakland Mills in Henry County, which is located at the junction of county roads H-46 and W-55 southwest of Mount Pleasant. No fossils were seen.

Site 100. Location: northern line of sec. 4, T71N, R7W. A road cut exposing the St. Louis Formation was examined along Highway 34 east of Rome in Henry County. The gray to brown limestone carries some white chert, but no fossils could be found.

Site 101. Location: NW¼/NW¼ sec. 30, T76N, R15W. The Ste. Genevieve Formation in Iowa offers an abundant fauna in places. In southeastern Iowa an exposure was examined north of Oskaloosa in Mahaska County. To reach the abandoned quarry, go north from Oskaloosa on Highway 63 for 5 miles. Turn east at the first gravel road north of the South Skunk River bridge. Cross a small creek and some railroad tracks. The old quarry will be seen to the south. Ask for permission to collect at the farmhouse on the hill around which the quarry was opened. The Ste. Genevieve Formation is overlain by sandstone, shale, and coal of the Pennsylvanian Cherokee Group. Some plant fossils occur in the Cherokee here. Although most of the quarry face is inaccessible because of deep water, a few piles of gray shale and limestone in the northwest part provide excellent fossil collecting in the Ste. Genevieve. This fauna is listed under Site 102, where a similar type was collected.

Site 102. Location: SW¼ sec. 20, T89N, R28W. The Ste. Genevieve Formation was also examined in Fort Dodge, Webster County. The site is located several hundred feet east of a grain elevator at the south end of Loomis Park, which lies on the east side of the Des Moines River in the northern part of town. An abundance of brachiopods occurs here. Like the Oskaloosa fauna, many fossils are fragmented or disarticulated, but the smaller specimens are generally entire. No clusters of species were seen. The fossils appear to be fairly evenly spread throughout certain zones. In

Fort Dodge, the formation is composed of poorly fossiliferous gray and red shales with units of fossiliferous yellowish shale. The red shale is well exposed at this site, but the area is badly overgrown. The faunas found in Fort Dodge and Oskaloosa exposures of the Ste. Genevieve Formation are described below; notice how much more diverse the Oskaloosa fauna appears to have been than the Fort Dodge:

IDENTIFICATION	OSKALOOSA	FORT DODGE
Brachiopods		
Linoproductus ovatus (productid)	6.71	...
Pugnoides ottumwa (rhynchonellid)	4.69	29.89
Spirifer pellaensis (spiriferid)	16.77	57.73
Composita trinuclea (spiriferid)	13.42	11.34
Orthotetes kaskaskiensis (strophomenid)	5.36	1.03
Girtyella indianensis (terebratulid)	3.02	...
Bryozoans		
Branching	7.71	...
Encrusting	4.02	...
Lacy	0.67	...
Corals		
"Zaphrentis" pellaensis (solitary)	13.42	...
Crinoid columns	19.12	...
Sponge borings	2.34	...
Worm tubes		
Spirorbis sp. (annelid)	2.68	...

Source: Moore 1965, Rose 1967, Shimer and Shrock 1972.

A total of 298 fossils were found at Oskaloosa and 97 at Fort Dodge. Bulk samples were taken from both exposures. A 25-pound sample of the Fort Dodge exposure contained small bryozoans, trilobite pygidia (*Phillipsia*), and immature brachiopods. Several years of collecting by hand here never yielded a single branching bryozoan or trilobite pygidium. A 60-pound bulk sample of the Oskaloosa site contained immature brachiopods, blastoids, trilobite pygidia (*Phillipsia*), small bryozoans, and three times more crinoid columns than found by hand sampling. The blastoid *Pentremites conoidea* can sometimes be found in the field after a heavy rain, but not very often because of its small size.

The only abundant Mississippian commensals found in this study occur in the Ste. Genevieve Formation. Encrusting bryozoans at Oskaloosa are found on the spiny coral *"Zaphrentis" pellaensis* (note: *Zaphrentis* is a Devonian genus), the spiriferids *Spirifer pellaensis* and *Composita trinuclea*, the rhynchonellid *Pugnoides ottumwa*, and most often on crinoid columns. In some cases the colony has completely encrusted the host. *Spirorbis* tubes were found on all the same species as the encrusting bryozoans, but apparently that species preferred the anterior portions of the brachial and pedicle valves of *C. trinuclea*.

Commensals (bryozoans and *Spirorbis*) also occur on *S. pellaensis* in the Fort Dodge fauna, but none of these were found when compiling the faunal list. Rarely do commensals occur on *C. trinuclea* or *P. ottumwa* at Fort Dodge. Additional collecting at both exposures yielded a few specimens of the pelecypod *Allorisma*. At Oskaloosa, sponge borings were seen on *S. pellaensis, C. trinuclea,* and *"Zaphrentis" pellaensis.*

Site 103. Location: near the southern line of the SW¼ sec. 24, T89N, R29W. Badly eroded and overgrown shales of the Ste. Genevieve Formation were seen in a slope overlooking Lizard Creek west of Fort Dodge in Webster County. They are mostly reddish, but a few units of fossiliferous yellowish shale were found. These occur on the west side of the Highway 169 bridge over the creek. There are two ravines on that side; the exposures occur on the south slope of the northern ravine. Brachiopods are abundant. The St. Louis Formation is exposed along the creek here and at several other places to the east and west (see Sites 104, 105). Another exposure of the Ste. Genevieve occurs at Site 110, Chapter 6.

Site 104. Location: near the center of sec. 24, T89N, R29W. The St. Louis Limestone is well exposed along the northern bank of Lizard Creek at this site, located west of the Lizard Creek junction with the Des Moines River (west of the south end of Loomis Park) in Fort Dodge, Webster County. No fossils were seen. Minor exposures of the Ste. Genevieve Shale were also seen, but no fossils were found.

Site 105. Location: near the center of the northern line of sec. 26, T89N, R29W. To reach the site, begin at the intersection of Highways 169 and 7 in western Fort Dodge, Webster County. Take a paved road west next to a cemetery. Pass the Fort Dodge Limestone Quarry entrance (no collecting permitted) and continue westerly to a bridge over a stream. This is Lizard Creek. Upstream from the bridge is an exposure of soft sandstone, probably of the Cherokee Group (Pennsylvanian). It is best to visit this site when the water level in the creek is at a minimum. Farther upstream, sandy limestone of the St. Louis Formation is well exposed. The dense, brown bedded limestone in the creek bed is probably of the Spergen Formation. Fossils were not found here. Exposures of the Ste. Genevieve Formation may occur still farther upstream.

7

Pennsylvanian Period
DESMOINESIAN AND MORROWAN SERIES

THE PENNSYLVANIAN PERIOD began 310 million years ago and ended 280 million years ago, a span of 30 million years. The Pennsylvanian System is divided into five series: the Morrowan (Lower), Atoken (lower middle), Desmoinesian (mid Middle), Missourian (upper Middle), and Virgilian (Upper). In Iowa, the Pennsylvanian System includes more formations than the rest of the Paleozoic combined. For this reason, three chapters of this book are devoted to the Pennsylvanian. The stratigraphic column for the Desmoinesian Series used here is based on a discussion by Orville J. Van Eck (Landis and Van Eck 1965). The Iowa Geological Survey is revising the Desmoinesian stratigraphic column for Iowa. Exposures occur in the central and southern parts of the state. The Cherokee Group is well exposed in many areas, and plant fossils are present at several sites. The Morrowan Series occurs in Scott and Muscatine counties and also offers excellent plant fossils.

SERIES	GROUP	FORMATION	MEMBER	DESCRIPTION
Desmoinesian	Marmaton	Lenapah	Cooper Creek	limestone
		Nowata		shale, sandstone, coal
		Altamont	Worland	limestone
			Lake Neosho	shale
			Amoret	limestone
		Bandera		shale (Lonsdale Coal)
		Pawnee	Coal City	limestone
			Mine Creek	shale
			Myrick Station	limestone
			Anna	shale
		Labette		shale (Mystic Coal)
		Fort Scott	Higginsville	limestone
			(unnamed)	shale

PENNSYLVANIAN PERIOD: DESMOINESIAN AND MORROWAN SERIES

SERIES	GROUP	FORMATION	MEMBER	DESCRIPTION
Desmoinesian	Marmaton	Ft. Scott (cont.)		
			Houx	limestone
			(unnamed)	shale
			Blackjack	limestone
	Cherokee		(unnamed)	shale
			Mulky	coal, shale
			Pleasantview	sandstone
			(unnamed)	shale
			Bevier	coal, shale
			Wheeler	coal, shale
			Ardmore	limestone
			(unnamed)	shale, limestone
			(unnamed)	shale, coal (Croweburg Coal of Missouri)
			Whitebreast	coal
			(unnamed)	shale, coal, siltstone (Greenbrush and Abingdon coals of Illinois)
			Wiley	coal, shale
			Seahorn	limestone
			(unnamed)	shale, coal
			Munterville	limestone, coal, shale
			(undifferentiated)	shale, sandstone, coal, thin limestones
Morrowan		Caseyville		shale, sandstone

Construction work virtually removed a small hill of Cherokee Shale and Sandstone in Fort Dodge, Webster County. As a result, an abundant flora was seen and collected. The Ste. Genevieve–Cherokee contact was also exposed temporarily. The Cherokee flora included petrified wood of *Cordaites* (one piece weighed over 200 pounds); leaves of *Cordaites;* pith cores (*Artistia*) of *Cordaites;* various seeds and nuts, including *Trigonocarpus* and *Cordaicarpus;* cones (*Lepidostrobus*); "leaves," limbs, and "bark" of several species of *Lepidodendron, Sigillaria,* and related genera; a wide variety of seed ferns, including *Alethopteris, Caulopteris,* and *Mariopteris;* many species of *Neuropteris, Odontopteris, Pecopteris,* and *Sphenopteris* and the bark of a seed fern tree (*Ptychopteris*); cones and stems of *Calamites;* and other plant fossils (Fenton and Fenton 1958, Janssen 1965, Langford 1963, Tidwell 1975).

There are several other exposures of the lower, undifferentiated beds of the Cherokee Group in the Fort Dodge area. A few of these, containing some plant fossils, are listed in this chapter.

Site 106. Location: S½ sec. 27, T77N, R1W. The Caseyville Formation of the Morrowan Series is well exposed at Wyoming Hill in Muscatine County. The hill is located 2 miles west of Fairport on Highway 22 east of Muscatine. The exposure is a remnant of an ancient delta that extended into an inland sea in Illinois. Plant fossils are common here.

Site 107. Location: NE¼/NW¼/NW¼/NW¼ sec. 24, T89N, R29W. In Fort Dodge, Webster County, on a high slope overlooking Lizard Creek west of its conjunction with the Des Moines River, is an exposure of Cherokee Sandstone that carries a few plant fossils and varies in color from gray to brown. The site is located just west of old Highway 7, which runs adjacent to the creek and intersects Highway 169 farther west.

Site 108. Location: NE¼/NE¼/SE¼/SE¼ sec. 12, T87N, R28W. The Cherokee Group is well exposed in the vicinity of Lehigh in Webster County. One site is northeast of the bridge over the Des Moines River.

Site 109. Location: SW¼/SW¼/SW¼ sec. 16, T87N, R26W. The Cherokee Group is also exposed at Bell's Mill Park along the Boone River north of Stratford in Hamilton County. One way to reach the site is to begin in the town of Stratford and take county road R-21 (paved) north for 2.5 miles to the junction with county road D-56. Turn east on D-56 (paved) and continue for 2.5 miles to the first north-bearing gravel road. Turn north on this road and continue for a little over 2 miles to the bridge over the Boone River. Bell's Mill Park is located to the south. The exposures begin at the bridge and continue north along the eastern bank. Coal and shale are well exposed here. Pyrite, partially petrified wood, selenite crystals, and cone-in-cone calcite can be collected.

Site 110. Location: SE¼ sec. 7, T89N, R29W. About 1 mile north of Loomis Park along the river road (paved) on the eastern side of the Des Moines River just north of Fort Dodge in Webster County is an exposure of Cherokee Coal. Specimens of *Stigmaria:* the roots of *Lepidodendron* and *Sigillaria* trees as well as a few other fossils can be found, but these are not well preserved. A little over 0.5 mile south of this exposure is a road cut in the Cherokee Sandstone. A few plant fossils can be found here also. The St. Louis Limestone is exposed along the river here; the Ste. Genevieve Formation is mostly covered but can still be found in the deepest parts of the road ditch.

Site 111. Location: C sec. 17, T88N, R28W. One of the best series of Cherokee Group exposures in Webster County occurs west of Coalville. Part of this series of road cuts occurs along the east side of county road P-59 (paved) just north of the bridge over the Des Moines River. A highly eroded slope of Cherokee Sandstone is present here.

Site 112. Location: NE¼/SW¼ sec. 17, T88N, R28W. To reach this site, proceed south from Site 111. Cross the Des Moines River and turn west on a paved road. The road curves to the north. Continue in a northwest direction to the high bluffs (up to 60 feet) along the southwest side of the road. Shale and sandstone of the lower Cherokee Group are well exposed here. The coal near the top of the first high slope is equivalent to the Rock Island Number 1 Coal of Illinois. In another high slope just to the northwest, this coal becomes a dark carbonaceous shale with thin dark limestone lenses. These also occur, but in lesser numbers, in the first high slope. Plant fossils can be found in these bluffs, but most are only small fragments, requiring careful searching. Some of the more common specimens include petrified wood, seeds, and small blade-shaped "leaf" bits of lycopod trees and seed ferns. The lower levels of these bluffs are covered by talus.

Site 113. Location: NW¼/NE¼/NE¼ sec. 18, T88N, R28W. The limestone lenses near the top of the sequence at Site 112 thicken to form a 14-inch, dense, fossiliferous black limestone ledge here. To reach the site, continue north from Site 112 on the paved road and turn west on a gravel road. Continue west for about 0.5 mile. Exposures of shale and some sandstone occur in the north ditch; these correspond to those at the previous site but are not as well revealed. The limestone forms a ledge in the ditch toward the western end of the sequence. A wide variety of marine fossils occurs in this unit. Fossil plant bits occur in the shale above and below this limestone and are most noticeable after a rainstorm. Boulders of the limestone can also be found in the deep ditch on the south side of the road.

Site 114. Location: W½ sec. 8, T88N, R28W. To reach this site from Site 113, backtrack to the paved road and turn north; continue for about 0.5 mile. The road then curves west and eventually intersects Highway 169 2 miles farther west. A long road cut begins at the curve and continues west for part of a mile. The dark, carbonaceous fissile shale exposed at the eastern end of the sequence is equivalent to the upper part of the bluffs seen at Site 112. Claystone concretions are abundant and contain various minerals, some rare, making this a popular site among mineral collectors. The black limestone (14 inches thick) also occurs here but is badly slumped. It is best seen in the eastern end of the southern slope. A wide variety of marine fossils can be found in the unit. A 25-pound bulk sample of the underlying dark shale yielded a few pyrite nodules and some fossil plant bits. The light-colored shales and sandstones above the dark shale exposed in the middle of the sequence carry a fairly abundant flora. A method used by this collector is to look along the south ditch in the middle of the sequence where the rock has slumped down and is cleaned by the water in the ditch. The thick reddish and brown sandy shales and sandstones exposed at the western end of the sequence, on both sides of the road and in an abandoned quarry to the north, do not appear to be fossiliferous. A 25-pound bulk sample also failed to uncover any fossils. A thin coal bed occurs on the northern slope here and in the base of the quarry (Lemish et al. 1981).

Black limestone was examined at two other places in Webster County and seems to be much more fossiliferous at this site. Some of the fossils were found in pyrite nodules. The top of the unit contains cone-in-cone calcite appearing as short horizontal pillars. Ripple marks can be seen in the lower portion. A total of 289 fossils were found. Fish fragments are fairly common, but most are quite small. Look for brown, shiny, odd-looking bits that come in a wide variety of types and shapes. The fauna found by the author is listed below; specimens marked with an asterisk (*) have not been found at Site 115 despite several years of collecting there:

IDENTIFICATION	PERCENT
Brachiopods	
Eolissochonetes sp. (chonetid)	3.80
Orbiculoidea sp. (inarticulate)	0.69
Dictyoclostus sp. (productid)	0.34
Cancrinella sp. (productid)	48.78
Linoproductus sp.* (productid)	0.69
Desmoinesia sp. (productid)	0.69
Wellerella sp. (rhynchonellid)	1.73
Ambocoelia sp.* (spiriferid)	1.03
Neospirifer cameratus (spiriferid)	2.07
Composita sp. (spiriferid)	4.15
Phricodothyris sp.* (spiriferid)	0.34
Derbyia sp. (strophomenid)	2.44
Bryozoans, lacy	0.34
Burrows	2.44
Corals	
Lophophyllum proliferum	0.34
Crinoid columns	7.26
Fish fragments	5.88
Gastropods	
Straparollus sp.	0.34
Trepospira discoidalis	0.34
Donaldina stevensana	0.34
Donaldina robusta	2.07
?*Bellerophon* sp.	0.34
Nautiloids	
?*Ephippioceras* sp.	0.34
Dolorthoceras circulare	4.15
Metacoceras sp.	0.34
Unidentified	1.73
Pelecypods	
Clinopistha radiata	1.73
Aviculopecten providencesis	1.03
?*Wilkingia* sp.	0.34
Unidentified	1.38
Trilobite pygidia*	1.03
Unidentified fossils	0.69

Source: Dunbar and Condra 1932, Miller et al. 1933, Moore 1965, Pabian 1970, Shimer and Shrock 1972.

Most of the bivalves here are disarticulated and/or fragmented, with the exception of the smaller brachiopods. Most specimens of the pelecypod *Aviculopecten* are broken and badly worn. The gastropods are generally entire, but most of the nautiloids are fragmented, with some fragments measuring up to 1 inch in diameter.

Site 115. Location: SW¼/SW¼/SW¼/SW¼ sec. 32, T89N, R29W. The black limestone examined at the previous sites also occurs here. Although the deposit is considerably thicker, it is badly disturbed and partially covered and the associated shales are not exposed. The exposure occurs along the east bank of the Des Moines River in Fort Dodge, Webster County. Although a wide variety of marine fossils can be found, these are not as numerous as at the previous locations. To reach the site, begin at the intersection of 21st Street and Highway 20 in Fort Dodge. Turn south on 21st Street and curve to the east, picking up South 22nd Street. Continue south on this street for about 1.25 miles to the southern part of town. Mines exposing the Fort Dodge Gypsum and associated shales (Jurassic in age) can be seen here. Collecting is not permitted, but the beds can be viewed along Soldier Creek in Snell-Crawford Park in Fort Dodge. Cross a small wooden bridge and turn west on the first gravel road; the road curves north. Turn west on 18th Avenue South. The old Coleman School is to the east of the corner. Come to a T intersection on 18th Avenue South and turn north on South 15th Street. Continue north on this street for less than 0.25 mile. Park in the area and proceed on foot to the west, to abandoned tracks of the Chicago and Northwestern Railroad near the Des Moines River. Depending on where you emerge from the brush, walk either up or down the tracks a short distance until the sewage treatment plant is directly west across the river. The exposure occurs in this area, in the slope below the tracks, and may be difficult to spot in the heavy brush. Although one hour of collecting yielded only 36 fossils, the author has collected at the site for many years and the faunal list below is fairly representative. The fossils found included:

IDENTIFICATION	PERCENT
Brachiopods	
Eolissochonetes sp. (chonetid)	8.33
Cancrinella sp. (productid)	25.00
Neospirifer cameratus (spiriferid)	2.77
Corals	
Lophophyllum proliferum	2.77
Crinoid columns	19.44
Fish fragments	5.54
Gastropods	
Donaldina stevensana	2.77
Straparollus sp.	2.77
Nautiloids	
?*Ephippioceras* sp.	2.77
Dolorthoceras circulare	13.88
Pelecypods	
Aviculopecten providencesis	5.54
Clinopistha radiata	8.33

Source: Dunbar and Condra 1932, Miller et al. 1933, Moore 1965, Pabian 1970, Shimer and Shrock 1972.

Nodules of pyrite a few inches across can be found in the limestone here, and some contain an abundant fauna of very young or small brachiopods, young pelecypods, and nautiloid fragments. As in most Pennsylvanian faunas, the productids and chonetids are the most common brachiopods here. Nautiloids and gastropods are more common (and in the same type of rock at Site 114) than in most of the Pennsylvanian faunas examined for this study, and some very excellent specimens can be found. Unlike several other Pennsylvanian faunas, branching bryozoans were not found. Most of the fossils at this site are fragmented or disarticulated.

Site 116. Location: along the southern part of the boundary between sections 29 and 28, T72N, R13W. There is a series of road cuts exposing shale, sandstone, and coal of the Cherokee Group along Highway 34 in Monroe and Wapello counties. The best exposure seen occurs in eastern Ottumwa along a gravel road intersecting the highway. Shales of the Cherokee are well exposed here. No plant fossils were seen, but a thin layer of selenite crystals, at least up to 3 inches in length, occurs in the northern end of the eastern slope.

Site 117. Location: C sec. 23, T76N, R18W. The abandoned mines south of Pella in Marion County also expose fossiliferous shales and sandstones of the Cherokee Group. Plant fossils are fairly common here. Plant fossils of the Cherokee were also found in a quarry north of Oskaloosa in Mahaska County (see Site 101).

Site 118. Location: NE¼ sec. 35, T75N, R21W. A road cut north of Dallas in Marion County exposes shale, sandstone, and conglomerate believed to be of the Cherokee Group. The cut occurs on the west side of Highway 181; no fossils were seen.

Site 119. Location: SW¼/SE¼ sec. 29, T83N, R26W. Another exposure of the Cherokee Group was examined south of Boone in Boone County. The exposure occurs high on the western slope of the valley overlooking the Des Moines River on the north side of county road E-57 (paved). Exposed here and in the ditches along the road are grayish and brown soft sandstones. No fossils were seen.

Site 120. Location: S½ sec. 4, T78N, R29W. The beds exposed in the pit of the Redfield Brick and Tile Company are probably of the Cherokee Group. The plant is located on the north side of Highway 6 on the eastern edge of Redfield in Dallas County. Exposed above the water level is blue gray, nonfossiliferous silty shale. This is overlain by various reddish yellow shales, minor deposits of grayish limestones, and some sandstone. Plant fossils reportedly occur here, but none were seen.

Site 121. Location: SW¼/SW¼/NW¼ sec. 25, T69N, R19W. An abandoned clay pit is located just north of Highway 2 about 4 miles west of Centerville in Appanoose County southwest of Mystic. Exposed here are thick gray and yellowish shales and a limestone that varies from grayish and dense to reddish brown and shaly. The limestone carries an abundant fauna of small brachiopods. The exposure is probably from the upper part of the Cherokee Group. In a brief stop (half an hour) a total of 264 fossils were found in the limestone, mostly small brachiopods. This fauna is described below:

IDENTIFICATION	PERCENT
Brachiopods	
Marginifera sp. (productid)	0.37
Ambocoelia sp. (spiriferid)	60.60
Phricodothyris sp. (spiriferid)	19.69
Punctospirifer kentuckyensis (spiriferid)	1.89
Composita sp. (spiriferid)	6.81
Crurithyris planoconvexi (spiriferid)	0.37
Derbyia sp. (strophomenid)	3.78
Unidentified	0.37
Crinoid columns	2.27
Pelecypods	
Aviculopecten sp. (pelecypod)	3.78

Source: Dunbar and Condra 1932, Moore 1965, Pabian 1970, Shimer and Shrock 1972.

Fossils appear to be fairly evenly spread, with no clusters of any particular species seen. The specimens of *Derbyia* and *Aviculopecten* were very small.

Madison County contains many excellent Pennsylvanian exposures; the Cherokee Group occurs in the northeast corner. The following groups are also present: Marmaton, Pleasanton, Kansas City, Lansing, and Douglas; the Virgilian Series occurs in the extreme west-central part of the county. Exposures of the Douglas Group are rare, however. They have been known to occur near the Madison-Adair county line, but the shales are quickly eroded and covered.

Site 122. Location: near C sec. 15, T77N, R26W. The Cherokee-Marmaton contact is exposed in the northeastern part of Madison County. To reach the exposure, take Highway 169 north out of Winterset for 2.5 miles to the intersection of county road G-4R (paved). The intersection is not marked. Turn right (east). Follow this road as it curves in a generally northeastern direction. The exposure is about 15 miles northeast of the corner. It occurs on the east side of county road G-4R just south of the intersection with county road G-14 (also paved). This is south of the Badger Creek bridge. The site is overgrown, and collectors should wear boots as a precaution against rattlesnakes. The following is a general description of the exposure (modified from Stark 1973):

I. Marmaton Group
   A. Fort Scott Formation
      1. Estimated 5 feet of yellow shale
      2. Estimated 4 feet of reddish brown shale
      3. Estimated 5 feet of gray platy shale
      4. Blackjack Creek Member: estimated 4 feet of brown limestone exposed toward the northern end of the cut
II. Cherokee Group

A. At least 8 feet of gray green shale exposed at the northern end of the cut

Site 123. Location: near C sec. 27, T75N, R26W. Several exposures of the Marmaton Group occur south of St. Charles in Madison County. To reach one exposure, take county road G-50 (paved) west out of St. Charles. Turn south on the first gravel road. Continue south to a T intersection; there, turn right (west) on a narrow dirt road. Go west for about 1 mile. The exposures can best be seen in the ditches in a slope east of a small bridge. The following stratigraphic column is generalized by the author from field estimates of poor exposures:

I. Altamont Formation
   A. Worland? Member: around 10 feet covered at the top of the slope; a few minor exposures of limestone
   B. Lake Neosho? Member: around 10 feet of yellow to gray shale exposed near the top of the north ditch; several beds
II. Bandera? Formation
   A. Around 10 feet of poorly exposed red shale
   B. Five feet of green shale with sandstone
   C. Around 10 feet of green shale
III. Pawnee? Formation
   A. Coal City? Member: around 2 feet of red brown limestone with some fossils; exposed in both ditches, in the roadbed, and in a cut near the middle of the slope
   B. Mine Creek? Member: around 20 feet of partially exposed shales, vary in color from gray to brown; a coal smut present near the top; lower levels best exposed in the north ditch; upper levels best exposed under the Coal City Limestone in the south ditch
   C. Myrick Station? Member: 1 foot of brown limestone with gray areas; small fossils
   D. Anna? Member
     1. A few inches of brown shale
     2. Two feet of gray shale
     3. At least 1 foot of black fissile shale
IV. Labette? Formation
   A. Mystic? Coal: 1 foot thick
   B. Brown, thin-bedded shaly sandstone; at least 5 feet exposed; best seen in the south ditch near the base of the slope

Although a major part of the Marmaton is present here, most of the beds in this sequence are not well exposed. Careful searching and some digging may be required.

Site 124. Location: S½ of boundary between sec. 25 and 30, T78N, R28-R27W. An exposure believed to be of the Mine Creek Member of the Pawnee Formation occurs along Highway 169 just north of the Madison County line in Dallas County. The cut occurs on both sides of the road north of the intersection of Highways 169 and 90 south of De Soto. Partially covered by considerable Pleistocene till on the slopes is at least 20 feet of gray shale with a thin black zone in the middle. There is also a considerable amount of brown weathered sandstone in the lower portions of the slopes. Limestone fragments at the base of the slopes contain a few brachiopods and crinoid columns, but these are the only fossils found here for this survey.

Site 125. Location: SE¼ sec. 34, T77N, R27W. The Worland Member of the Altamont Formation is exposed in several places in eastern Madison County. A good exposure was examined in the northeastern part of the county. To reach the road cut, begin at the intersection of Highway 169 and county road G-4R (paved). The intersection is not marked but is about 2.5 miles north of Winterset. Turn east on G-4R and continue for about 4.5 miles to the fourth left-bearing gravel road. Turn north on this road and continue for about 2 miles to the grassed-over cut south of a bridge. The brown to gray Worland Limestone occurs on both sides of the road and carries a fair abundance of fossils, including brachiopods and fusulinids (Stark 1973).

Site 126. Location: SW¼ sec. 17, T75N, R26W. A sandstone exposure was examined on the north side of county road G-50 about 4 miles west of Saint Charles in Madison County. Exposed is around 10 feet of soft brown sandstone with red brown denser zones, particularly near the top. This is believed to belong to the Nowata Formation. In Madison County the Nowata contains considerable sandstone (Landis and Van Eck 1965).

Site 127. Location: SE¼ sec. 1, T75N, R27W. The only member of the Lenapah Formation presently recognized in Iowa is the Cooper Creek Limestone. It is commonly seen at the base of exposures of the Pleasanton Group in eastern Madison County. A high road cut east of East Peru once included the Pleasanton–Cooper Creek contact, but the Cooper Creek is now covered (see Chap. 8, Site 129). A good exposure of the Cooper Creek was seen southwest of Patterson. To reach it, take county road G-50 west out of St. Charles for about 5.5 miles to the third north-bearing gravel road. Turn north and continue for about 1.5 miles. The cut is on the western side. The exposure is described below (modified from Stark 1973):

I. Kansas City Group
   A. Hertha Formation: 3 feet of grayish brown dense limestone with fossils and shale seams; exposed at the top of the cut
II. Pleasanton Group: 15 feet of shales and minor amounts of limestone; partially overgrown
III. Marmaton Group
   A. Lenapah Formation
      1. Cooper Creek Member: a few feet of brown limestone exposed in the ditch at the base of the cut

The Pleasanton is also exposed in another cut 0.5 mile north of this exposure and on the eastern side of the road. The Cooper Creek may also be present at that cut, but it was not seen. A thick limestone exposure was examined in another cut along a gravel road 1 mile west of these two cuts (SW¼ sec. 1, T75N, R27W). That cut is believed to expose the Bethany Falls Member of the Swope Formation (Kansas City Group).

8

Pennsylvanian Period
MISSOURIAN SERIES

THE MISSOURIAN SERIES is upper Middle Pennsylvanian in age and comprises three groups: the Lansing; Kansas City, and Pleasanton. Eighteen formations of the Missourian are recognized in southwest Iowa, and many of these have abundant faunas. The stratigraphic column for the Missourian in Iowa is listed below:

GROUP	FORMATION	MEMBER	DESCRIPTION
Lansing	Stanton		limestone
	Vilas		shale
	Plattsburg		limestone
Kansas City	Bonner Springs		shale
	Wyandotte	Farley	limestone
		Island Creek	shale
		Argentine	limestone
		Quindaro	shale
		Frisbie	limestone
	Lane		shale
	Iola	Raytown	limestone
		Muncie Creek	shale
		Paola	limestone
	Chanute		shale
	Drum	Corbin City	limestone
		Cement City	limestone
	Quivira		shale
	Westerville		limestone
	Cherryvale	Wea	shale
		Block	limestone
		Fontana	shale

GROUP	FORMATION	MEMBER	DESCRIPTION
Kansas City (*cont.*)			
	Dennis	Winterset	limestone
		Stark	shale
		Canville	limestone
	Galesburg		shale
	Swope	Bethany Falls	limestone
		Hushpuckney	shale
		Middle Creek	limestone
	Ladore		shale
	Hertha		limestone
Pleasanton			shale, coal, limestone, sandstone

Because some exposures and quarries of the Missourian Series in Nebraska are included in this field guide and because variations do occur between the Pennsylvanian of Iowa and Nebraska, the stratigraphic column for the Missourian Series in Nebraska is listed here:

GROUP	FORMATION	MEMBER	DESCRIPTION
Lansing	Stanton	South Bend	limestone
		Rock Lake	shale
		Stoner	limestone
		"Kiewitz"	shale
		"Dyson Hollow"	limestone
		Eudora	shale
		Captain Creek	limestone
	Vilas		shale
	Plattsburg	Spring Hill	limestone
		Hickory Creek	shale
		Merriam	limestone
Kansas City	Bonner Springs		shale
	Wyandotte	Farley	limestone
		Island Creek	shale
		Argentine	limestone
		Quindaro	shale
		Frisbie	limestone
	Lane		shale
	Iola	Raytown	limestone
	Chanute		shale
	Drum	Corbin City	limestone
		Cement City	limestone
		Richfield	shale
		P.W.A.	limestone
	Quivira		shale
	Sharpy	Westerville	limestone
		Wea	shale
		Block	limestone
	Fontana		shale
	Dennis	Winterset	limestone
		Stark	shale

GROUP	FORMATION	MEMBER	DESCRIPTION
Kansas City	Dennis (cont.)		
		Canville	limestone
	Galesburg		shale
	Swope	Bethany Falls	limestone
		Hushpuckney	shale
	Ladore		shale
	Hertha		limestone
Pleasanton			shale

The Pennsylvanian System is dominated by cyclic deposits termed cyclothems, which reflect changing water depths during deposition, which were possibly caused by relatively minor waxing and waning of polar glaciers during a time that Iowa was at very low latitudes (Phillip Heckel and Brian Witzke, personal communications). Although cyclothems can be made up of as many as ten members, those in Madison County usually consist of four: a nearshore marine shale (usually the sandy shale marking the end of one cyclothem and the upper shale marking the start of another, sometimes containing nonmarine shales with plant fossils), a transgressive or middle limestone deposited in open water below the waves, an offshore deeper water deposit or middle shale, and a regressive limestone that is generally much thicker than the transgressive limestone.

Site 128. Location: E¼ sec. 1, T75N, R27W. The Pleasanton Group marks the base of the Missourian Series. Exposures were seen southwest of Patterson in Madison County. To reach them, take county road G-50 (paved) west out of St. Charles for about 6 miles to the third north-bearing gravel road. Turn north and continue for about 1.5 miles. The first cut occurs on the western side of the road and includes a few feet of limestone of the Cooper Creek Member of the Lenapah Formation at the base. About 15 feet of shales of the Pleasanton Group are exposed here, but the site is partially overgrown. A few feet of Hertha Limestone are present at the top of the cut. Another cut occurs along the east side of the road about 0.5 mile further north. The Pleasanton Group and Hertha Formation are also exposed here, but the Cooper Creek Limestone was not seen. The Bethany Falls Limestone Member of the Swope Formation is probably the unit exposed in another cut along a gravel road located 1 mile west of these exposures.

Site 129. Location: NW¼ sec. 12, T74N, R27W. Just east of East Peru in Madison County a high bluff is exposed on the north side of county road R-21 (paved). Use caution here, for rattlesnakes have been seen. The exposure is described below (modified from Heckel 1980):

I. Kansas City Group
  A. Swope Formation
    1. Bethany Falls Member: regressive limestone of the Swope Cyclothem; around 5 feet of brown fossiliferous limestone exposed at the top of the cut and on the eastern end

2. Hushpuckney Member: offshore shale of the Swope Cyclothem; 2 feet of nonfossiliferous shale
   a. Half a foot of yellow shale
   b. Half a foot of gray shale
   c. One foot of black fissile shale
3. Middle Creek Member: transgressive limestone of the Swope Cyclothem; 1 foot of dense dark gray limestone; no fossils
   B. Ladore Formation: nearshore shale of the Hertha-Swope cyclothems. Around 20 feet of yellowish gray shale partially covered; silty near the top and sandy near the base; burrows found in the sandstone
   C. Hertha Formation: regressive limestone of the Hertha Cyclothem; 8 feet of dense grayish limestone with shaly seams and pockets; thin-bedded with a thick bed near the top; many fossils, including productid brachiopods in life position
II. Pleasanton Group: nearshore shale of the Hertha Cyclothem
   A. Fifteen feet of gray shale; a few *Chonetinella flemingi;* base covered
   B. At least 5 feet of brown sandstone exposed at the western end of the cut
III. Marmaton Group
   A. Lenapah Formation
      1. Cooper Creek Member: limestone present under the Pleasanton sandstone at the western end of the cut, but no longer exposed

A fauna (130 fossils) was collected from the Hertha Formation at this site and is described below:

IDENTIFICATION	PERCENT
Brachiopods	
aff. *Productella* sp. (productid)	25.38
Desmoinesia sp. (productid)	0.76
Composita subtilita (spiriferid)	24.61
Neospirifer sp. (spiriferid)	1.53
Phricodothyris sp. (spiriferid)	1.53
Dielasma sp. (terebratulid)	0.76
Bryozoans, unidentified branching	1.53
Corals	
Lophophyllum proliferum (solitary)	3.70
Crinoid columns	36.15
Gastropods	
Donaldina sp.	4.61

Source: Dunbar and Condra 1932, Moore 1965, Pabian 1970, Shimer and Shrock 1972.

A productid brachiopod related to *Productella* is abundant here; the majority of specimens are in life position, their spiny pedicle valves embedded in the dense limestone. They, like most fossils in this fauna, are more numerous in clusters. The crinoid columns seem to be most common in the more argillaceous zones of the Hertha Limestone, and the branching bryozoans apparently occur only at the top of the formation.

Site 130. Location: S½ sec. 27, T76N, R27W. The Bethany Falls Limestone Member of the Swope Formation is quarried at the E. I. Sargent Quarries located around 3 miles east of Winterset in Madison County on Highway 92. Among the fossils found were large pelecypods; one specimen was over 7 inches long. These occur in the upper brown limestone. The Hushpuckney Member, gray shale, and black fissile shale can be seen in the deepest parts of the quarries. Occasional clusters of fossils can be found in the black fissile shale, including pelecypods, crinoid columns, and the productid brachiopod *Marginifera*. Collectors are asked to visit the quarry on Sunday. Stop at the house near the main gate for permission.

Site 131. Location: C sec. 6, T75N, R27W. The Swope Formation is also exposed south of Winterset in Madison County on old Highway 169. It is represented by thin-bedded, mostly grayish limestone of the Bethany Falls Member (about 15 feet) and by gray shale and black fissile shale of the Hushpuckney Member. The Bethany Falls Limestone carries a few fossils with a zone of reddish brown limestone near the top that contains crinoid columns. The Hushpuckney Shale can be found in the ditch.

Site 132. Location: NW¼ sec. 12, T75N, R28W. Another exposure of the Bethany Falls Limestone occurs along county road P-69 (gravel) beginning about 1 mile south of Winterset in Madison County and continuing until 0.5 mile east of Highway 169. P-69 intersects Highway 169 just north of the Middle River. Some large productid brachiopods were found here. Shale of the Hushpuckney Member was also seen.

There are several other exposures of the Swope Formation in Madison County. The Devils Backbone Tunnel (the only automobile tunnel in the state) is located in Pammel State Park and is opened up under the Bethany Falls Member.

Site 133. Location: SE¼/SE¼/NW¼ sec. 17, T75N, R28W. An exposure believed to be of the Winterset Limestone Member of the Dennis Formation was examined west of Pammel Park near the Middle River. To reach the site, begin where Highways 169 and 92 split west of Winterset in Madison County. Go west on Highway 92 for about 3 miles; then turn south on a gravel road. Continue south for 1.5 miles to a T intersection. Turn west and then south on another gravel road. This road curves and bears east to Pammel Park; however, turn west just before the curve. This gravel road then curves south and continues to the Middle River. The Winterset? Limestone exposed along the road north of the bridge was found to have a fairly abundant fauna of fusulinids and the spiriferid brachiopod *Crurithyris* as well as bryozoans, pelecypods, echinoid spines, crinoid columns, and the brachiopods *Meekella* and *Dielasma*.

Site 134. Location: C sec. 11, T75N, R28W. Some of the best Pennsylvanian fossil collecting in Iowa or Nebraska, in the opinion of this collector, can be done along Highway 169 southwest of Winterset in Madison County. The first exposure occurs at the base of the high slope on both sides of the highway north of the Middle River bridge. The best exposure occurs at the southern end of the eastern slope and is described below (Heckel 1980 and the author):

I. Cherryvale Formation
   A. Wea Member:
      1. Limestone, dark gray and dense; only a thin zone present, poorly exposed; pelecypods and brachiopods seen but not as abundant as in level 2
      2. Limestone, dark gray and dense; 2 feet present with abundant pelecypods, brachiopods, and gastropods
      3. Shale, 3 feet thick; varies in color from gray to tan; some pelecypods
   B. Block Member: limestone, tan and shaly at the top, gray and dense at the base, 4 feet thick; no fossils seen
   C. Fontana Member: blue gray siltstone, 5 feet thick; abundant fauna in a zone in the middle of the unit; includes well-preserved brachiopods, pelecypods, bryozoans, and some trilobite pygidia; best seen north of the Winterset Limestone in both slopes
II. Dennis Formation
   A. Winterset Member: regressive limestone of the Dennis Cyclothem; tan to gray limestone around 5 feet thick; shaly seams; best exposed in the middle of the western slope; badly disturbed on the eastern side; some fossils
   B. Stark Member: offshore shale of the Dennis Cyclothem
      1. Yellowish gray shale; maximum thickness 2.5 feet; best exposed near the south end of the eastern cut, just north of a private driveway; only a few inches thick in the western cut; excellently preserved and abundant fauna of corals, brachiopods, crinoid columns, and nearly microscopic enrolled trilobites
      2. Blue gray shale, maximum thickness 1 foot; contains a varied but not very abundant fauna; a few pyrite nodules
      3. Black fissile shale, 2.5 feet thick; contains a few inarticulate brachiopods and vertebrate (fish) fragments; some pyrite
   C. Canville Member: transgressive limestone of the Dennis Cyclothem; thin, intermittent limestone nodules near the base of the black fissile shale of the Stark Member reportedly found by Heckel (1980) in the eastern cut, but not common
III. Galesburg Formation: nearshore shale of the Swope-Dennis cyclothems
   A. Blue gray shale becoming nearly black fissile shale near the top, which is difficult to distinguish from the overlying Stark Shale; 4 feet thick; no fossils even in a bulk sample; much pyrite
   B. Yellowish gray shale at least 4 feet thick; no fossils seen; best seen in the southern end of the eastern cut, south of a private driveway

IV. Swope Formation
   A. Bethany Falls Member: regressive limestone of the Swope Cyclothem; yellowish orange at the top and gray toward the base of the exposure; 3 feet exposed in the ditch at the southern end of the western cut; some crinoid columns and brachiopods

Along both slopes of Highway 169, north of the top of the Cherryvale exposure, is a thick deposit of gray shale with closely spaced, red oxidized zones. These are believed to be tidal flat deposits from the Chanute Formation (Heckel, personal communication). The Drum Formation is covered here.

The black shale of the Stark Member (and similar black shales) was laid down in the deepest waters of the cyclothem deposition and contains a meager fauna of small pelecypods, inarticulate brachiopods, and small fish remains. The Winterset Limestone at this site is composed of two fairly distinctive beds. The lower, more shaly, bedded unit indicates a rough-water environment. The upper unit is more massive and finer grained and indicates a quieter water environment (Heckel 1980).

Abundant faunas were collected from units 1 and 2 of the Stark Member here. One hour of collecting yielded 85 fossils from unit 1 and 602 fossils from unit 2. The fossils found included:

IDENTIFICATION	UNIT 1	UNIT 2
	(%)	(%)
Brachiopods		
Chonetes granulifer (chonetid)	...	0.16
Chonetinella flemingi (chonetid)	2.35	1.65
Orbiculoidea missouriensis (inarticulate)	17.64	0.66
Dictyoclostus portlockianus (productid)	9.41	9.63
Hystrinculina sp. (productid)	2.35	6.64
Juresania nebrascensis (productid)	...	0.66
Linoproductus meniscus (productid)	...	0.16
Marginifera sp. (productid)	9.41	12.79
Desmoinesia sp. (productid)	...	0.66
Wellerella truncata (rhynchonellid)	...	0.16
Ambocoelia planoconvexa (spiriferid)	3.52	1.82
Punctospirifer kentuckyensis (spiriferid)	1.17	0.66
Composita ovata (spiriferid)	24.70	12.95
Neospirifer latus (spiriferid)	1.17	1.82
Crurithyris planoconvexa (spiriferid)	5.88	2.15
Neospirifer triplicatus (spiriferid)	...	0.49
Derbyia crassa (strophomenid)	2.35	5.81
Bryozoans		
Branching, unidentified (small)	1.17	0.66
Branching, unidentified (average)	...	0.16
Corals		
Pleurodictycum sp. (colonial)	...	0.49
Lophophyllum sp. (solitary)	1.17	10.13
Crinoid calyx		
Polusocrinus sp.	...	0.16
Crinoid columns	17.64	29.40

Source: Conservation and Survey Division Field Guides 1969, Dunbar and Condra 1932, Miller et al. 1933, Moore 1965, Pabian 1970, Shimer and Shrock 1972.

The uppermost Stark Shale at this site has the highest concentration of corals of any Pennsylvanian fauna examined in this study. This level of the Stark is very similar to the upper level of the Cherryvale? Formation exposed south of the Middle River bridge (Site 135). A 25-pound bulk sample of the uppermost Stark yielded 2,204 fossils, mostly small brachiopods but also a few very small enrolled specimens of the trilobite *Ditomopyge scitula*. Fossils in this unit can be cleaned from matrix simply with water and a stiff brush.

Three members of the Cherryvale Formation are recognized in parts of Iowa, but not in Madison County. However, in this book, the formation at the Highway 169 exposures has been divided into members merely for convenience. The Cherryvale Formation in the northern cut offers several abundant faunas. One occurs in the middle of the Fontana Member. The majority of the brachiopods are articulated; all the pelecypods are disarticulated and several are fragmented. One hour of collecting in this level of the Fontana Member yielded 502 fossils; types are listed below:

IDENTIFICATION	PERCENT
Brachiopods	
Juresania nebrascensis (productid)	0.79
Linoproductus meniscus (productid)	0.99
Ambocoelia planoconvexa (spiriferid)	2.39
Composita trilobata (spiriferid)	29.48
Crurithyris sp. (spiriferid)	2.39
Derbyia crassa (strophomenid)	16.53
Bryozoans	
Branching, unidentified (small)	1.39
Branching, unidentified (medium)	0.99
Encrusting	5.79
Lacy	2.19
Crinoid columnals	0.19
Burrows	9.96
Pelecypods	
Wilkingia sp.	24.30
Yoldia sp.	0.39
Acanthopecten carboniferus	0.19
Trilobites	
Ameura sp. (pygidia)	0.39
Worm tubes, annelid	
Spirorbis sp.	1.19

Source: Conservation and Survey Division Field Guides 1969, Dunbar and Condra 1932, Miller et al. 1933, Moore 1965, Pabian 1970, Shimer and Shrock 1972.

The productid brachiopods, so abundant in many Pennsylvanian faunas, are only minor elements in this, which is one of the few Pennsylvanian faunas in this survey that was dominated by spiriferid brachiopods and pelecypods. Commensals (including the only Pennsylvanian *Spirorbis* tubes found by this collector) are more common in this fauna than in most others of the Pennsylvanian examined for this study. *Composita trilobata*, *Derbyia crassa*, and the pelecypod *Wilkingia* served as hosts for the commensals. A few large, excellently preserved specimens of the pelecypod *Acanthopecten carboniferus* can be found in this fauna.

The upper two levels of the Wea Member of the Cherryvale Formation exposed here contain faunas that are very similar in content and preservation. Both levels are composed of gray to brown, silty limestone. The majority of the bivalves are disarticulated, and the pelecypods and gastropods are represented by casts. In level 2, dense clusters of pelecypods are numerous, and most of the brachiopods occur near the top. Smaller clusters of *Derbyia* and the gastropod *Bellerophon* were also found. One hour of collecting in this unit yielded 1,581 fossils. No clusters were observed in level 1, which yielded 43 specimens during one hour. These two faunas included the following:

IDENTIFICATION	LEVEL 1	LEVEL 2
	(%)	(%)
Brachiopods		
Linoproductus meniscus (productid)	9.30	1.58
Linoproductus platyumbonus (productid)	...	0.06
Derbyia crassa (strophomenid)	4.65	6.83
Gastropods		
Bellerophon crassus	...	8.98
Nautiloids		
Metaceras sp.	...	0.18
Pelecypods		
Wilkingia sp.	11.62	27.95
Yoldia sp.	32.55	33.64
Parallelodon tenuistriatus	41.86	17.64
Aviculopecten (*Fasciculiconcha*) *providencesis*	...	3.03

Source: Dunbar and Condra 1932, Miller et al. 1933, Moore 1965, Pabian 1970, Shimer and Shrock 1972.

The beds at this site are quite different from those exposed just south of the Middle River bridge at Site 135.

Site 135. Location: C sec. 14, T75N, R28W. Excellent exposures of the Kansas City Group also occur south of the Middle River bridge along both sides of Highway 169 southwest of Winterset in Madison County. However, this author has been unable to definitely correlate any of the beds exposed at this site with those just to the north (see Site 134) or any other deposits of the Kansas City Group seen in the Winterset area. The series of exposures is described below by the author:

I. Drum? Formation: a few feet of brown limestone poorly exposed at the top of the southernmost slope of the sequence and on the east side of the road; the top of the Winterset? Limestone can still be seen in the deep ditch on the west side
II. Quivira? Formation: exposed under the Drum? Limestone in the same slope
   A. Two feet of red shale

B. Two feet of gray shale
III. Westerville? Formation: 4 feet of brown limestone exposed at the base of the southernmost slope; crinoid columns and a few brachiopods seen
IV. Cherryvale? Formation: various shales and limestones exposed in the slope just north of the slope exposing the above beds, also on the eastern side of the highway; excellent fossils
   A. Wea? Member
      1. Shale, varies from tan to gray; at least 5 feet exposed with abundant brachiopods, bryozoans, crinoid calyces, nautiloids, large pelecypods, and a few large gastropods
      2. Limestone, blue gray and dense; slightly oolitic; less than 1 foot thick with many brachiopods, pelecypods, fusulinids, bryozoans, nautiloids; not well exposed
      3. Shale, dark gray to black and thin-bedded; 5 feet exposed; many brachiopods, crinoid columnals, and bryozoans
   B. Block? Member: Limestone, gray at the base, yellowish near the top; 4 feet exposed; many brachiopods and pelecypods with a dense, thin zone of *Derbyia crassa* near the top
   C. Fontana? Member: Gray shale; 5 feet exposed near the base of the eastern slope overlying a minor outcrop of the Winterset? Limestone; contains a fairly abundant brachiopod fauna

The following beds are exposed in a ravine on the western side of Highway 169 south of the Middle River bridge:

I. Dennis? Formation
   A. Winterset? Member: at least 12 feet of yellow to gray limestone excellently exposed in a bluff; few fossils seen
   B. Stark? Member: poorly exposed; probably over 5 feet thick; black fissile shale and gray shale; a bluish gray shale with abundant fossil fragments also present, probably belonging to the Stark
   C. Canville? Member: not well exposed; brown limestone, probably 1 foot thick
II. Galesburg? Formation: at least 10 feet of green gray silty shale, including a brown silty limestone deposit in the middle; no fossils; excellently exposed at the northern base of the ditch below the limestone bluff

Collecting in the Cherryvale? at this site has declined steadily in quality since it was first examined in 1976, but this collector has yet to find any other Pennsylvanian exposure with faunas equal to these. The best collecting can be done on the east-side slope in the drainage cuts. A 25-pound bulk sample of unit 1 of the Wea? Member here yielded an excellent specimen of the trilobite *Amerua sangamonensis*. The specimen was almost entirely encased in a small limestone nodule that prevented it from being spotted in the field. Some larger than usual brachiopods occur here, and a few very large specimens can be found in unit 2 of the Wea?. Faunas were collected

PENNSYLVANIAN PERIOD: MISSOURIAN SERIES

from all three units of the Wea? here and also from the Fontana? and Block? members of the Cherryvale?. In all, five distinct faunas are present, and they are quite different from the Cherryvale? faunas collected north of the Middle River bridge.

The Fontana? fauna at this site is fairly abundant, but some fossils are fragmented. One hour of collecting yielded 151 specimens. The Block? fauna here has a greater abundance of large brachiopods than the Fontana?, and most fossils are undamaged. One hour of collecting yielded 146 fossils. These two faunas included:

IDENTIFICATION	FONTANA?	BLOCK?
	(%)	(%)
Brachiopods		
Chonetinella flemingi (chonetid)	9.93	...
Chonetes granulifer (chonetid)	1.32	...
Orbiculoidea missouriensis (inarticulate)	0.66	0.68
Dictyoclostus portlockianus (productid)	12.58	0.68
Marginifera sp. (productid)	7.94	...
Linoproductus meniscus (productid)	3.97	4.97
Linoproductus platyumbonus (productid)	...	0.68
Juresania nebrascensis (productid)	...	0.68
Neospirifer latus (spiriferid)	0.66	0.68
Punctospirifer kentuckyensis (spiriferid)	0.66	...
Composita ovata (spiriferid)	...	4.10
Composita trilobata (spiriferid)	3.31	2.05
Derbyia crassa (strophomenid)	31.78	74.65
Bryozoans		
Branching, unidentified (small)	0.66	1.36
Branching, unidentified (medium)	4.63	0.68
Branching, unidentified (large)	...	1.36
Encrusting, unidentified	0.66	...
Coral		
Lophophyllum sp. (solitary)	2.64	...
Crinoid columnals	17.88	2.73
Pelecypods		
Septimyalina sp.	...	0.68
Wilkingia sp.	...	4.10

Source: Dunbar and Condra 1932, Moore 1965, Pabian 1970, Shimer and Shrock 1972.

A 25-pound bulk sample of the Fontana? Member at this site yielded 68 fossils, mostly crinoid columnals and the brachiopods *Derbyia*, *Chonetes*, and *Chonetinella*. Fusulinids, commonly found in bulk samples of most Pennsylvanian shales, were not present. A few crinoid plates shaped like shark teeth were also found and occur in several other Pennsylvanian shales.

All three units of the Wea? Member at this site are very fossiliferous; most of the fossils are entire and excellently preserved. Some large specimens of lacy bryozoans free from matrix are present but fragile. The pelecypods are generally quite large but usually poorly preserved, and the crinoid calyces are worn. The faunas of these three units are described below. The numbers at the top of the columns refer to the number of fossils found.

IDENTIFICATION	(340) UNIT 1	(530) UNIT 2	(860) UNIT 3
	(%)	(%)	(%)
Brachiopods			
Chonetinella flemingi (chonetid)	5.88	0.75	67.09
Chonetes granulifer (chonetid)	29.41	...	17.55
Linoproductus meniscus (productid)	0.88	0.56	1.16
Linoproductus platyumbonus (productid)	...	0.18	0.11
Marginifera sp. (productid)	1.47	1.32	0.11
Desmoinesia sp. (productid)	0.58	...	...
Dictyoclostus portlockianus (productid)	9.11	1.88	0.58
Juresania nebrascensis (productid)	1.17	1.32	0.69
Juresania symmetrica (productid)	...	...	0.34
Composita ovata (spiriferid)	...	0.37	0.46
Composita trilobata (spiriferid)	3.52	0.37	...
Neospirifer triplicatus (spiriferid)	1.17	0.37	0.34
Neospirifer latus (spiriferid)	2.05	0.94	0.46
Phricodothyris perplexa (spiriferid)	0.29	...	...
Meekella striatoscostata (strophomenid)	2.64	1.88	0.23
Derbyia crassa (strophomenid)	7.35	1.32	...
Bryozoans			
Branching, unidentified (small)	1.76	10.00	6.74
Branching, unidentified (medium)	10.58	...	0.69
Branching, unidentified (large)	2.35	0.56	0.11
Encrusting, unidentified	0.29	0.18	...
Lacy, unidentified	1.76	1.69	...
Coral			
Lophophyllum proliferum (solitary)	...	0.18	...
Crinoid calyx			
Polusocrinus sp.	0.58	...	0.11
Crinoid columns	12.05	18.86	2.90
Echinoid spines	...	0.37	...
Fusulinids	...	56.60	...
Gastropods			
Anematina sp.	0.58	...	...
Green algae?	0.58	...	...
Nautiloids			
Metacoceras sp.	0.29	...	...
Domatoceras lasallense	0.29	...	...
Pelecypods			
Aviculopecten sp.	...	...	0.11
Wilkingia sp.	3.52	0.18	...
Unidentified	...	...	0.11

Source: Conservation and Survey Division Field Guides 1969, Dunbar and Condra et al. 1932, Miller et al. 1933, Moore 1965, Pabian 1970, Pabian and Fagerstrom 1972, Shimer and Shrock 1972.

A 25-pound bulk sample of unit 3 of the Wea? Member contained 2,702 fossils, mostly *Chonetes* and *Chonetinella,* and crinoid columns. A 25-pound bulk sample of unit 1 contained 536 fossils, mostly crinoid columns and small branching bryozoans. Both samples also yielded fusulinids and echinoid spines, neither of which were identified in the field except in the limestone (unit 2).

If this sequence is correctly identified, there is considerable variation in faunas and rock type between this exposure of the Cherryvale? Formation and the exposure north of the Middle River bridge. Also, other exposures of the Cherryvale? Formation in the Winterset area seem to be quite different from this one.

Site 136. Location: NE¼/NE¼/NE¼ sec. 15, T75N, R28W. A brown to tan dense limestone with shaly seams, believed to belong to the Winterset Member of the Dennis Formation, was examined southwest of Winterset in Madison County. To reach the exposure, take Highway 169 south to the Middle River and turn west on county road P-69 (gravel) just north of the bridge. The road is marked with a "state park" arrow. The outcrop occurs a fraction of a mile west of the highway on the north side of P-69. Fossils are abundant here, and some productid brachiopods are preserved in life position. Most of the fossils are entire and well preserved. Spiriferid brachiopods are more common than in most Pennsylvanian faunas included in this study. One hour of collecting provided a total of 228 fossils, which included the following:

IDENTIFICATION	PERCENT
Brachiopods	
Chonetinella flemingi (chonetid)	1.31
Marginifera sp. (productid)	6.14
Desmoinesia sp. (productid)	0.87
aff. *Productella* sp. (productid)	2.19
Linoproductus meniscus (productid)	0.87
Dictyoclostus portlockianus (productid)	0.87
Crurithyris planoconvexa (spiriferid)	19.73
Phricodothyris perplexa (spiriferid)	2.19
Ambocoelia planoconvexa (spiriferid)	1.31
Neospirifer triplicatus (spiriferid)	0.43
Composita ovata (spiriferid)	10.52
Meekella striatoscostata (strophomenid)	10.08
Dielasma bovidens (terebratulid)	1.75
Bryozoans, unidentified branching (small)	1.31
Burrows	0.87
Corals	
Lophophyllum sp. (solitary)	1.75
Crinoid columns	8.33
Echinoid spines	
Archeocidaris sp.	5.70
Fusulinids	21.92
Pelecypods	
Edmondia sp.	0.43
Wilkingia sp.	1.31

Source: Conservation and Survey Division Field Guides 1969, Dunbar and Condra 1932, Moore 1965, Pabian 1970, Shimer and Shrock 1972.

This fauna contains the greatest concentration of the strophomenid brachiopod *Meekella* found in this study. Although not rare, this brachiopod is uncommon and is usually not well preserved. Most of the specimens here are small but in good condition. The most common Pennsylvanian strophomenid, *Derbyia,* was not found at this site.

Site 137. Location: E½/NW¼ sec. 22, T75N, R28W. The lower Kansas City Group is well exposed west of Site 136. Continue in a westerly direction from the previous site along the same gravel road (county road P-69) for about 2.5 miles. Cross a stream and look north. A high bluff will be seen. Ask at the house just up the road and to the north for permission to collect. The lower beds in the bluff are exposed near the bridge, and the upper beds at the top of the bluff on the northern end. Rattlesnakes frequent the area, so caution is advised. Be on constant watch for them and move slowly; wear boots. The exposure is described below (Heckel 1980 and the author):

I. Dennis Formation
   A. Winterset Member: regressive limestone of the Dennis Cyclothem; 5 feet of tan thin-bedded limestone exposed at the northern top of the bluff
   B. Stark Member: offshore shale of the Dennis Cyclothem
      1. Two feet of gray shale
      2. One foot of black fissile shale
II. Galesburg Formation: nearshore shale of the Dennis-Swope cyclothems; 6 feet of shale; covered
III. Swope Formation
   A. Bethany Falls Member: regressive limestone of the Swope Cyclothem; 20 feet of limestone; various beds with a few thin shale zones; tan with some fossils
   B. Hushpuckney Member: offshore shale of the Swope Cyclothem
      1. A few inches of brown shale
      2 Less than 1 foot of gray shale
      3. Two feet of black fissile shale
   C. Middle Creek Member: transgressive limestone of the Swope Cyclothem; 1 foot of brown limestone with a few large pelecypods
IV. Ladore Formation: the nearshore shale of the Swope-Hertha cyclothems
   A. Brown shale, 1 foot thick; many fragmented fossils
   B. Gray shale, 2 feet thick
   C. Sandy limestone, 2 feet thick with ripple marks and burrows
   D. Four feet of gray shale exposed at the southern end of the bluff near the bridge
   E. A few feet of sandstone poorly exposed near the bridge

Fossils are present in several beds here, but only the lower ones are easily accessible. An abundant fauna was seen in unit A of the Ladore Formation. One hour of collecting yielded 49 specimens, but most of the fossils are highly fragmented and not every fragment was counted. The fossils found are listed below:

IDENTIFICATION	PERCENT
Brachiopods	
Linoproductus meniscus (productid)	2.04
Composita ovata (spiriferid)	24.48
Crurithyris planoconvexa (spiriferid)	2.04
Derbyia crassa (strophomenid)	65.30
Crinoid calyces	
Polusocrinus sp.	6.12

Source: Dunbar and Condra 1932, Pabian 1970, Moore 1965.

The fossils appear to be evenly scattered throughout the unit; no small fossils were found, just fragments of larger ones. Also notice that no crinoid columns were seen despite the abundance of crinoid calyces.

Site 138. Location: SW¼/NW¼ sec. 22, T75N, R28W. The middle beds of the Kansas City Group are exposed south of Pammel State Park in a road cut. To reach the exposure, begin at Site 137 along county road P-69. Continue west for about 0.5 mile and turn north on another gravel road. The cut will appear on the east side. Parts of the cut are slumped, but the Dennis and Iola cyclothems are present. The exposure is described below (Heckel 1980):

I. Iola Formation
   A. Raytown Member: regressive limestone of the Iola Cyclothem; 10 feet of brown limestone; massive at the top; bedded with a few shale zones at the base; part of the base covered; some fossils; exposed at the northern top of the cut
   B. Muncie Creek Member: offshore shale of the Iola Cyclothem; not well exposed here
      1. One foot of fossiliferous gray shale
      2. One foot of black fissile shale
      3. Half a foot of gray shale
   C. Paola Member: transgressive limestone of the Iola Cyclothem; around 3 feet of brown limestone
II. Chanute Formation: not well exposed here; a maximum of 5 feet of gray shale with a coal smut near the top
III. Drum Formation: around 8 feet of brown fossiliferous limestone (may be of the Westerville Formation)
IV. Cherryvale Formation: around 10 feet of gray shale and thin limestone beds; poorly exposed; fossiliferous
V. Dennis Formation
   A. Winterset Member: regressive limestone of the Dennis Cyclothem; around 5 feet of brown massive limestone exposed in the ditch at the south end of the cut; partially covered; some fossils

Site 139. Location: E½ sec. 8, T75N, R27W. An exposure believed to include the Raytown Member was examined southeast of Winterset in Madison County along county road G-50 (paved). The first exposures occur on the southern side of the road east of old Highway 169. Many of the beds are not well exposed. A description of the beds seen is given below by the author:

I. Iola? Formation
   A. Raytown? Member
      1. Fifteen feet of limestone and shale, badly slumped; seen on the northern slope at the eastern end of the sequence; many fossils in places
      2. Limestone, not measured; grayish to brown; poorly exposed in the ditch of the northern slope
      3. Siltstone, blue gray; around 1 foot thick; contains a few large productid brachiopods; not well exposed; seen in the ditch in the northern slope
   B. Muncie Creek? Member: best exposed in the ditch in the northern slope
      1. A few inches of brown shale
      2. One foot of gray shale
      3. Two feet of black fissile shale
II. Chanute? Formation: best exposed in the ditch of the northern slope; several feet of gray green poorly fossiliferous shale; entire unit exposed above the limestone and below the black fissile shale in the southern slope at the eastern end of the sequence
III. Drum? Formation: 5 feet of brown poorly fossiliferous limestone; exposed in the middle of the southern slope
IV. Cherryvale? Formation: a thick deposit of brown and gray nonfossiliferous shale well exposed in two slopes at the western start of the sequence on the south side of the road

A brief search (0.5-hour) was made of the most fossiliferous unit exposed here (unit 1 of the Raytown?). A total of 97 fossils were found. They seem to occur in clusters in the more shaly units of the Raytown?. These fossils included:

IDENTIFICATION	PERCENT
Brachiopods	
Neospirifer sp. (spiriferid)	1.03
Composita sp. (spiriferid)	3.09
Crurithyris sp. (spiriferid)	2.06
Ambocoelia planoconvexa (spiriferid)	4.12
Derbyia sp. (strophomenid)	27.83
Bryozoans	
Branching	3.09
Encrusting	4.12
Lacy, unidentified	1.03

PENNSYLVANIAN PERIOD: MISSOURIAN SERIES

IDENTIFICATION	PERCENT
Pelecypods	
Myalina sp.	17.52
Wilkingia sp.	15.46
Aviculopecten sp.	4.12
Nucula sp.	2.06
Septimyalina sp.	9.27
Parallelodon sp.	1.03
Yoldia sp.	4.12

Source: Dunbar and Condra 1932, Moore 1965, Pabian 1970, Shimer and Shrock 1972.

The majority of the pelecypods here are fragmented, and the specimens of *Derbyia* are all quite small.

Site 140. Location: C sec. 10, T75N, R28W. The Iola and Wyandotte cyclothems are exposed north of Pammel State Park in Madison County. To reach the exposure, take Highway 162 south from Highway 92 en route to the park. Exposures occur to the west and east of the highway about 1 mile south of Highway 92 on property owned by Paul Bruett, R.R. 3, Winterset, IA, 50273. Collecting is allowed by permission only. The eastern exposure along a creek includes the following (Heckel 1980):

I. Iola Formation
   A. Raytown Member: regressive limestone of the Iola Cyclothem; around 10 feet of brown limestone; massive at the top, bedded with shaly zones near the base
   B. Muncie Creek Member: offshore shale of the Iola Cyclothem
      1. Two feet of gray shale
      2. Two feet of black fissile shale
   C. Paola Member: transgressive limestone of the Iola Cyclothem; 3 feet of brown limestone
II. Chanute Formation: gray shale with a coal smut near the top; only a few feet poorly exposed along the creek

The creek exposure on the west side of the road contains the following (Heckel 1980):

I. Wyandotte Formation
   A. Argentine Member: regressive limestone of the Wyandotte Cyclothem; only a few feet of brown limestone exposed here; other exposures of the Argentine a little farther west
   B. Quindaro Member: offshore shale of the Wyandotte Cyclothem
      1. One foot of gray shale; no fossils seen
      2. Two feet of black fissile shale, with a fair abundance of fish fragments
      3. Half a foot of gray shale; no fossils seen
   C. Frisbie Member: transgressive limestone of the Wyandotte Cyclothem; 1 foot of brown limestone

II. Lane Formation: nearshore shale of the Iola-Wyandotte cyclothems; poorly exposed gray shale

Site 141. Location: S½/NE¼ sec. 5, T75N, R29W. The operating Stanzel Quarry in western Madison County exposes the upper part of the Kansas City Group and the lower part of the Lansing. To reach the quarry, begin at the junction of Highways 92 and 169 west of Winterset. Go west on Highway 92 for 10 miles to the quarry entrance east of the Middle River bridge. The unmarked entrance is located on the north side of the road. Contact the Schildberg Construction Company, Greenfield, IA 50849; full safety equipment and advance permission is required. The following beds are exposed here (Heckel 1980 and the author):

I. Lansing Group
   A. Stanton Formation
      1. Stoner Member: regressive limestone of the Stanton Cyclothem; a few feet of brown limestone with some chert and fusulinids exposed along a gravel road north of the quarry
   B. Vilas Formation: nearshore shale of the Stanton-Plattsburg cyclothems; estimated thickness of 15 feet; gray shale with red shale at the base and a few thin limestone beds near the top; partially exposed above the Plattsburg Limestone in the northern part of the quarry and south of the quarry face, where a few brachiopods and trilobite fragments were seen
   C. Plattsburg Formation: a cycle in itself, but members not evident here; 3 feet of grayish brown poorly fossiliferous limestone exposed above the Bonner Springs Shale in the northern end of the quarry
II. Kansas City Group
   A. Bonner Springs Formation: nearshore shale of the Plattsburg-Wyandotte cyclothems; 10 feet of red shale, turning gray at the top and base; exposed along the third level of the quarry north of the Island Creek–Farley level
   B. Wyandotte Formation
      1. Farley Member: 3 feet of red brown limestone exposed above the Island Creek; no fossils seen
      2. Island Creek Member: 5 feet of gray shale exposed along the second level of the quarry north of the quarry face; no fossils seen
      3. Argentine Member: regressive limestone of the Wyandotte Cyclothem; comprises the quarry face; around 15 feet of grayish to brown limestone exposed above the water level. The upper level of the Argentine in this quarry is very similar in appearance to the upper level of the Bethany Falls Limestone exposed in the other three operating quarries in Madison County. The Argentine contains a few fossils.

Site 142. Location: SW¼/SW¼/NW¼ sec. 7, T75N, R29W. The Stanton Formation of the Lansing Group is well exposed west of Site 141.

To reach the site, go west on Highway 92 for about 2 miles west of the Stanzel Quarry entrance. Turn south on the second south-bearing gravel road west of the quarry. Continue south for 0.5 mile. The exposure occurs along a stream to the east on the Madison-Adair county line. This is on private property belonging to Eugene Drake, R.R. 4, Winterset, IA 50273. Permission is needed. The exposure is described below (Heckel 1980):

I. Stanton Formation
   A. Stoner Member: regressive limestone of the Stanton Cyclothem; 15 feet of fossiliferous brown shale with shaly, fossiliferous brown limestone at the top and base; exposed in a bluff east of the stream. The Stoner of Iowa contains much more shale than the Stoner of Nebraska.
   B. Eudora Member: offshore shale of the Stanton Cyclothem
      1. Two feet of gray shale
      2. One foot of black fissile shale
      3. Half a foot of gray shale
   C. Captain Creek Member: transgressive limestone of the Stanton Cyclothem; 1 foot of brown limestone
II. Vilas Formation: nearshore shale of the Stanton-Plattsburg cyclothems; around 8 feet of gray shale with fossils near the top (*Chonetes*, bryozoans, other brachiopods); red shale present below this zone, but covered

Site 143. Location: NW¼/NW¼/SE¼ sec. 26, T76N, R30W. The Stoner Member of the Stanton Formation is also exposed around 3 miles to the northwest of this exposure in Adair County. To reach the site, begin on Highway 92 at the Madison-Adair county line. Go west for about 2 miles. Turn right (north) on the third north-bearing gravel road (county road P-39). Continue north for 2 miles and turn right (east) on another gravel road (county road G-39). Continue east for less than 1 mile to the first exposure on the southern side of the road. The following beds are exposed in the ditch here (described by the author):

I. Stanton Formation
   A. Stoner Member
      1 Limestone, 2 or 3 feet exposed; also found in the talus on the north side of the road; uneven bedding; greenish gray; no fossils seen
      2. Limestone, at least 2 feet thick; gray with many fusulinids; shaly at the base; forms a ledge in the ditch
      3. Shale, 3 feet thick, brown; exposed under the unit 2 limestone ledge; fossiliferous
      4. Limestone; reddish, with many fusulinids; very poorly exposed

To the east of this exposure, just west of the bridge over the Middle River and on the north side of the road, is an exposure of reddish limestone with dark gray pockets. It is around 5 feet thick and contains a few fossils, mostly fragmented brachiopods. This is believed to be part of the Stoner Member also.

Half an hour was spent collecting in unit 3 of the Stoner Member here, and a preliminary fauna list was compiled. The fossils included:

IDENTIFICATION	PERCENT
Brachiopods	
Chonetes granulifer (chonetid)	1.82
Chonetinella flemingi (chonetid)	4.10
Desmoinesia sp. (productid)	0.91
Meekella sp. (strophomenid)	0.45
Bryozoans, encrusting	0.45
Crinoid columns	0.91
Fusulinids	91.32

Source: Dunbar and Condra 1932, Moore 1965, Pabian 1970.

A total of 219 fossils were found here, 200 of which were fusulinids. Several of the brachiopods are fragmented, especially *Meekella*.

Nebraska offers many excellent and fossiliferous exposures of the Pennsylvanian and Permian. Burchett and Eversoll (1974) list a few thousand pits, quarries, and mines in that state. Most of these are abandoned, and quite a few have apparently changed hands since 1974, but their book is still a valuable reference. Over 300 limestone quarries and clay pits are included, which expose Pennsylvanian, Permian, and Cretaceous formations. The only quarries that this collector could locate in Nebraska that still allow collecting are owned by the Hopper brothers. Two inactive old WPA quarries exposing the Kansas City Group are in Sharpy County (S½/NW¼ sec. 28, T13N, R12E). For permission to collect contact Hopper Brothers' Quarries, Weeping Water, NB 68463. The Iola-Winterset limestones were quarried at both sites.

Site 144. Locations: road cut—S½/NW¼/SW¼ sec. 18, T12N, R11E; Goodrich Quarry—Center of eastern line, sec. 13, T12N, R10E; Carter Quarry—SW¼/SW¼/SW¼ sec. 12, T12N, R10E. The Lansing Group of the Missouri Series and part of the Douglas Group of the Virgilian Series are well exposed south of Gretna, Nebraska, in Sharpy County. The exposures occur in a series of road cuts and in two abandoned quarries, beginning at the southeastern edge of the Gretna State Fish Hatchery (slightly over 5 miles south of Gretna along Highway 31) on the east side of Highway 31 (gravel here), with the Platte River to the west. The sequence continues for about 1 mile south, with various units occurring at road level. It is best to continue south to the southern end of the sequence, where the lower beds are well exposed in a bluff just before the road curves east. After visiting this exposure, identification of the others in the sequence becomes easier. The section exposed in the road cut and in the abandoned Goodrich Quarry to the east is described below (Burchett and Reed 1967, Conservation and Survey Division Field Guide, Sharpy County 1969):

PENNSYLVANIAN PERIOD: MISSOURIAN SERIES

I. Lansing Group
   A. Stanton Formation
      1. South Bend Member: 5.5 feet of gray limestone with fossils
      2. Rock Lake Member: 6.5 feet of reddish shale with a thin gray zone at the top
      3. Stoner Member: up to 16 feet of grayish tan limestone in various beds; fossils; exposed at the top of the cut
      4. "Kiewitz" Member: 2.5 feet of blue gray claystone; quite fossiliferous
      5. "Dyson Hollow" Member: blue gray limestone; 2 feet thick with fossils
      6. Eudora Member: 1.5 feet of gray shale with 0.5 foot of black fissile shale at the base
      7. Captain Creek Member: 0.5 foot of dark gray limestone with fossils
   B. Vilas Formation: up to 8 feet of mostly greenish gray shale; partially exposed in the road ditch
   C. Plattsburg Formation
      1. Spring Hill Member: 1.5 feet of poorly exposed yellowish limestone and 13 feet of covered shales present above the water level of the Platte River; exposed west of the road

The following sequence is exposed at the abandoned Carter Quarry 0.5 mile south of the Gretna State Fish Hatchery on the east side of the road (Burchett and Reed 1967):

I. Virgilian Series
   A. Douglas Group
      1. Cass Formation
         a. Haskell Member: 6.5 feet of gray limestone exposed at the top of the quarry; fossils
         b. Little Pawnee Member: 1.5 feet of gray shale with a black fissile shale zone at the base; both beds of equal thickness
         c. Shoemaker Member: 1 feet of dark gray limestone
      2. Plattford Formation: 15.5 feet of poorly exposed red and green shales
II. Missourian Series
   A. Lansing Group
      1. Stanton Formation
         a. South Bend Member: 9 feet of gray limestone with a gray shale deposit near the base; not well exposed
         b. Rock Lake Member: 6 feet of reddish shale with a thin gray zone at the top
         c. Stoner Member: 9.5 feet of gray limestone; variable bedding; fossils
         d. "Kiewitz" Member: 2 feet of grayish claystone with fossils
         e. "Dyson Hollow" Member: 1 foot of gray limestone with fossils

At the southeastern end of the Gretna State Fish Hatchery (NE¼/SE¼/NW¼ sec. 12, T12N, R10E), the Stanton Formation is exposed. The beds include the lower part of the South Bend, Rock Lake, Stoner, and "Kiewitz" members, with a minor exposure of the "Dyson Hollow" Member (Burchett and Reed 1967).

Faunas were collected from the "Dyson Hollow," "Kiewitz," and Stoner Members of the Stanton Formation in this area. The fauna of the "Dyson Hollow" is fairly abundant, and most specimens are not damaged. The most abundant elements in the "Dyson Hollow" are the crinoid columns and spiriferid brachiopods. Branching bryozoans and productid brachiopods can also be found.

The fauna of the "Kiewitz" is evenly scattered and abundant, but the majority of the fossils are fragmented or disarticulated. Unlike the "Dyson Hollow" fauna, the "Kiewitz" is dominated by crinoid columns and productid brachiopods.

The fauna of the Stoner Member was collected from the upper half of the unit. The majority of the fossils are fragmented or disarticulated and generally occur in or near the shaly seams. Fossils are not particularly abundant. The fauna is dominated by spiriferid brachiopods, crinoid columns, and productid brachiopods.

Fossils found in these three members include the following specimens; numbers at the top of the columns indicate the number found after one hour of searching:

IDENTIFICATION	(191) "DYSON HOLLOW"	(232) "KIEWITZ"	(96) STONER
	(%)	(%)	(%)
Brachiopods			
Chonetes granulifer (chonetid)	2.09	6.03	...
Chonetinella flemingi (chonetid)	1.04	10.34	1.04
Dictyoclostus portlockianus (productid)	0.52	6.89	7.29
Dictyoclostus americanus (productid)	...	1.29	...
Hystrinculina sp. (productid)	0.52	4.31	5.20
Pulchratia sp. (productid)	...	3.01	...
Juresania nebrascensis (productid)	...	1.29	...
Linoproductus meniscus (productid)	3.66	...	1.04
Punctospirifer kentuckyensis (spiriferid)	...	...	1.04
Ambocoelia planoconvexa (spiriferid)	10.47	...	5.20
Composita ovata (spiriferid)	2.09	4.74	39.58
Composita trilobata (spiriferid)	14.13	...	...
Phricodothyris perplexa (spiriferid)	...	1.29	4.16
Neospirifer triplicatus (spiriferid)	...	1.72	...
Neospirifer latus (spiriferid)	1.57	...	...
Crurithyris planoconvexa (spiriferid)	1.57	...	...
Derbyia crassa (strophomenid)	1.04	0.86	5.20
Bryozoans			
Branching (small)	5.23	2.15	5.20
Branching (average)	2.09	2.15	...
Branching (large)	...	0.86	...
Encrusting	...	4.74	...
Lacy	0.52	1.72	...

IDENTIFICATION	(191) "DYSON HOLLOW" (%)	(232) "KIEWITZ" (%)	(96) STONER (%)
Burrows	...	1.72	2.08
Corals			
Lophophyllum sp. (solitary)	1.04	0.86	5.20
Crinoid columns	52.35	43.10	14.58
Echinoid spines			
Archeocidaris sp.	...	0.86	5.20
Gastropods			
Straparollus (*Euomphalus*) sp.	...	...	1.04

Source: Conservation and Survey Division Field Guides 1969, Dunbar and Condra 1932, Moore 1965, Pabian 1970, Shimer and Shrock 1972.

Echinoid plates also occur in the "Kiewitz" and Stoner members but were found only after additional collecting, so they were not included in the faunal list. The encrusting bryozoans of the "Kiewitz" fauna were found on echinoid spines; lacy bryozoans; crinoid columns; the spiriferid brachiopod *Composita ovata*; the productid brachiopods *Dictyoclostus portlockianus*, *Hystriculina*, and *Pulchratia*; and a few other brachiopods. A 25-pound bulk sample of the "Kiewitz" Member yielded 1,969 fossils. The most abundant elements were crinoid columns (28 percent) *Chonetinella* (22 percent); fusulinids (13 percent); branching bryozoans (12 percent), and *Chonetes* (11 percent).

9

Pennsylvanian Period
VIRGILIAN SERIES

BEDS of the Virgilian Series (upper Pennsylvanian) lie at or near the surface in southwestern Iowa. The eastern boundary lies in Ringgold, Union, and western Madison counties. The northern boundary lies in Adair, Cass, and Pottawattamie counties. Outcrops of the Virgilian occur west and south of this boundary as well as in southeastern Nebraska. The stratigraphic column for the Virgilian Series in Iowa is described below:

GROUP	FORMATION	MEMBER	DESCRIPTION
Wabaunsee	French Creek		shale
	Jim Creek		limestone
	Friedrich		shale
	Grandharen		limestone
	Dry		shale
	Dover		limestone
	Langdon		shale (Nyman Coal)
	Maple Hill		limestone
	Wamego		shale
	Tarkio		limestone
	Willard		shale
	Elmont		limestone
	Harveyville		shale
	Reading		limestone
	Auburn		shale
	Wakarusa		limestone
	Soldier Creek		shale

PENNSYLVANIAN PERIOD: VIRGILIAN SERIES

GROUP	FORMATION	MEMBER	DESCRIPTION
Wabaunsee (*cont.*)			
	Burlingame		limestone
	Silver Lake		shale
	Rulo		limestone
	Cedar Vale		shale (Elmo Coal)
	Happy Hollow		limestone
	White Cloud		shale
	Howard		limestone
	Severy		shale (Nodaway Coal)
Shawnee	Topeka	Coal Creek	limestone
		Holt	shale
		Dubois	limestone
		Turner Creek	shale
		Sheldon	limestone
		Jones Point	shale
		Curzon	limestone
		Iowa Point	shale
		Hartford	limestone
	Calhoun		shale
	Deer Creek	Ervine Creek	limestone
		Burroak	shale
		Haynies	limestone
		Larsh	shale
		Rock Bluff	limestone
		Oskaloosa	shale
		Ozawkie	limestone
	Tecumseh	Rakes Creek	shale
		Ost	limestone
		Kenosha	shale
	Lecompton	Avoca	limestone
		King Hill	shale
		Beil	limestone
		Queen Hill	shale
		Big Springs	limestone
		Doniphan	shale
		Spring Branch	limestone
	Kanwaka	Stull	shale
		Clay Creek	limestone
		Jackson Park	shale
	Oread	Kereford	limestone
		Heumader	shale
		Plattsmouth	limestone
		Heebner	shale
		Leavenworth	limestone
		Snyderville	shale
		Toronto	limestone
Douglas	Lawrence		shale
	Stranger		shale
	Iatan		limestone
	Weston		shale

Exposures and quarries of the Virgilian Series in Nebraska are included in this text, but variations occur between the Virgilian of Iowa and that of Nebraska. Therefore, the stratigraphic column for the Virgilian Series of Nebraska is given below:

GROUP	FORMATION	MEMBER	DESCRIPTION
Wabaunsee	Wood Siding	Brownville	limestone
		Pony Creek	shale
		Grayhorse	limestone
		Plumb	shale
		Nebraska City	limestone
	Root	French Creek	shale
		Jim Creek	limestone
		Friedrich	shale
	Stotler	Grandhaven	limestone
		Dry	shale
		Dover	limestone
	Pillsbury		shale, sandstone
	Zeandale	Maple Hill	limestone
		Wamego	shale
		Tarkio	shale, limestone
	Willard		shale
	Emporia	Elmont	limestone
		Harveyville	shale
		Reading	limestone
	Auburn		shale
	Wakarusa		limestone
	Soldier Creek		shale
	Burlingame	South Fork	limestone
		Winnebago	shale
		Taylor Branch	limestone
	Scranton	Silver Lake	shale
		Rulo	limestone
		Cedarvale	shale
		Happy Hollow	limestone
		White Cloud	shale, sandstone
	Howard		limestone
	Severy		shale
Shawnee	Topeka	Coal Creek	limestone
		Holt	shale
		DuBois	limestone
		Turner Creek	shale
		Sheldon	limestone
		Jones Point	shale
		Curzon	limestone
		Iowa Point	shale
		Hartford	limestone
	Calhoun		shale
	Deer Creek	Ervine Creek	limestone
		Larsh	shale

PENNSYLVANIAN PERIOD: VIRGILIAN SERIES

GROUP	FORMATION	MEMBER	DESCRIPTION
Shawnee	Deer Creek (cont.)		
		Rock Bluff	limestone
		Oskaloosa	shale
		Ozawkie	limestone
	Tecumseh	Rakes Creek	sandy shale, sandstone
		Ost	limestone
		Kenosha	shale
	Lecompton	Avoca	limestone
		King Hill	shale
		Beil	limestone, shale
		Queen Hill	shale
		Big Springs	limestone
		Doniphan	shale, limestone
		Spring Branch	limestone
	Kanwaka	Stull	shale
		Clay Creek	limestone
		Jackson Park	shale
	Oread	Kereford	limestone
		Heumader	shale
		Plattsmouth	limestone
		Heebner	shale
		Leavenworth	limestone
		Snyderville	shale
		Toronto	limestone
Douglas	Lawrence		shale
	Cass	Haskell	limestone
		Little Pawnee	shale
		Shoemaker	limestone
	Plattford	(unnamed)	shale
		Nehawka	limestone
		(unnamed)	shale

The Virgilian-Missourian contact can be seen south of the Gretna State Fish Hatchery in Sharpy County, Nebraska. The Cass and Plattford formations of the Douglas Group (Virgilian) overlie the Stanton Formation of the Lansing Group (Missourian). This exposure was discussed more fully in Chapter 8 (Site 144).

The following Hopper brothers' quarries expose the Virgilian Series in Nebraska. These and others are listed in Burchett and Eversoll (1974). Prior permission and safety equipment are required. The formations listed below are those quarried and are not necessarily the only units exposed (courtesy Conservation and Survey Division, University of Nebraska):

LOCATION	COUNTY	FORMATION[a]	QUARRY NAME	STATUS	ADDRESS[b]
N½/NE¼/NW¼ sec. 2, T10N, R11E	Cass	1		Abandoned	A
SE¼/NW¼ sec. 2, T10N, R11E	Cass	2	Jameson, near Weeping Water	Inactive	A
NW¼/SE¼/NW¼ sec. 2, T10N, R11E	Cass	1	Jameson, near Weeping Water	Active	A

LOCATION	COUNTY	FORMATION[a]	QUARRY NAME	STATUS	ADDRESS[b]
W½/NW¼ sec. 2, T10N, R11E	Cass	1	Domingo, near Weeping Water	Active	A
S½/SE¼/NE¼ sec. 3, T10N, R11E	Cass	2	Olsen, near Weeping Water	Inactive	A
N½/NE¼ sec. 3, T10N, R11E	Cass	1	Olsen, near Weeping Water	Active	A
NW¼/NW¼ sec. 3, T10N, R11E	Cass	1	Dwinell, near Weeping Water	Active	A
S½/SE¼/NW¼ sec. 3, T10N, R11E	Cass	1	Bates, near Weeping Water	Active	A
NE¼/SE¼ sec. 16, T10N, R12E	Cass	2	Elliott, near Weeping Water	Inactive	A
SW¼/NE¼/SE¼ sec. 20, T10N, R13 E	Cass	2	Schwaberer, near Nehawka	Active	A
SE¼/SE¼ sec. 34, T11N, R11E	Cass	1	Clements, near Weeping Water	Inactive	A
SW¼/SE¼ sec. 9, T12N, R10E	Cass	3	Feede, near South Bend	Active	A
N½/NW¼ sec. 6, T12N, R10E	Cass	5	Beetison, near Ashland	Inactive	C
S½ sec. 6, T12N, R10E	Cass	6	Carlson, near Ashland	Active	C
SW¼/NW¼ sec. 15, T12N, R10E	Cass	3	Jones Estate, near South Bend	Inactive	A
NE¼/NW¼ sec. 13, T2N, R11E	Pawnee	4	McClintock, near Pawnee City	Inactive	B

[a] Formation quarried: 1 = Kereford to Plattsmouth limestones, 2 = Ervine Creek Limestone, 3 = Cass Limestone, 4 = Tarkio Limestone, 5 = Toronto to Cass limestones, 6 = Cass to Stoner limestones.

[b] Address: A = Hopper Brothers' Quarries, Weeping Water, NB 68463; B = Hopper Brothers' Quarries, Pawnee City, NB 68420; C = Ashland Stone Company Division, Hopper Brothers' Quarries, Ashland, NB 68003.

Site 145. Location: SW¼/NE¼ sec. 27, T73N, R38W. A good exposure of the Plattsmouth Member of the Oread Formation was examined in Montgomery County, Iowa, where there are reportedly many quarries exposing the Oread and other formations. Black chert peppered with white fusulinids occurs in the Plattsmouth Member in several of these quarries. Only one could be located in two separate field trips to the area; this (located near Stennett) is evidently the only operating quarry left in the county. Collecting is not permitted, but a road cut occurs there. To reach the cut, take Highway 48 north of Red Oak to county road H-20 (paved). Turn east and continue east on H-20 for 1 mile. Then turn north on the first gravel road. Continue north for 0.5 mile, coming to another gravel road. Turn east on this road, which curves to the north and continues to the quarry. The cut occurs south of the quarry on the western side of the road. Exposed here is shale and limestone of the Plattsmouth Member of the Oread Formation. The black chert with fusulinids can be found in fair abundance here. Also found in the shale was a specimen of the colonial coral *Cladochonus*, one of only two Pennsylvanian colonial corals found during this study.

Site 146. Location: NW¼/NW¼/NW¼ sec. 25, T73N, R38W. This site occurs along the east side of county road H-20 (gravel) north of Stennett in Montgomery County, east of Site 145. A few feet of blue gray limestone were seen here, but the area is partially overgrown. The Leavenworth Member of the Oread Formation is probably the unit exposed.

Site 147. Location: SE¼/SE¼ sec. 34, T11N, R11E. Like several southeastern Nebraska towns, Weeping Water, Cass County, is surrounded by many rock quarries. The Hopper brothers' Clements Quarry is located about 1.5 miles west of Weeping Water, north of Highway 50A. (Note: There are two road cuts in the area; they are described under Sites 148 and 149.) Prior permission is required to collect in the quarries, and full safety equipment is needed. For permission, contact Hopper Brothers' Quarries, Weeping Water, NB 68463 and specify the Clements Quarry. The following beds are exposed (Burchett 1971):

I. Shawnee Group
   A. Lecompton Formation
      1. Avoca Member: 1.5 feet of grayish tan limestone with a thin shale seam in the middle; some fossils
      2. King Hill Member: 10 feet of red brown shale; green zones at the top and base
      3. Beil Member
         a. One foot of grayish tan limestone with fossils
         b. One and a half feet of grayish tan shale with fossils
         c. Three feet of grayish tan limestone with fossils
      4. Queen Hill Member
         a. Four feet of greenish shale
         b. Half a foot of black fissile shale
      5. Big Springs Member: 2 feet of gray limestone with fossils
      6. Doniphan Member: 2.5 feet of bluish gray shale with fossils
      7. Spring Branch Member: 7.5 feet of gray limestone with fossils
   B. Kanwaka Formation: a few inches of green shale with fossils
   C. Oread Formation
      1. Kereford Member: 7 feet of blue gray limestone in two beds with fossils
      2. Plattsmouth Member: 18 feet of bluish gray limestone; variable bedding with fossils

Site 148. Location: SW¼/SE¼/SW¼ sec. 35, T11N, R11E. The site is a road cut along Highway 50A a little over 0.5 mile west of Weeping Water, Cass County, Nebraska. The cut occurs on the north side of the road just east of a railroad crossing. Truck traffic is quite heavy along the road. Most of the beds exposed here are also exposed in the upper levels of the

Clements Quarry (see Site 147). The following beds are present in the cut (Conservation and Survey Division Field Guide 1969):

I. Shawnee Group
   A. Tecumseh Formation
      1. Rakes Creek Member: shale poorly exposed at the very top of the cut
      2. Ost Member: about 3 feet of brown limestone
      3. Kenosha Member: at least 2 feet of red shale
   B. Lecompton Formation
      1. Avoca Member: 1.5 feet of grayish tan limestone with a thin shale seam in the middle; some fossils
      2. King Hill Member: 10 feet of red brown shale; green zones at the top and base
      3. Beil Member
         a. One foot of grayish tan limestone with fossils, including corals
         b. One and a half feet of grayish tan shale with fossils, including corals; partially covered at the base of the cut
         c. Three feet of grayish tan limestone with fossils, poorly exposed

The upper beds of this site are included in another road cut (see Site 149). Fossils were collected from the upper part of the Beil and Avoca members at this site. Both units appear to be similar in lithology and fossil content. The fossils in the Beil fauna are generally entire, but some brachiopods are disarticulated. Some excellent corals have been found in the Beil, but this collector found only small specimens and fragments of larger ones. The Avoca fauna is very similar to that of the Beil, but the majority of the fossils were found to be fragmented or disarticulated. One hour of collecting yielded 471 fossils in the Beil and 429 fossils in the Avoca. These two faunas included:

IDENTIFICATION	BEIL	AVOCA
	(%)	(%)
Brachiopods		
Enteletes sp. (orthid)	0.42	...
Juresania nebrascensis (productid)	1.06	0.46
Chonetes granulifer (productid)	0.63	...
Composita subtilita (spiriferid)	2.12	0.46
Composita elongata (spiriferid)	0.42	...
Hustedia mormoni (spiriferid)	1.27	1.16
Neospirifer triplicatus (spiriferid)	0.63	0.46
Ambocoelia planoconvexa (spiriferid)	...	0.69
Punctospirifer kentuckyensis (spiriferid)	0.21	...
Derbyia crassa (strophomenid)	...	0.46
Bryozoans, lacy	0.42	...
Burrows	...	0.93
Crinoid columns	21.23	23.31
Echinoid spines		
Archeocidaris sp.	1.27	0.23

IDENTIFICATION	BEIL	AVOCA
	(%)	(%)
Fusulinids	63.69	69.93
Corals		
Lophophyllum proliferum (solitary)	6.79	1.86

Source: Conservation and Survey Division Field Guides 1969, Dunbar and Condra 1932, Moore 1965, Pabian 1970, Shimer and Shrock 1972.

Some of the largest fusulinids found during this study occur in the Beil and Avoca faunas at this site. The bulk of both faunas consists of fusulinids, occurring in clusters in the Beil but more evenly spread in the Avoca.

Site 149. Location: SW¼/SW¼/SW¼ sec. 35, T11N, R11E. To reach the site, proceed west from Site 148 along Highway 50A for a fraction of a mile and turn north on a gravel road. A road cut will appear on the east side; the Tecumseh Formation is exposed here. Older beds can be seen in a quarry to the west and in another road cut southeast of this one (see Sites 147, 148). The following beds are included in the cut (Conservation and Survey Division Field Guide 1969):

I. Shawnee Group
   A. Deer Creek Formation
      1. Rock Bluff Member: about 1 foot of blue gray limestone with a few fossils; exposed at the very top of the cut
   B. Tecumseh Formation
      1. Rakes Creek Member
         a. At least 25 feet of yellowish sandstone
         b. Two feet of greenish gray, sandy shale
         c. Two and a half feet of brown shale
      2. Ost Member: 3 feet of light brown limestone
      3. Kenosha Member: 2 feet of red shale poorly exposed in the road ditch at the base of the bluff

Site 150. Location: NW¼/NW¼ sec. 17, T77N, R31W. There is a pair of quarries on the northwest end of a string of eight, all of which are owned by the Schildberg Construction Company of Greenfield, IA 50849. Permission and safety equipment are required. These two are located just east of Highway 25 about 12 miles north of Greenfield in Adair County. The quarry on the south side of the gravel road was examined, and the beds are described below:

I. Shawnee Group
   A. Topeka? Formation
      1. Iowa Point? Member
         a. Gray shale poorly exposed at the top of the face
         b. Black fissile shale, roughly 5 feet poorly exposed
         c. A thin zone of gray shale
      2. Hartford? Member: 5 feet of brown limestone; shaly, with fossils
   B. Calhoun? Formation

1. At least 2 feet of black fissile shale
2. Three feet of gray shale
C. Deer Creek Formation
   1. Ervine Creek Member: at least 10 feet of gray bedded limestone; shaly near the top, shaly seams; some fossils

The Ervine Creek fauna in this quarry does not seem to be as fossiliferous as an Ervine Creek exposure examined north of Thurman in Fremont County. However, the Hartford? Limestone carries a fairly abundant fauna, but no faunal list was compiled.

Site 151. Location: SE¼/SE¼ sec. 17, T77N, R31W. A fairly abundant fauna of brachiopods was found in the Ervine Creek Member at this exposure. This is Schildberg quarry near Greenfield in Adair County. To reach the site, backtrack on Highway 25 from Site 150 and turn east on a gravel road. Continue east for less than 1 mile to the quarry on the north side of the road.

Site 152. Location: NW¼/NW¼ sec. 26, T70N, R43W. Several exposures of the Pennsylvanian occur along the Missouri River in southwestern Iowa. Some of these are along county road L-44 (paved) north of Thurman in Fremont County. About 1.5 miles north of the town on the east side of the road is an exposure of shale believed to be of the Severy Formation of the Wabaunsee Group. Around 10 feet of shale are present in three beds: a lower unit of red shale, a middle unit of gray shale, and an upper unit of yellowish shale. Fossils are most numerous in the upper unit, but a few were also found in the middle. The majority of fossils found, here are fragmented and disarticulated. Only 36 fossils were found including the following:

IDENTIFICATION	PERCENT
Brachiopods	
Chonetes granulifer (chonetid)	8.57
Dictyoclostus sp. (productid)	2.85
Wellerella sp. (rhynchonellid)	5.71
Derbyia crassa (strophomenid)	2.85
Bryozoans	
Branching, unidentified (small)	5.71
Encrusting, unidentified	5.71
Lacy, unidentified	2.85
Crinoid columns	65.71

Source: Dunbar and Condra 1932, Moore 1965, Pabian 1970, Shimer and Shrock 1972.

Site 153. Location: SW¼/SW¼/SW¼ sec. 23, T70N, R43W. About 0.5 mile north of Site 152 near Thurman in Fremont County is an operating quarry. Collecting is not permitted there, but exposures do occur along the eastern side of county road L-44 (paved) south of the quarry. Although some of the exposures are privately owned, the bluffs along the road are on public property. At least 15 feet of yellowish gray limestone of the Ervine Creek Member of the Deer Creek Formation are exposed. It is dense with shaly seams and fairly fossiliferous. At the southern end of the cut are at least 2 feet of black fissile shale and 2 feet of gray shale believed to represent the Calhoun? Formation. Fragments of a highly fossiliferous dark gray limestone can be found in the talus and may be from the Topeka? Formation.

The majority of fossils found in this exposure of the Ervine Creek Limestone are fragmented and evenly scattered, although they seem to be more numerous near or in the shaly seams. The fusulinids, however, occur in clusters. A total of 353 fossils were found, including the following:

IDENTIFICATION	PERCENT
Brachiopods	
Chonetinella flemingi (chonetid)	0.28
Chonetes granulifer (chonetid)	1.41
Marginifera sp. (productid)	0.84
Wellerella sp. (rhynchonellid)	2.26
Ambocoelia planoconvexa (spiriferid)	9.34
Neospirifer sp. (spiriferid)	0.28
Composita ovata (spiriferid)	3.68
Crurithyris planoconvexa (spiriferid)	1.69
Punctospirifer kentuckyensis (spiriferid)	1.13
Derbyia crassa (strophomenid)	2.26
Meekella sp. (strophomenid)	1.13
Bryozoans	
Branching (small size)	1.69
Branching (average size)	0.56
Encrusting, unidentified	0.28
Lacy, unidentified	0.28
Corals	
Lophophyllum sp. (solitary)	1.69
Crinoid columns	42.49
Echinoid spines	
Archeocidaris sp.	1.98
Fusulinids	17.56
Green algae	9.06

Source: Conservation and Survey Division Field Guides 1969, Dunbar and Condra 1932, Moore 1965, Pabian 1970, Shimer and Shrock 1972.

Site 154. Location: NW¼/NW¼ sec. 31, T70N, R42W. To reach the exposure, take Highway 145 west on route to Thurman, Fremont County. On the eastern edge of town, turn north on a paved county road. The road curves east and then takes a northeastern route. Follow the road for about 1 mile and turn east on the first east-bearing gravel road; cross Plum Creek. The exposure occurs on the south side of the road. Exposed here are around 3 feet of brown dense limestone probably of the Howard Formation. A few fossils were seen.

Site 155. Location: SE¼/SW¼ sec. 2, T8N, R10E. Exposures of the Wabaunsee Group were examined at the Little Nemaha State Wayside

Area located just east of Unadilla, Nebraska, in Otoe County. The exposures occur along both sides of Highway 2, but the northern slope provides the best fossil collecting. The exposure is described below (Conservation and Survey Division Field Guide, Otoe County, 1969):

I. Auburn Formation
 A. Brown limestone, badly eroded; at least 1 foot present; exposed near the top of the northern slope; contains a few fossils in pockets
 B. Three shale zones, difficult to distinguish from one another in the eroding slopes; combined thickness less than 20 feet; the two lower zones composed of grayish shale; the upper zone brown shale; no fossils, but cone-in-cone calcite present
II. Wakarusa Formation: grayish limestone that weathers to brown; badly eroded; 3 feet exposed at the western end of the northern slope; fossiliferous

The fauna of the Wakarusa Formation is fragmented or disarticulated and evenly scattered. The fauna of the upper Auburn is much less abundant, but fossils occur in fairly dense, small clusters and only rarely as individuals. One hour of collecting yielded 205 fossils from the Wakarusa but only 50 from the Auburn. These two faunas included the following specimens:

IDENTIFICATION	WAKARUSA	AUBURN
	(%)	(%)
Brachiopods		
Chonetes granulifer (chonetid)	9.75	...
Chonetinella flemingi (chonetid)	4.87	...
Juresania sp. (productid)	0.48	...
Dictyoclostus sp. (productid)	0.48	...
Cancrinella boonensis (productid)	...	48.00
Punctospirifer kentuckyensis (spiriferid)	0.97	2.00
Neospirifer sp. (spiriferid)	0.97	...
Neospirifer triplicatus (spiriferid)	...	2.00
Ambocoelia expansa (spiriferid)	...	18.00
Derbyia sp. (strophomenid)	0.48	6.00
Bryozoans		
Branching, unidentified (small)	2.92	12.00
Branching, unidentified (average)	0.97	...
Encrusting, unidentified	0.97	2.00
Lacy, unidentified	2.92	...
Crinoid columns	73.65	6.00
Fusulinids	0.48	...
Gastropods		
Anomphalus sp.	...	2.00
Pelecypods, unidentified	...	2.00

Source: Conservation and Survey Division Field Guides 1969, Dunbar and Condra 1932, Moore 1965, Pabian 1970, Shimer and Shrock 1972.

In the Wakarusa fauna, bryozoans were found encrusting crinoid columns and lacy bryozoans. However, the fragmented nature of this fauna hampered precise identification in some cases.

PENNSYLVANIAN PERIOD: VIRGILIAN SERIES

Site 156. Location: SW¼/SE¼/SW¼ sec. 30, T3N, R12E. Just west of Table Rock, Nebraska, in Pawnee County on the north side of Highway 4 is an exposure slightly younger than that at Unadilla. This is described below (Conservation and Survey Division Field Guide, Pawnee County, 1969):

I. Emporia Formation
   A. Harveyville Member: grayish shale; badly eroded with only a few feet exposed; best seen immediately overlying the Reading; abundant fossils
   B. Reading Member
      1. Limestone, 2 feet thick, reddish brown; dense with fossils
      2. Shale, 1 foot thick, grayish; no fossils; best seen underlying the upper Reading
      3. Limestone, around 1 foot thick, grayish but weathers to brown; no fossils seen; poorly exposed
      4. Limestone, poorly exposed; a little over 1 foot thick and dark gray; no fossils seen
II. Auburn Formation: greenish shale, poorly exposed; no fossils seen

Better exposures of the Auburn Formation can be found in the area (NW¼/SW¼/SW¼ sec. 29, T3N, R12E). To reach them, continue west on Highway 4 from Table Rock and turn right (north) on the first gravel road. Exposures of various shales occur in places, sometimes on both sides of the road. This is the upper part of the Auburn; fossils were not seen.

Faunas of the upper Reading (unit 1) and the lower Harveyville members were collected in the highway exposure. These are the youngest units of the Pennsylvanian System examined in this survey. One hour of collecting in the Harveyville yielded a total of 570 fossils, and in the Reading a total of 414 fossils. These two faunas included the following:

IDENTIFICATION	READING (%)	HARVEYVILLE (%)
Brachiopods		
Chonetes granulifer (chonetid)	4.58	25.61
Chonetinella flemingi (chonetid)	1.69	2.28
Enteletes hemiplicatus (orthid)	0.72	...
Hystriculina sp. (productid)	0.48	...
Dictyoclostus portlockianus (productid)	0.72	...
Reticulatia sp. (productid)	1.20	...
Linoproductus sp. (productid)	0.72	...
Juresania nebrascensis (productid)	...	1.22
Cancrinella boonensis (productid)	...	0.35
Ambocoelia planoconvexa (spiriferid)	23.67	11.92
Punctospirifer kentuckyensis (spiriferid)	0.72	3.15
Composita ovata (spiriferid)	0.72	0.87
Neospirifer sp. (spiriferid)	0.48	0.35
Hustedia mormoni (spiriferid)	...	0.17
Derbyia crassa (strophomenid)	3.14	9.82
Meekella sp. (strophomenid)	0.48	...
Bryozoans		
Branching (small)	9.66	16.49
Branching (average)	...	2.10

IDENTIFICATION	READING	HARVEYVILLE
	(%)	(%)
Lacy	0.24	5.61
Encrusting	...	0.70
Corals		
Lophophyllum sp.	1.44	...
Crinoid columns	24.15	10.00
Echinoid spines		
Archeocidaris sp.	0.48	0.52
Fusulinids	24.15	8.77
Green algae	0.48	...

Source: Conservation and Survey Division Field Guides 1969, Dunbar and Condra 1932, Moore 1965, Pabian 1970, Shimer and Shrock 1972.

The fauna of the Reading Member is generally composed of entire and articulated fossils. A few individuals are fragmented, and a few brachiopods are disarticulated. Fossils are evenly scattered.

The fauna of the Harveyville Member at this site is remarkably similar to the Reading fauna, considering that two completely different rock types are involved. The smaller fossils of the Harveyville are complete and articulated, whereas the larger specimens are disarticulated and/or broken. The lacy bryozoans of this fauna are all highly fragmented. Fusulinids occur in small but dense clusters. All other fossils are evenly scattered.

There are many other exposures of the Virgilian and Missourian series near the Missouri River in southwestern Iowa and throughout southeastern Nebraska. Along the Missouri River in Nebraska the Pennsylvanian-Permian contact is exposed in a few places (see Burchett and Reed 1967, Burchett 1970, Burchett 1971, Burchett and Eversoll 1974, and Conservation and Survey Division Field Guides, 1969).

10

Permian Period

THE PERMIAN PERIOD began 280 million years ago and ended 225 million years ago. The Permian System is absent in Iowa, but several formations of the Cimarron and the Big Blue series of the lower Permian occur in the subsurface throughout Nebraska. Many excellent exposures occur in the southeastern part of the state. The stratigraphic column for the Permian in Nebraska is listed below:

CIMARRON SERIES

GROUP	FORMATION	MEMBER	DESCRIPTION
Kiger	Freezeout		limestone
	Forelle		limestone
	Glendo		shale
Salt Fork	Dog Creek		shale
	Blaine	(Minnekahata)	(limestone)
			shale, gypsum
	Flowerpot	(Opeche)	(shale)
			shale
	Cedar Hills		sandstone
	Salt Plains		sandstone, siltstone
	Harper		sandstone
	Stone Corral		anhydrite
	Ninnescah		sandstone, shale

BIG BLUE SERIES

GROUP	FORMATION	MEMBER	DESCRIPTION
Wellington	Afton		limestone
	Slate Creek		limestone
	Highland		shale
	Carlton		limestone
	Chisholm Creek		shale
	Annelly		gypsum, shale

GROUP	FORMATION	MEMBER	DESCRIPTION
Wellington (cont.)			
	Geuda Springs		salt, shale, gypsum
	Hollenberg		limestone
	Pearl		shale
Chase	Nolans	Herington	limestone
		Paddock	shale
		Krider	limestone
	Odell		shale
	Winfield	Cresswell	limestone, shale
		Grant	shale
		Stovall	limestone
	Gage		shale
	Towanda		limestone
	Holmesville		shale
	Barneston	Fort Riley	limestone
		Oketo	shale
		Florence	limestone
	Blue Springs		shale
	Kinney		limestone
	Wymore		shale
	Wereford	Schroyer	limestone
		Harvensville	shale
		Threemile	limestone
Council Grove	Speiser		shale
	Funston		limestone, shale
	Blue Rapids		shale
	Crouse		limestone, shale
	Easly Creek		shale
	Bader	Middleburg	limestone
		Hosser	shale
		Eiss	limestone, shale
	Stearns		shale
	Beattie	Morrill	limestone
		Florena	shale
		Cottonwood	limestone
	Eskridge		shale
	Grenola	Neva	limestone
		Salem Point	shale
		Burr	limestone
		Legion	shale
		Sallyards	limestone
	Roca		shale
	Red Eagle	Howe	limestone
		Bennett	shale
		Glenrock	limestone
	Johnson		shale
	Foraker	Long Creek	limestone
		Hughes Creek	shale

PERMIAN PERIOD

GROUP	FORMATION	MEMBER	DESCRIPTION
Council Grove	Foraker (cont.)		
		Americus	limestone
Admire	Hamlin	Oaks	shale
		Houchens Creek	limestone
		Stine	shale
	Five Point		limestone
	West Branch		shale
	Chicago Mound	Falls City	Rehmer Limestone
			Reserve Shale
			Miles Limestone
		Hawxby	shale
		Aspinwall	limestone
	Towle	Indian Cave	sandstone

The Flowerpot and Opeche formations of the Salt Fork Group are time equivalents as are the Blaine and Minnekahata formations.

The Pennsylvanian-Permian contact is exposed in the Missouri River bluffs around Peru, Nemaha County, Nebraska, and 20 miles north of Rulo, Richardson County, Nebraska. The Wabaunsee Group of the Pennsylvanian and the Admire Group of the Permian are exposed at these two localities (Burchett 1970).

Below is a list of Hopper brothers' quarries exposing the Permian System in Nebraska (Burchett and Eversoll 1974). No examination of any of these quarries was made. The owners require prior permission and safety equipment.

LOCATION	COUNTY	FORMATION[a]	QUARRY NAME	STATUS	ADDRESS[b]
W½/SW¼ sec. 32, T3N, R7E	Nemaha	1	Hopper Brothers', near Blue Springs	Inactive	A
W½/NE¼ sec. 23, T5N, R13E	Nemaha	2	Bowling East, near Auburn	Active	B
NE¼/NW¼ sec. 23, T5N, R13E	Nemaha	2	Bowling West, near Auburn	Active	B
NE¼/NW¼ sec. 25, T5N, R13E	Nemaha	2	Steffens, near Auburn	Abandoned	B
W½/NE¼ sec. 11, T7N, R9E	Otoe	2	Hunt, near Douglas	Active	A
C/E½/NW¼ sec. 11, T7N, R93	Otoe	2	Hopper Brothers', near Douglas	Inactive	A
NE¼/SE¼ sec. 8, T1N, R10E	Pawnee	3	Hopper and Spohr, near Pawnee City	Active	C
S½/NW¼ sec. 9, T1N, R10E	Pawnee	3	Giesman, near Pawnee City	Inactive	C

[a]Formation quarried: 1 = Fort Riley Limestone, 2 = Cottonwood Limestone, 3 = Morrill to Cottonwood Limestones.

[b]Address: A = Hopper Brothers' Quarries, Weeping Water, NB 68463; B = Hopper Brothers' Quarries, Auburn, NB 68305; C = Hopper Brothers' Quarries, Pawnee City, NB 68420.

Two exposures of Permian age were examined in Nebraska to obtain a glimpse of what life was like during that period. There are many other fossiliferous units of the Permian exposed in the state.

Site 157. Location: between the NE¼/NW¼ sec. 20 and the SE¼/SW¼ sec. 17, T1N, R6E. The two exposures examined are near Odell, Nebraska, in Gage County. The units exposed belong to the Chase Group. The first is located about 1.5 miles east of Odell on Highway 8. The following beds are exposed here (Conservation and Survey Division Field Guide, Gage County, 1969):

I. Odell Formation
  A. Red and greenish, nonbedded shales; best seen east of the first exposure; no fossils
II. Winfield Formation
  A. Cresswell Member: composed of two gray dense limestone deposits, each 1 foot thick with a middle zone of blue gray shale 2 feet thick; best seen to the east of the first exposure
  B. Grant Member: 15 feet of grayish shale; best seen in the first cut to the west and on the south side of the highway; fossiliferous

Site 158. Location: Between the NE¼/SE¼ sec. 9 and NW¼/SW¼ sec. 10, T1N, R6E. Continue east from site 157 on Highway 8, noting Permian exposures on both sides of the highway. Turn left (north) at the junction with Highway 112. Continue north for 1.5 miles. Exposures will be seen on both sides of the highway. The exposure is described below (Conservation and Survey Division Field Guide, Gage County, 1969):

I. Nolans Formation
  A. Herington Member: reddish brown limestone; badly weathered; no fossils seen; only a thin exposure seen overlying the Paddock
  B. Paddock Member: 10 feet of tan to gray shale exposed to the south of the eastern cut; no fossils seen
  C. Krider Member
    1. Approximately 2 feet total of two thin, tan claystones sandwiching a thin, tan shale deposit; no fossils seen
    2. Two feet of greenish shale; no fossils seen
    3. Two feet of silty, yellowish limestone with a fair abundance of pelecypods; best exposed in the middle of the eastern cut
II. Odell Formation
  A. Three feet of shale, greenish at the top and gray near the base; no fossils seen
  B. Red nonbedded shale; no fossils; contains several thin beds of greenish shale and two thin claystone beds, difficult to identify since they are frequently covered by the red shale that composes the bulk of the deposit; combined thickness around 20 feet
  C. Five beds of greenish to gray shale with a combined thickness of 8 feet; no fossils seen

The Cresswell and Grant members of the Winfield Formation have been exposed here but were not seen by this collector. The Odell Formation is best exposed at the northern end of the eastern cut.

Faunas were collected from the Grant Shale (Site 157) and unit 3 of the Krider Member (Site 158). The Grant fauna is highly fragmented and most bivalves are disarticulated, but fossils appear to be evenly scattered. Species found in the Grant Shale, as with other Permian faunas of Nebraska, are reminiscent of many Pennsylvanian species and represent a fauna that lived before the Middle Permian transformation that caused the extinction of many of these organisms. One hour of collecting in the Grant Shale yielded 264 fossils, including the following:

IDENTIFICATION	PERCENT
Brachiopods	
Reticulatia sp. (productid)	6.43
Peniculauris sp. (productid)	1.13
Juresania sp. (productid)	0.37
Composita subtilita (spiriferid)	3.78
Crurithyris sp. (spiriferid)	1.13
Derbyia multistriata (strophomenid)	51.89
Bryozoans	
Encrusting, unidentified	0.37
Lacy, unidentified	3.78
Burrows	9.84
Corals, unidentified solitary	1.13
Crinoid columns	13.26
Echinoid spines	1.89
Green algae?	2.27
Nautiloids	
Metacoceras sp.	0.37
Pelecypods	
Myalina copei	1.13

Source: Conservation and Survey Division Field Guides 1969, Dunbar and Condra 1932, Moore 1965, Pabian 1970, Shimer and Shrock 1972.

The most common fossil here, *Derbyia multistriata*, is highly fragmented. Entire valves are rare, but fragments indicate that some individuals must have been quite large. Some large specimens of the spiriferid *Composita subtilita* were found, but all were damaged. Some specimens (particularly some spiriferids, productids, and nautiloids) were badly worn, but a few large pieces of lacy bryozoans were found. A 25-pound bulk sample of the Grant Shale yielded 157 fossils, mostly crinoid columns (34.39 percent), as well as other fossils: echinoid spines (24.84 percent), *Derbyia* (21.65 percent), small branching bryozoans (13.37 percent), lacy bryozoans (5.09 percent), and a pelecypod (0.63 percent). Some echinoid plates can also be found.

The condition of the Krider fauna is much like that of the Grant. Fossils are not overly abundant but are evenly spread. The majority of specimens are fragmented and/or disarticulated. One hour of collecting yielded 124 fossils, including the following:

IDENTIFICATION	PERCENT
Brachiopods	
Orbiculoidia missouriensis (inarticulate)	3.22
Composita subtilita (spiriferid)	1.61
Derbyia multistriata (strophomenid)	0.80
Bryozoans, unidentified lacy	3.22
Green algae?	5.64
Nautiloid, unidentified	0.80
Pelecypods	
Myalina copei	66.93
Aviculopecten sp.	11.29
Acanthopecten coloradoensis	1.61
Wilkingia sp.	0.80
Nucula sp.	0.80
Aviculopinna peracuta	0.80
Unidentified	1.61

Source: Conservation and Survey Division Field Guides 1969, Dunbar and Condra 1932, Moore 1965, Pabian 1970, Shimer and Shrock 1972.

Note the abundance of pelecypods in the Krider fauna. Some of these are quite large, but preservation of many specimens is poor.

PLATES

PLATE 1. Orthid Brachiopods

1. *Plaesiomys* sp. Pedicle valve. Width: 2 cm. Ion Member, Decorah Formation, Churchtown. A fairly common genus of the Ordovician. Another common orthid, *Dinorthis*, is related to *Plaesiomys* but has fewer and more pronounced ribs.

2. *Glyptorthis* sp. Pedicle valve. Width: 3 cm. Spechts Ferry Member, Decorah Formation, Spook Cave near McGregor. There are several species of this genus in the Ordovician.

3. *Mimella* sp. Pedicle valve. Width: 1.5 cm. Ion Member, Decorah Formation, Churchtown. An uncommon genus of the Ordovician.

4. *Pionodema subuequata.* Pedicle valve. Width: 2.5 cm. Spechts Ferry Member, Decorah Formation, McGregor. Also found in a few other Ordovician deposits.

5. *Doleroides pervetus.* Pedicle valve. Width: 2.5 cm. Spechts Ferry Member, Decorah Formation, McGregor. A fairly common genus of the Ordovician.

6. *Hesperorthis tricenaria.* (a) Pedicle valve from the Platteville Formation of Spring Grove, Minnesota; (b) profile; (c) brachial valve. Width: around 2 cm. McGregor Member, Platteville Formation, McGregor. This genus can be found in several Ordovician and Silurian formations.

7. *Paucicrura rogata.* Pedicle valve. Width: 1 cm. Spechts Ferry Member. Decorah Formation, Spook Cave near McGregor. A common genus of the Ordovician. *Diceromyonia* is another common genus similar to but larger than *Paucicrura*.

8. *Platystrophia trentonensis.* Pedicle valve. Width: 2 cm. Ion Member, Decorah Formation, Churchtown. A common genus of the Ordovician with a few species also occurring in the Silurian.

9. *Finkelnburgia* sp. (a) internal mold and (b) external mold of two individuals. Pedicle valves. Width: 8 mm. Lodi Member, St. Lawrence Formation, Cambrian Period, Allamakee County. A primitive orthid rarely found at most Iowa exposures.

Most drawings in the plates are at or near life size.

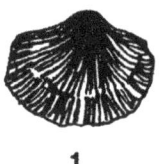
1

2

3

4

5

6a

6b

6c

7

8

9a

9b

1

PLATE 2. Orthid and Strophomenid Brachiopods

Orthids

1. *Schizophoria iowensis.* Pedicle valve. Width: 3 cm. Cerro Gordo Member, Lime Creek Formation, Rockford.

2. *Schizophoria* sp. Brachial valve. Width: 3 cm. Solon Member, Cedar Valley Formation, Independence. A common genus of the Devonian, with a few post-Devonian species also.

3. *Rhipidomella* sp. Pedicle valve. Width: 1.5 cm. Chapin Member, Hampton Formation, Le Grand. A common genus, with many species (from the Silurian to the Pennsylvanian) found by this author. Most common in the lower Mississippian. This is a small species; a few species are much larger.

4. *Enteletes hemiplicatus.* Pedicle valve. Width: 1.5 cm. Reading Formation, Table Rock, Nebraska. An uncommon genus of the Pennsylvanian with very fine ribbing.

Strophomenids

5. *Strophomena* sp. (a) Brachial valve, (b) pedicle valve. Width: 3.5 cm. Dunleith Member, Galena Formation, near Spook Cave near McGregor. A fairly common Ordovician genus. Similar to *Rafinesquina* but with a concave pedicle valve and a convex brachial valve.

6. *Sowerbyella curdsvillensis.* Pedicle valve. Width: 1.5 cm. Ion Member, Decorah Formation, Churchtown. A very common genus of the Ordovician.

7. *Rafinesquina* sp. (a) Brachial valve, (b) pedicle valve. Width: 3.5 cm. Spechts Ferry Member, Decorah Formation, Spook Cave, near McGregor. A fairly common genus of the Ordovician. Resembles *Strophomena* but with a convex pedicle valve and a concave brachial valve.

8. *Leptaena* sp. Pedicle valve. Width: 3 cm. Coralville Member, Cedar Valley Formation, Coralville Reservoir. An uncommon genus occurring in a few Silurian and Devonian deposits. A more common species was found in the lower Mississippian.

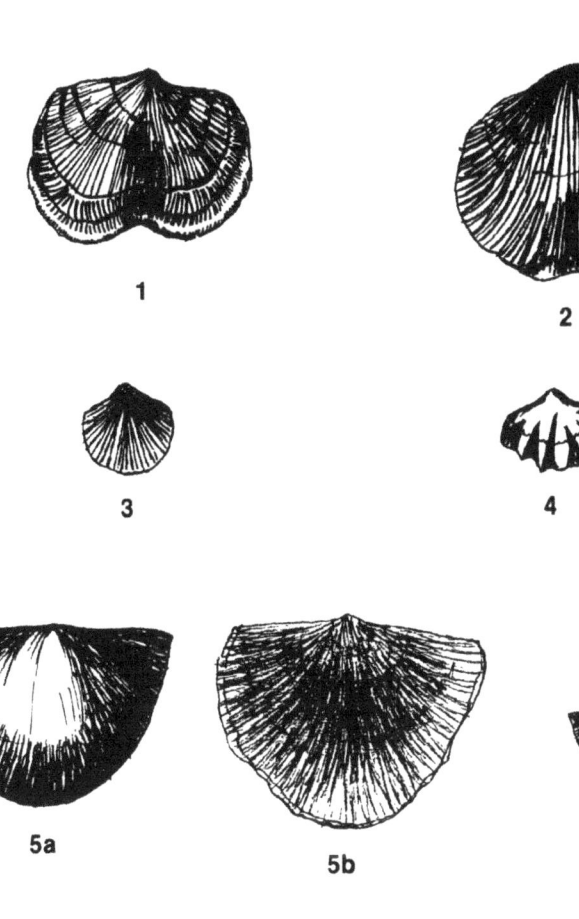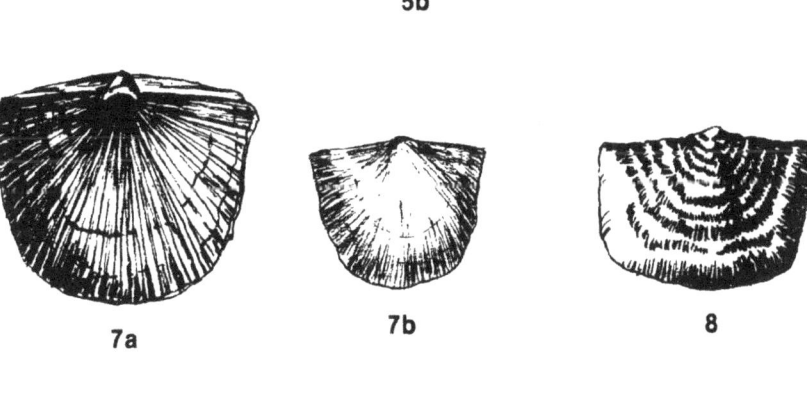

PLATE 3. Strophomenid Brachiopods

1. *Douvillina arcuata.* Pedicle valve. Width: 2 cm. Cerro Gordo Member, Lime Creek Formation, Rockford. Common in the Cerro Gordo but much less numerous in other Devonian deposits.

2. *Strophonelloides reversa.* Pedicle valve. Width: 2 cm. Cerro Gordo Member, Lime Creek Formation, Rockford. Fairly common in the Cerro Gordo but rare in other Devonian deposits.

3. *Nervostrophia* sp. Pedicle valve. Width: 1.5 cm. Cerro Gordo Member, Lime Creek Formation, Bird Hill. Apparently restricted to the Cerro Gordo. A much larger species was also found at Rockford.

4. *Strophodonta* sp. Pedicle valve. Width: 2 cm. Cerro Gordo Member, Lime Creek Formation, Rockford. A fairly common genus of the Devonian.

5. *Leptaena analoga.* Pedicle valve. Width: 1.5 cm. Wassonville Member, Hampton Formation, Wellman.

6. *Orthotetes kaskaskiensis.* (a) Pedicle valve, (b) brachial valve. Width: 4 cm. Ste. Genevieve Formation, Fort Dodge.

7. *Orthotetes keokuk.* A small brachial valve. Width: 5 cm. Keokuk Formation, Augusta. A common Mississippian genus. Some individuals of this species are among the largest brachiopods of the Mississippian System in Iowa.

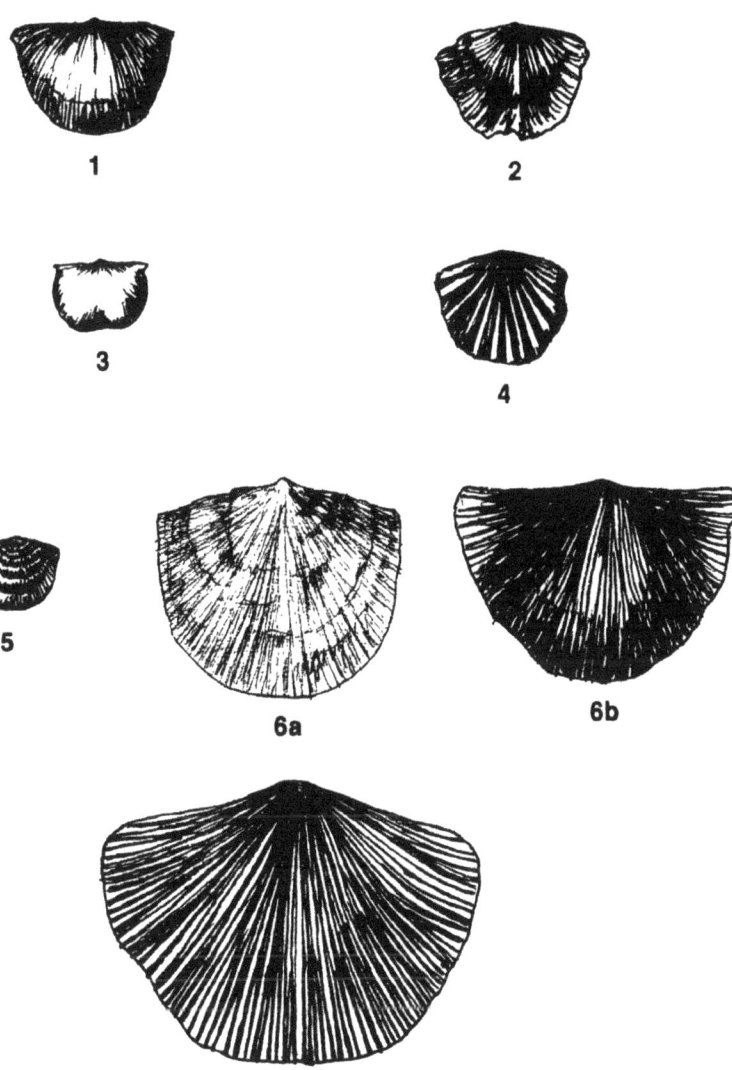

PLATE 4. Strophomenid and Terebratulid Brachiopods

Strophomenids

1. *Schuchertella lens.* Brachial valve. Width: 3.5 cm. Maynes Creek Member, Hampton Formation, Le Grand. Also found in the Gilmore City Formation.

2. *Schuchertella lens.* Pedicle valve. Width: 4 cm. Maynes Creek Member, Hampton Formation, Le Grand. An irregularly shaped brachiopod.

3. *Derbyia multistriata.* Pedicle valve. Width: 4 cm. Krider Member, Nolans Formation, Odell, Nebraska. A common brachiopod of the Permian.

4. *Derbyia crassa.* Pedicle valve. Width: 4.5 cm. Cherryvale Formation, Winterset. A very common genus of the Pennsylvanian and Permian.

5. *Meekella striatoscostata.* Pedicle valve. Width: 3 cm. Cherryvale Formation, Winterset. A fairly common genus of the Pennsylvanian but usually smaller than this specimen and fragmented.

Terebratulids

6. *Cranaena romingeri.* Pedicle valve. Width: 6 mm. Coralville Member, Cedar Valley Formation, Coralville Reservoir. A similar but larger species, *C. iowensis*, also occurs in the Cedar Valley. This genus occurs in several Devonian and Mississippian deposits but is generally not abundant.

7. *Girtyella indianensis.* Pedicle valve. Width: 6 mm. Ste. Genevieve Formation, Oskaloosa. Fairly common in parts of the Ste. Genevieve but not found in other formations.

8. *Dielasma bovidens.* Pedicle valve. Width: 6 mm. Winterset Member, Dennis Formation, Winterset. An uncommon genus of the Pennsylvanian.

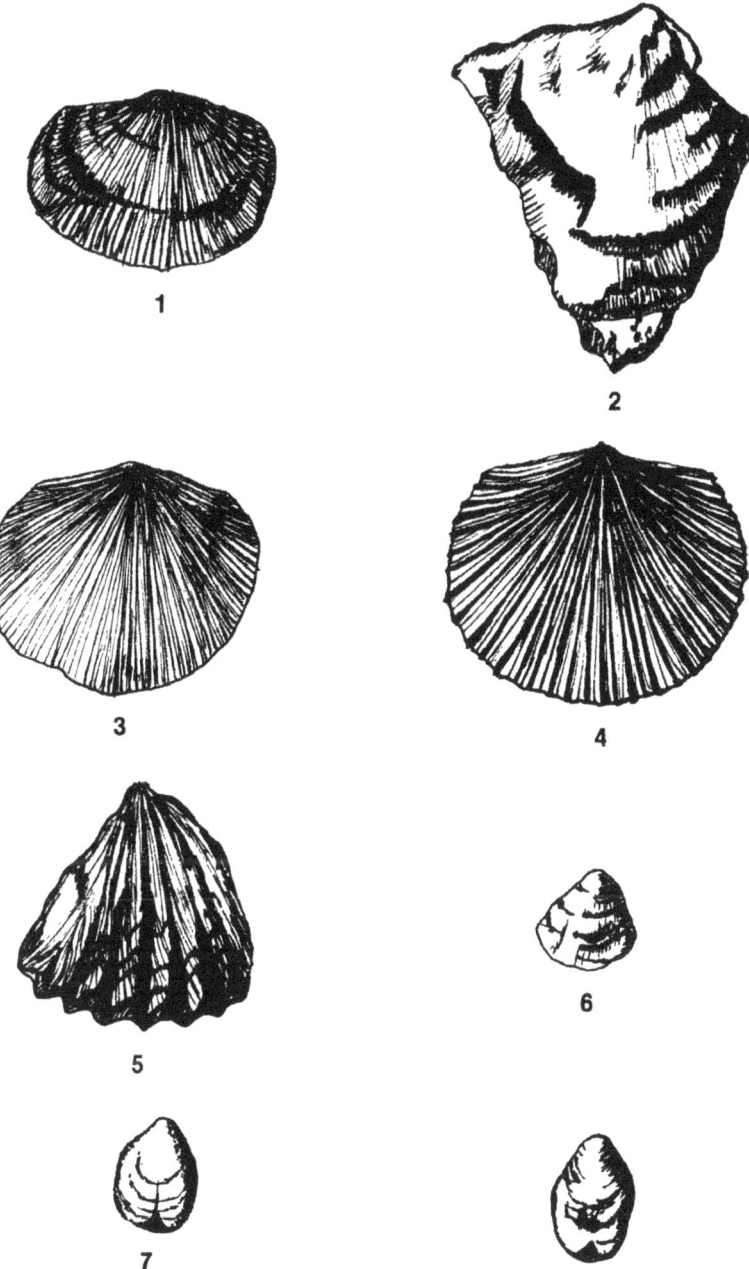

PLATE 5. Pentamerid and Spiriferid Brachiopods

Pentamerids

1. *Pentamerus oblongus.* Pedicle valve (internal mold). Width: 3.5 cm. Hopkinton Formation, Maquoketa. A small but complete specimen. A similar genus, *Pentameroides,* is common in parts of the Scotch Grove Formation.

2. *Constistricklandia* sp. Pedicle valve (internal mold). Width: 2 cm. Scotch Grove Formation, Scotch Grove. Not a very common genus.

3. *Gypidula typicalis.* Pedicle valve. Width: 2.5 cm. Solon Member, Cedar Valley Formation, Independence. Fairly common in the Cedar Valley with a very similar species in the Shell Rock Formation.

4. *Stricklandia* sp. Pedicle valve. Width: 3 cm. A common genus of the Silurian System in Iowa.

Spiriferids

5. *Atrypa waterlooensis* Brachial valve. Width: 4.5 cm. Coralville Member, Cedar Valley Formation, Coralville Reservoir. Most common in the Coralville.

6. *Spinatrypa bellula.* Pedicle valve. Width 1.5 cm. A spiny spiriferid from the Solon Member of the Cedar Valley Formation at Vinton. A small individual. This is a common genus of the Devonian System in Iowa.

7. *Atrypa independensis.* Brachial valve. Width: 2.5 cm. Coralville Member, Cedar Valley Formation, Coralville Reservoir. An average sized individual; some specimens are much larger. A common genus throughout the Devonian System in Iowa.

8. *Atrypa rockfordensis.* Brachial valve. Width: 2.5 cm. Cerro Gordo Member, Lime Creek Formation, Rockford.

9. *Spinatrypa devoniana.* Pedicle valve. Width: 2.5 cm. Cerro Gordo Member, Lime Creek Formation, Bird Hill. A spiriferid brachiopod with spines.

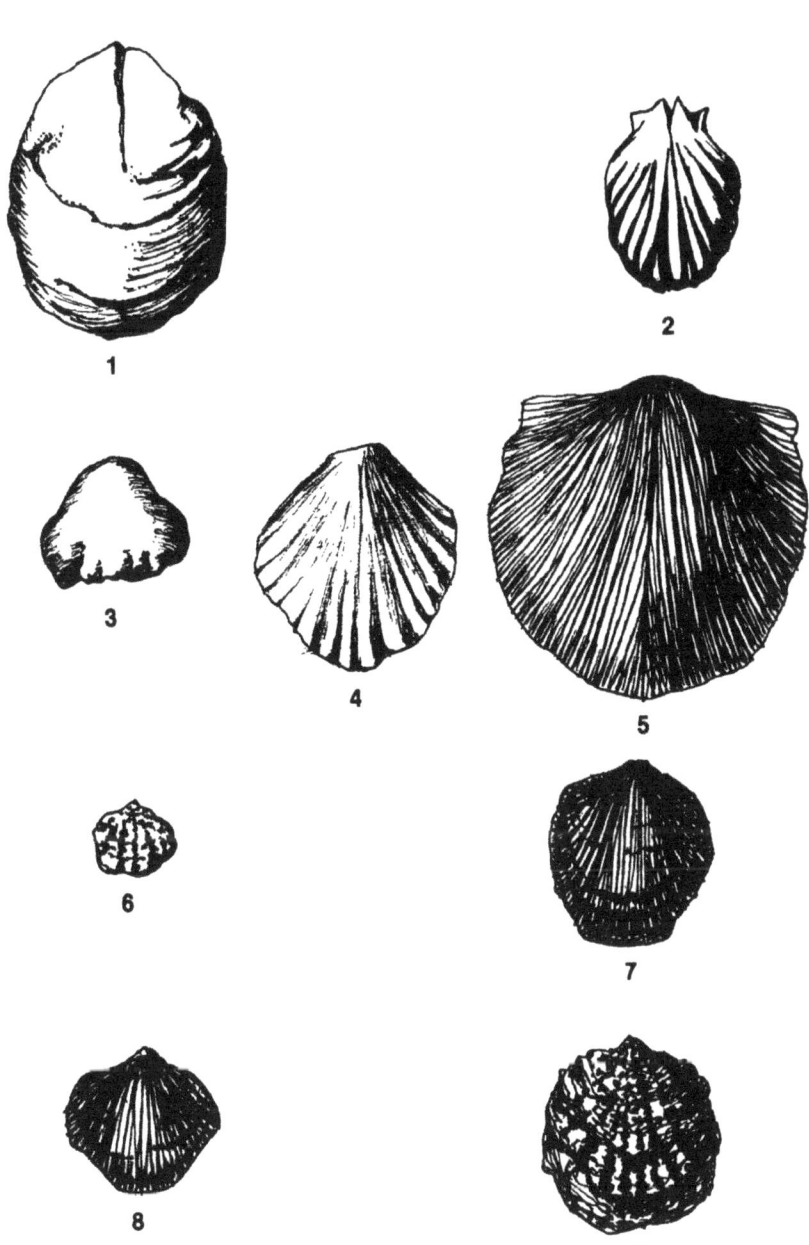

PLATE 6. Spiriferid Brachiopods

1. *Composita* sp. Pedicle valve. Width: 1.5 cm. Aplington Formation, Aplington. A common genus of the later Paleozoic. Although generally not abundant in the Devonian, the genus is common in the Aplington.

2. *Composita trinuclea.* Pedicle valve. Width: 1.5 cm. Ste. Genevieve Formation, Oskaloosa. A genus most common in the Pennsylvanian and Permian.

3. *Composita elongata.* Pedicle valve. Width: 1.5 cm. Beil Member, Lecompton Formation, Weeping Water, Nebraska. An uncommon species of the Pennsylvanian.

4. *Composita trilobata.* Brachial valve. Width: 3 cm. Cherryvale Formation, Winterset. A large individual. Common in the Pennsylvanian.

5. *Composita ovata.* Brachial valve. Width: 2.5 cm. Stark Member, Dennis Formation, Winterset. A large individual. Common in the Pennsylvanian.

6. *Composita subtilita.* Brachial valve. Width: 2.5 cm. Hertha Formation, East Peru. A fairly common species of the Pennsylvanian and Permian.

1

2

3

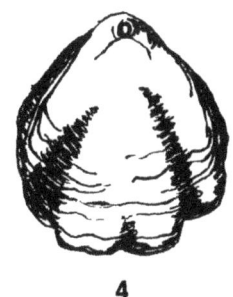

4

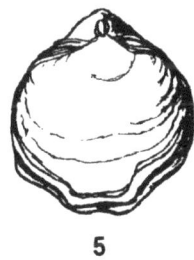

5

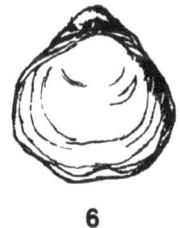

6

6

PLATE 7. Spiriferid Brachiopods

1. *"Spirifer" orestes.* Pedicle valve. Width: 1.5 cm. Cerro Gordo Member, Lime Creek Formation, Bird Hill. A similar species was found in the Aplington Formation. Although this species appears to be a *Spirifer*, the genus is considered to be restricted to the Mississippian.

2. *Tenticospirifer cyrtiniformis.* (a) Anterior view of both valves, (b) brachial valve, (c) profile. Width: about 1 cm. Cerro Gordo Member, Lime Creek Formation, Rockford. A large individual. The brachial valve, like the pedicle valve, generally has a fold that is not evident on the specimen illustrated. The genus is common in the Devonian.

3. *Spinocyrtia macbridei.* Pedicle valve. Width: 2 cm. Solon Member, Cedar Valley Formation, Vinton. An average sized individual. Fairly common in the Solon but not found in other deposits. Profile like *Tenticospirifer.* A similar but smaller and more common spiriferid of the Solon is *Acutatheca propria.*

4. *Spinocyrtia iowensis.* Pedicle valve. Width: 6 cm. Solon Member, Cedar Valley Formation, Vinton. An average sized individual. Some specimens are larger with long "wings" as seen in *Mucrospirifer.* However, unlike *Mucrospirifer*, the fold of *Spinocyrtia* is bald. A common genus of the Devonian.

5. *Cyrtospirifer whitneyi.* Pedicle valve. Width: 2.5 cm. Cerro Gordo Member, Lime Creek Formation, Rockford. A fairly common genus of the Devonian with a large species in the Aplington Formation.

6. *Mucrospirifer* sp. Pedicle valve. Width: 2.5 cm. English River Formation, Burlington. A small individual. Similar to *Spinocyrtia* but with ribs on the fold. A fairly common genus of the Devonian.

7. *Spirifer* sp. Pedicle valve. Width: 4 cm. Gilmore City Formation, Gilmore City. Only one of several very similar species of *Spirifer* common throughout the Mississippian.

8. *Spirifer keokuk.* Pedicle valve. Width: 2 cm. Keokuk Formation, Augusta. A small individual.

9. *Syringothyris* sp. (a) Profile; (b) pedicle valve, both of an internal mold. Width: 4 cm. Maynes Creek Member, Hampton Formation, Chapin, Iowa. Although there are several species of this genus in the Mississippian, particularly in the Hampton, Burlington, and Keokuk formations, none are very abundant.

 1

 2a

 2b

 3

 2c

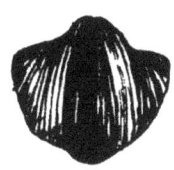 5

 4

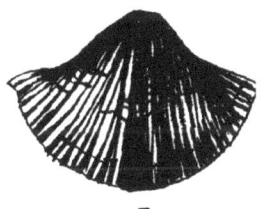 7

6

 8

 9a

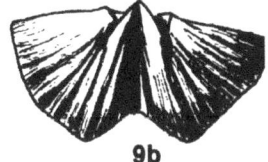 9b

7

PLATE 8. Spiriferid Brachiopods

1. *Spirifer pellaensis.* (a) Pedicle valve, Ste. Genevieve Formation, Fort Dodge; (b) brachial valve, Ste. Genevieve Formation, Oskaloosa. Width: 3 cm.

2. *Neospirifer triplicatus.* Pedicle valve. Width: 6.5 cm. Cherryvale Formation, Winterset. A large individual. Common in the Pennsylvanian.

3. *Neospirifer latus.* Pedicle valve. Width: 7 cm. Cherryvale Formation, Winterset. A large individual. Common in the Pennsylvanian.

4. *Neospirifer cameratus.* Pedicle valve. Width: 4 cm. Cherokee Group, Fort Dodge. A less common Pennsylvanian species.

5. *Spirifer grimesi.* Pedicle valve. Width: 9 cm. Haight Creek Member, Burlington Formation, near Mediapolis. A very large spiriferid restricted to the Burlington.

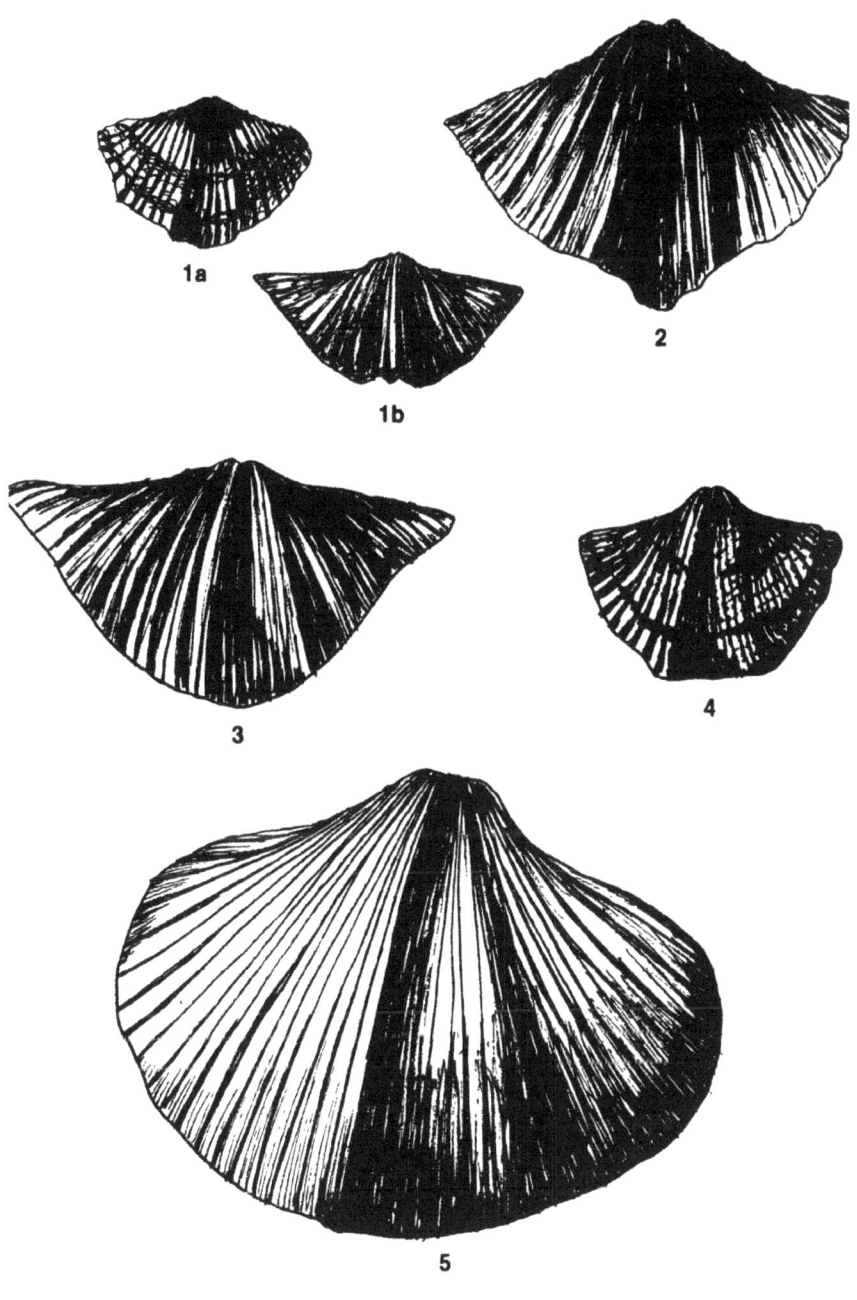

PLATE 9. Spiriferid Brachiopods

1. *Theodossia hungerfordi*. Pedicle valve. Width: 3 cm. Cerro Gordo Member, Lime Creek Formation, Rockford. A common Devonian genus.

2. *Eumetria verneuiliana*. Pedicle valve. Width: 1 cm. Gilmore City Formation, Gilmore City. Although found in several Mississippian formations, the genus is most common in the Gilmore City.

3. *Torynifer pseudolineata*. Profile. Width: 2.5 cm. Keokuk Formation, Augusta. *Torynifer* closely resembles *Athyris* but has an opening for the pedicle in the gap between the beaks of the pedicle and brachial valves. In *Athyris* the pedicle opening occurs in the beak of the pedicle valve.

4. *Athyris lamellosa*. Pedicle valve. Width: 5 cm. Keokuk Formation, Augusta. Closely resembles *Torynifer* but with a different pedicle opening. Also found in the Burlington Formation. A large individual.

5. *Phricodothyris perplexa*. (a) Pedicle valve, Mertha Formation, East Peru; (b) brachial valve, Kiewitz Member, Stanton Formation, Gretna, Nebraska. Width: around 1.3 cm. A fairly common brachiopod of the Pennsylvanian.

6. *Crurthyris planoconvexa*. (a) Pedicle valve, (b) brachial valve. Width: around 1.2 cm. Dyston Hollow Member, Stanton Formation, Gretna, Nebraska. A small individual. Common in the Pennsylvanian.

7. *Hustedia mormoni*. Pedicle valve. Width: 1 cm. Beil Member, Lecompton Formation, Weeping Water, Nebraska. Not a common genus.

8. *Ambocoelia planoconvexa*. (a) Pedicle valve, (b) brachial valve. Width: 3 mm. Stark Member, Dennis Formation, Winterset. Very common in the Pennsylvanian. A large individual. A less common but larger species is *A. expansa*.

9. *Punctospirifer kentuckyensis*. Pedicle valve. Width: 1.5 cm. Stark Member, Dennis Formation, Winterset. A large individual. Common in the Pennsylvanian.

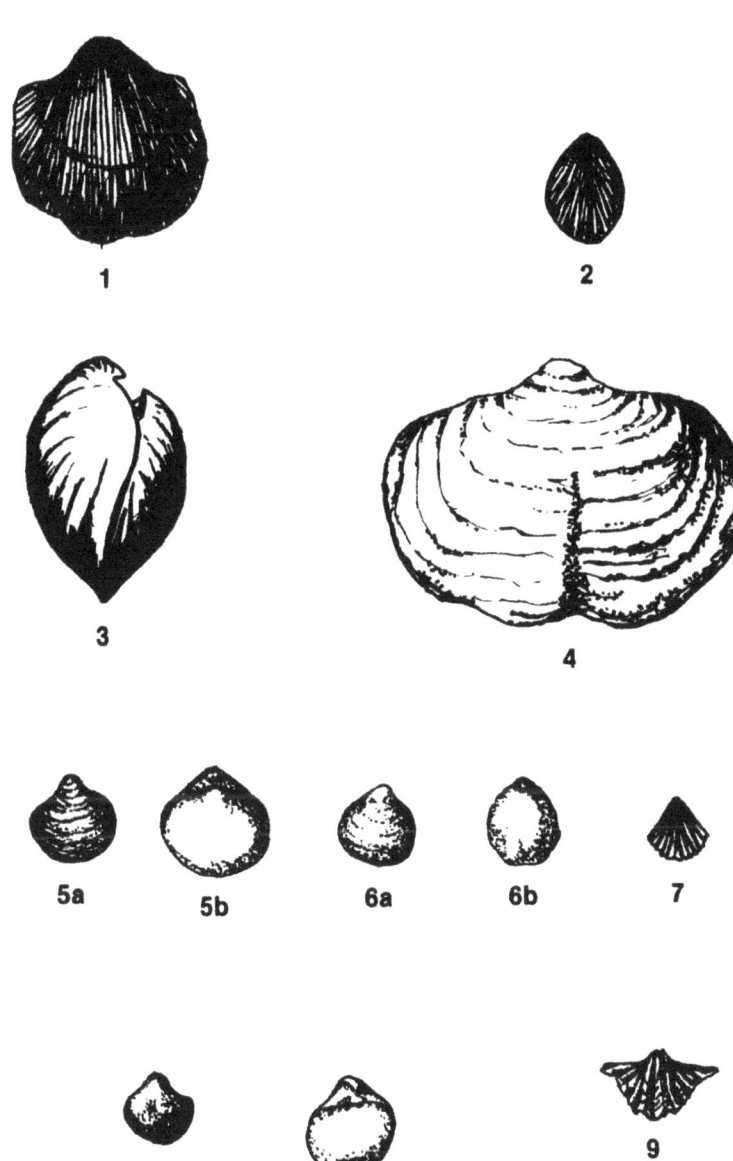

PLATE 10. Rhynchonellid Brachiopods

1. *Rhynchotrema increbescens.* Pedicle valve. Width: 1.3 cm. Ion Member, Decorah Formation, Churchtown. A fairly common genus in the Ordovician.

2. *Stegerhynchus* sp. Pedicle valve. Width: 1 cm. Palisades-Kepler Facies, Scotch Grove Formation, Hunt Quarry, north of Cedar Bluff. This and similar rhynchonellids are common in parts of the Silurian.

3. *Camarotoechia contracta.* Pedicle valve. Width: 1 cm. Aplington Formation, Aplington. Common in the Aplington but rarer in other Devonian formations. The genus also occurs in the Mississippian.

4. *Paryphorhynchus* sp. Pedicle valve. Width: 2.5 cm. English River Formation, Burlington. Fairly common in the English River but rarer in other deposits.

5. *Rhynchopora cooperensis.* Pedicle valve. Width: 1.6 cm. Gilmore City Formation, Gilmore City. Common in the Gilmore City and also found in a few other Mississippian deposits.

6. *Allorhynchus heteropsis.* Pedicle valve. Width: 1.5 cm. Eagle City Member, Hampton Formation, Iowa Falls. Common in the Eagle City at some sites.

7. *Pugnoides ottumwa.* Pedicle valve. Width: 1.2 cm. Ste. Genevieve Formation, Oskaloosa, Iowa. Common in the Ste. Genevieve but rare in other deposits.

8. *Wellerella truncata.* Pedicle valve. Width: around 1 cm. Not a very common Pennsylvanian genus.

9. *Rhynchopora illinoisensis.* Pedicle valve. Width: 1.5 cm. Stark Member, Dennis Formation, Winterset. Not a very common brachiopod of the Pennsylvanian.

1

2

3

4

5

6

7

8

9

10

PLATE 11. Chonetid and Productid Brachiopods

1. *Chonopectus fischeri.* Chonetid strophomenid. Width: 2 cm. English River Formation, Burlington. A large individual. Common in but restricted to the English River.

2. *Orbinaria* sp. Productid. Pedicle valve. Width: 2.6 cm. Aplington Formation, Aplington. Common in but apparently restricted to the Aplington.

3. *Devonoproductus walcotti.* Productid strophomenid. (a) Brachial valve, (b) pedicle valve. Width: 1.2 cm. Cerro Gordo Member, Lime Creek Formation, Rockford. Although occurring in several Devonian formations, the genus is not very abundant.

4. *Chonetes gregarius.* Chonetid strophomenid. Pedicle valve. Width: 1.4 cm. McCraney Formation, Burlington, Iowa. *Chonetes* is a common genus with many species ranging from the Devonian to the Pennsylvanian.

5. *Productellana bifaria.* Productid strophomenid. Pedicle valve. Width: 1 cm. Maynes Creek Member, Hampton Formation, Chapin. A small specimen. An uncommon genus.

6. *Chonetes logani.* Chonetid strophomenid. Brachial valve. Width: 2 cm. Wassonville Member, Hampton Formation, Wellman.

7. *Chonetes granulifer.* Chonetid strophomenid. Width: 1.5 cm. Cherryvale Formation, Winterset. A common Pennsylvanian genus. Similar to *Chonetinella* but with a flatter shell and a less prominent fold.

8. *Chonetinella flemingi.* Chonetid strophomenid. Width: 1 cm. Cherryvale Formation, Winterset, Iowa. Common in the Pennsylvanian. (See *Chonetes granulifer.*)

9. *Neochonetes* sp. Chonetid strophomenid. Width: 3 cm. Harveyville Formation, Table Rock, Nebraska. Fairly common in the upper Pennsylvanian.

10. aff. *Productella* sp. Productid strophomenid. Brachial valve. Width: 1 cm. Hertha Formation, East Peru. Identification uncertain. Found in a few Pennsylvanian limestones but most common in the Hertha. Usually found in life position with the pedicle valve sunk into the rock.

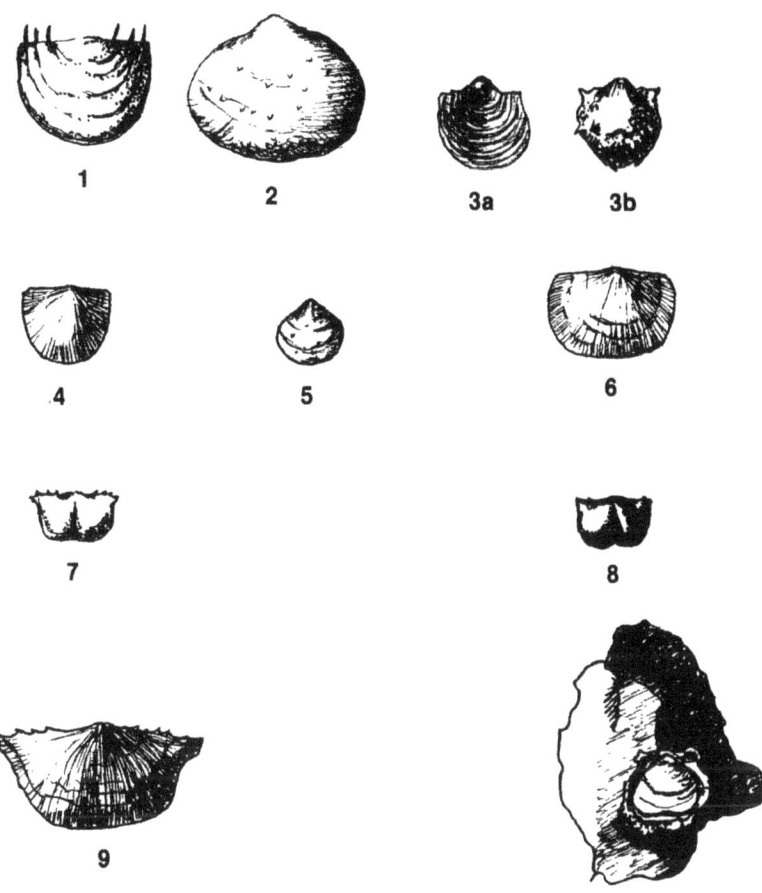

PLATE 12. Productid Brachiopods

1. *Linoproductus ovatus.* Pedicle valve. Width: 2 cm. Ste. Genevieve Formation, Oskaloosa. Restricted to the Ste. Genevieve but common in the Pennsylvanian.

2. *Linoproductus meniscus.* Pedicle valve. Width: 5 cm. Cherryvale Formation, Winterset. A large individual. A common genus of the Pennsylvanian.

3. *Linoproductus platyumbonus.* Pedicle valve. Width: 3.5 cm. Cherryvale Formation, Winterset. A slightly fragmented specimen. Similar to *L. meniscus* but more spiny and not as common.

4. *Juresania nebrascensis.* Pedicle valve. Width: 3 cm. Cherryvale Formation, Winterset. A common genus of the Pennsylvanian and Permian but usually fragmented.

5. *Juresania symmetrica.* Pedicle valve. Width: 4 cm. Similar to *J. nebrascensis* but larger with more and smaller spines. Not a common species. Reconstruction of a fragmented specimen of the Cherryvale Formation àt Winterset.

6. *Juresania* sp. Pedicle valve. Width: 4.5 cm. Grant Member, Winfield Formation, Odell, Nebraska. Reconstruction of a poorly preserved specimen.

1

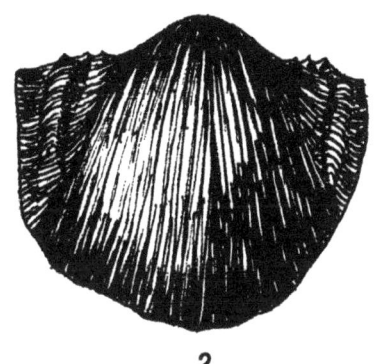

2

3

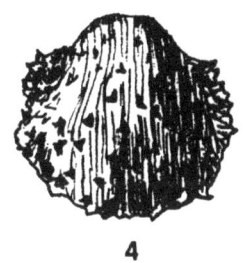

4

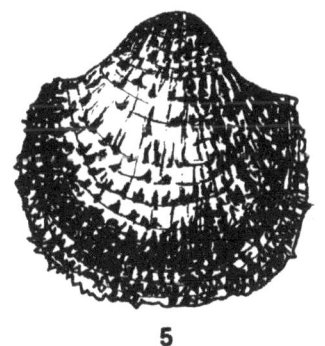

5

6

PLATE 13. Productid Brachiopods

1. *Setigerites setigerites.* Pedicle valve. Width: 3.8 cm. Keokuk Formation, Augusta. An uncommon genus occurring in several Mississippian formations but usually fragmented.

2. *Marginicinctus marginicinctus.* Brachial valve. Width: 3.5 cm. Keokuk Formation, Augusta. A fairly common genus of the Mississippian. The brachial valves of other productids, particularly *Dictyoclostus,* resemble *Marginicinctus* but lack the frill along the outside (anterior) margin of the shell.

3. *Cancrinella booensis.* Pedicle valve. Width: 1 cm. Auburn Formation, Unadilla, Nebraska. Generally not a very common genus in the Pennsylvanian.

4. *Dictyoclostus portlockianus.* Pedicle valve. Width: 4 cm. Cherryvale Formation, Winterset. A fairly common genus of the Pennsylvanian. A larger species is *D. americanus.*

5. *Hystrinculina* sp. Pedicle valve. Width: 1.5 cm. Stark Member, Dennis Formation, Winterset. Not a very common genus in the Pennsylvanian.

6. *Marginifera* sp. Pedicle valve. Width: 1.5 cm. Stark Member, Dennis Formation, Winterset. Fairly common in the Pennsylvanian.

7. *Desmoinesia* sp. Pedicle valve. Width: 2.5 cm. Cherryvale Formation, Winterset. Not a very common genus in the Pennsylvanian.

8. *Cancrinella* sp. Pedicle valve. Width: 1 cm. Cherokee Group, Fort Dodge. A large individual. Although the genus is not very common, this species is abundant in parts of the Cherokee.

9. *Reticulatia* sp. Pedicle valve. Width: 4 cm. Grant Member, Winfield Formation, Odell, Nebraska. Found only in the Permian by this collector. Not very common.

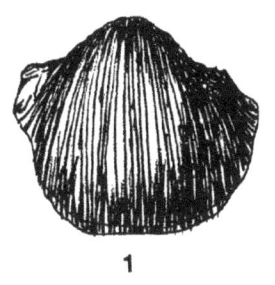

1

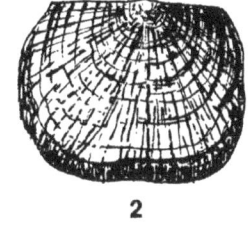

2

3

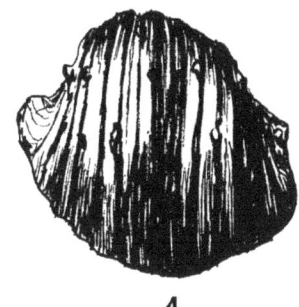

4

5

6

7

8

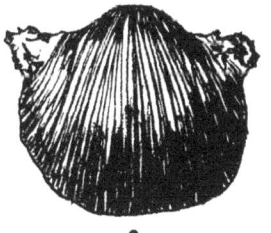

9

PLATE 14. Solitary Corals

1. *Lambeophyllum profundum.* Length: 4 cm. Ion Member, Decorah Formation, Churchtown. Fairly common in the Platteville and Decorah formations. Another solitary coral, *Streptelasma,* is fairly common in the Galena and Maquoketa formations. Both are generally fragmented.

2. *Zaphrentis* sp. Length: 8 cm. Coralville Member, Cedar Valley Formation, Coralville Reservoir. A common coral of the Devonian, with similar genera in the Silurian and Mississippian.

3. *Cystiphyllum vesiculosum.* Length: 9 cm. Solon Member, Cedar Valley Formation, Quasqueton. A common genus in the Devonian in Iowa. Composed of many small, globose plates.

4. *Heliophyllum halli.* Length: 6 cm. Rapid Member, Cedar Valley Formation, Palo. A rather small specimen. A common genus in the Devonian.

5. *Cyathophyllum.* Length: 4 cm. Gilmore City Formation, Gilmore City. Common in the upper part of the formation. A small, weathered specimen.

6. *"Zaphrentis" pellaensis.* Length: 3 cm. Ste. Genevieve Formation, Oskaloosa. A small but well-preserved specimen. An unusual spiny coral that is common in parts of the Ste. Genevieve but was not found in any other formation. The genus *Zaphrentis* is considered to be restricted to the Devonian.

7. *Lophophyllum profundum.* Length: 2 cm. Stark Member, Dennis Formation, Winterset. A fairly common coral of the Pennsylvanian. Some specimens are much larger.

8. *Cyathaxonia arcuata.* Length: 3 cm. Chapin Member, Hampton Formation, Chapin. A fairly common coral of the Chapin and Maynes Creek members.

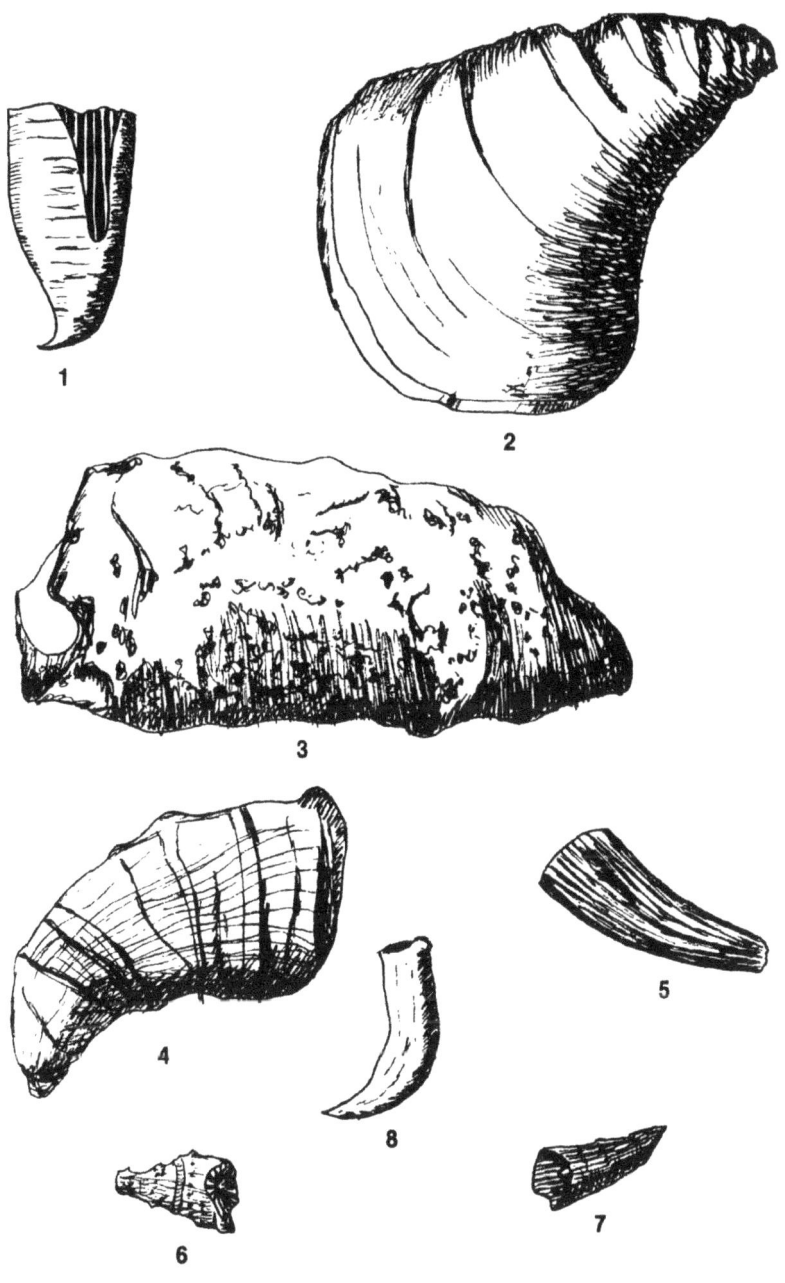
14

PLATE 15. Trilobites

1. *Ptychapsis* sp. Pygidium. Width: 3 cm. Franconia Formation, Reno, Minnesota. Only one of several fairly common trilobites of the Cambrian.

2. *Illaensis americanus*. Cephalon. Width: 2.5 cm. McGregor Member, Platteville Formation, Waukon. This species is restricted to the McGregor, but the genus also occurs in a few other Ordovician deposits.

3. Unidentified trilobite pygidium. Width: 1 cm. Elgin Member, Maquoketa Formation, Graf. Small pygidia such as this are common throughout the Paleozoic.

4. *Isotelus gigas*. Pygidium. Width: 4.5 cm. Elgin Member, Maquoketa Formation, Clermont. Common in the upper part of the Elgin. Similar species occur in other Ordovician deposits, including the Galena Formation. An average sized specimen. Surface features have been slightly enhanced.

5. *Flexicalymene meeki*. Cephalon. Width: 1.8 cm. Maquoketa Formation, Granger, Minnesota. Not a common trilobite. Sketched from a photo of a specimen in rock.

6. *Greenops* sp. Pygidium. Width: around 1 cm. Solon Member, Cedar Valley Formation, Vinton. Trilobite fragments are fairly numerous in the Solon at Vinton, but most are difficult to identify. Sketched from a photo of a specimen in rock.

7. *Phillipsia* sp. Pygidium. Width: 1 cm. Ste. Genevieve Formation, Oskaloosa.

8. Unidentified trilobite pygidium. Width: 1.3 cm. McCraney Formation, Burlington.

9. *Ameura* sp. Pygidium. Width: 1.5 cm. Cherryvale Formation, Winterset. Also found in a few other Pennsylvanian deposits.

10. *Ameura sangamonensis*. Complete specimen. Length: 4.5 cm. Cherryvale Formation, Winterset. Complete trilobites are uncommon in any formation in Iowa.

11. *Ditomopyge scitula*. Complete specimen, pygidium view. Width: 3 mm. Stark Member, Dennis Formation, Winterset. A very small, enrolled specimen.

12. *Dikelocephalus* sp. Spine from the cranidium. Lodi Member, St. Lawrence Formation, Cambrian Period, Allamakee County. Total length: 40 mm.

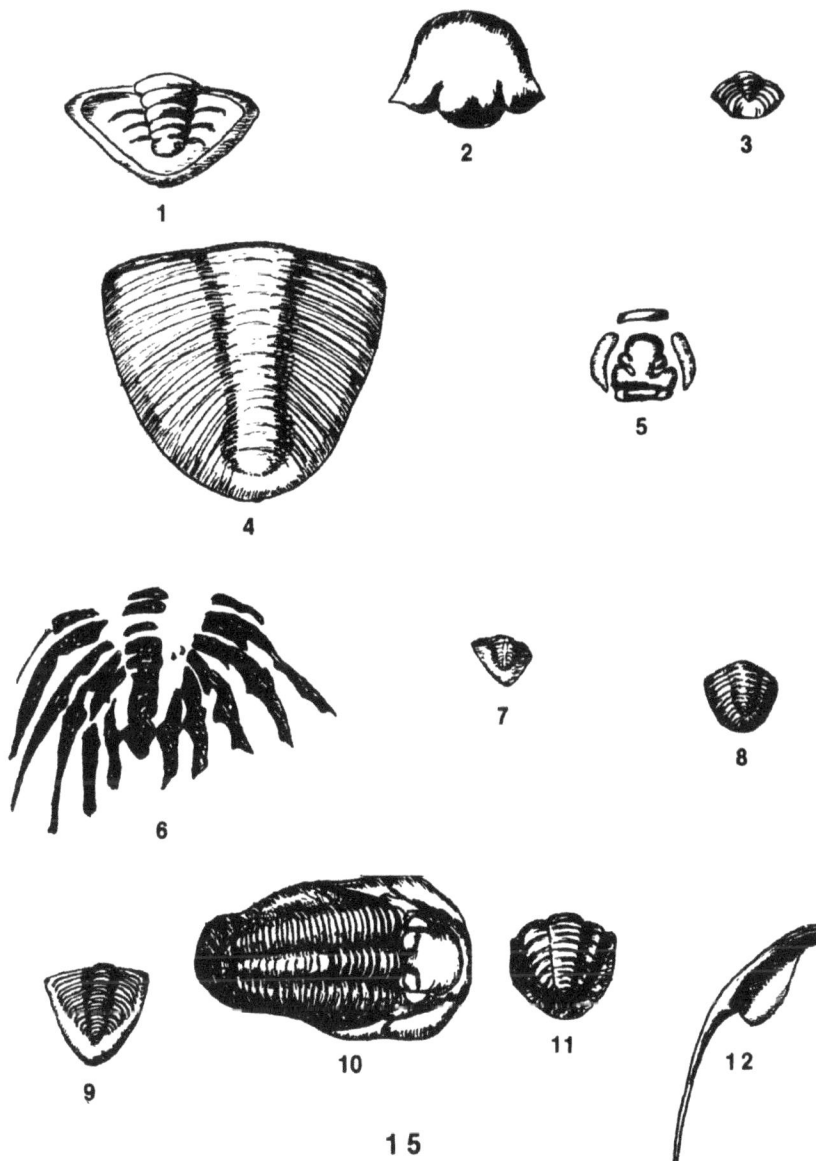

PLATE 16. Stromatoporoid

A large, mound-shaped stromatoporoid found in the Cedar Valley Formation at Garrison. Width: 14 cm. Stromatoporoids come in a wide variety of shapes and sizes, but basically there are three types: low mound, tall, and branching. This specimen was sketched from a rock and shows a cross-section of the colony; the concentric lines are layers that were built around the central mass. Stromatoporoids are most common in the Silurian and Devonian.

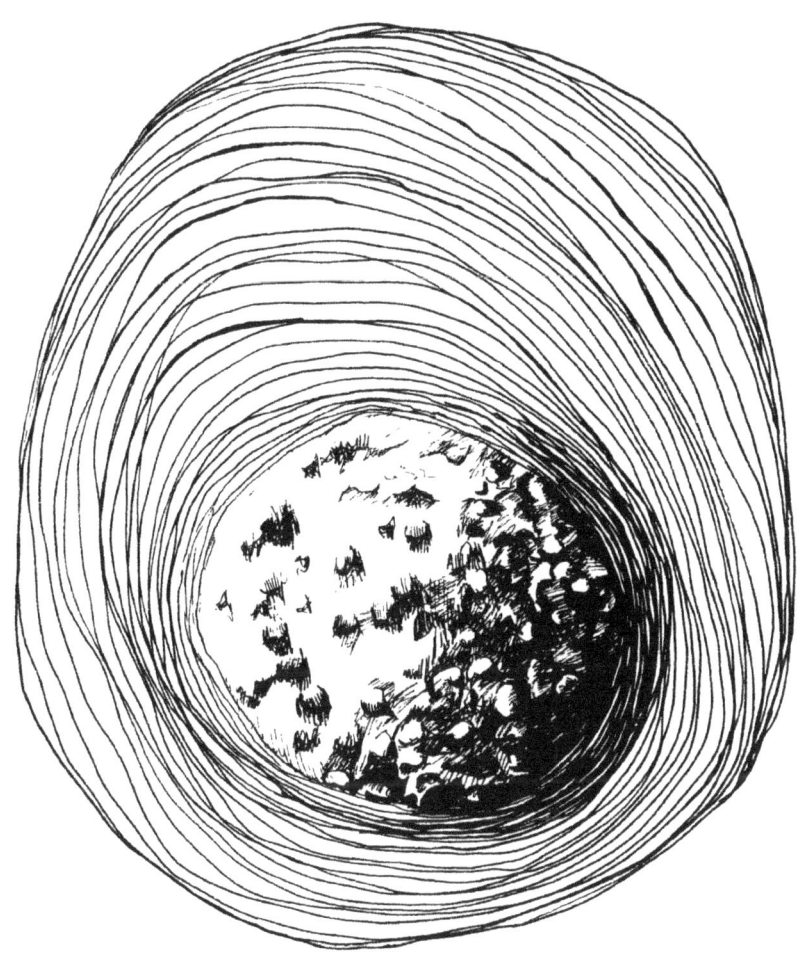

PLATE 17. Colonial Corals and Stromatoporoids

1. *Halysites catenulatus.* Colonial coral. (a) Top view, (b) side view of part of a colony. Length of colony shown: 3.5 cm. Hopkinton Formation, Maquoketa. Occurs in several Silurian formations; a related species occurs in a few Ordovician deposits. Individuals grew in rows of chains.

2. *Heliolites megastoma.* Colonial coral. Width of portion shown: 2.5 cm. La Porte City Facies, Hopkinton Formation, Manchester. Common in the La Porte City and also present in other Silurian deposits. This coral is composed of two sizes of individuals or corallites.

3. *Syringopora* sp. Colonial coral. Width of portion shown: about 2 cm. Hopkinton Formation, Maquoketa. Not very abundant in the Silurian. This colonial coral had short, horizontal bars connecting the corallites, which can be seen in this side view.

4. *Favosites* sp. Colonial coral. Width: 3 cm. Palisades-Kepler Facies, Scotch Grove Formation, Hunt Quarry, north of Cedar Bluff. A common genus of the Silurian and Devonian. A very small colony.

5. *Pachyphyllum woodmani.* Colonial coral. Width: 2.5 cm. Cerro Gordo Member, Lime Creek Formation, Rockford. A small colony. Similar species occur in the Cedar Valley and Shell Rock formations.

6. *Hexagonaria parvula.* Colonial coral. Width: 2.5 cm. Solon Member, Cedar Valley Formation, Vinton. Portion of a colony showing individual corallites marked by walls. Top view. Common in the Cedar Valley. A similar common Devonian genus, *Billingstratae*, lacks the walls between the corallites. A similar but not related colonial coral, *Lithostrotionella*, can be found in a few Mississippian formations.

7. *Aulopora* sp. Colonial coral. Width: 3.5 cm. Coralville Member, Cedar Valley Formation, Coralville Reservoir. Fairly common in the Devonian, it grew attached to a wide variety of organisms. Specimens were even seen on other corals. A large specimen.

8. Unidentified stromatoporoid. Width: 6 cm. Nora Member, Shell Rock Formation, Nora Springs. A small fragment of a colony displaying the layered texture. In some deposits, stromatoporoids make up the bulk of the rock. Most common in the Silurian and Devonian.

9. *Cladochonus* sp. Colonial coral. Width: 5 cm. Plattsmouth Member, Oread Formation, Stennett. Specimen is partially covered by rock. Not a common genus in the Pennsylvanian.

10. *Idiostroma* sp. Branching stromatoporoid. Width: 3 mm. Owen Member, Lime Creek Formation, Bird Hill. Cross-section through a single branch.

11. *Pleurodictyum eugeneae.* Colonial coral. Width: 2 cm. Stark Member, Dennis Formation, Winterset. Top view of a cone-shaped colony. Not common in the Pennsylvanian.

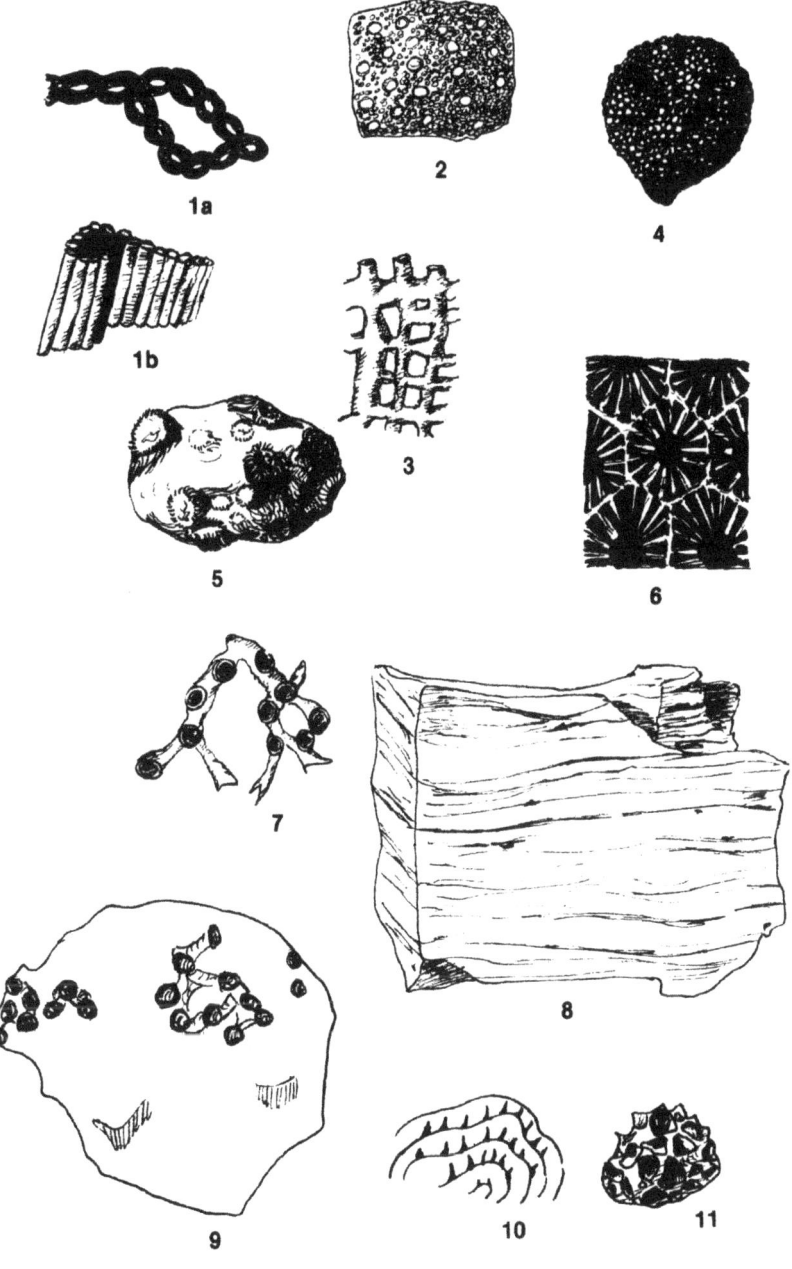

PLATE 18. Miscellaneous Fossils and Bryozoans

Miscellaneous

1. *Cornulites corrugatus.* Believed to be a type of mollusk. Length: 1 cm. Brainard Member, Maquoketa Formation, Dubuque. A large specimen. Restricted to the Brainard.

2. Believed to be a small, unidentified scolecodont (annelid worm jaw structure). Width: 2 mm. Solon Member, Cedar Valley Formation, Vinton. Because of their small size such fossils were rarely found in this study.

3. *Spirorbis* sp. Annelid worm tube from the stem of a crinoid. Diameter: 2 mm. Ste. Genevieve Formation, Oskaloosa. Such organisms usually occur on brachiopods, but they can be found on other fossils also. Fairly common from the Devonian to the Pennsylvanian.

4. *Tentaculites* sp. Believed to be a type of mollusk. Length: 5 mm. Cerro Gordo Member, Lime Creek Formation, Rockford. Also found in the Cedar Valley Formation.

Bryozoans

5. Unidentified branching bryozoan. Length: 4 cm. Ion Member, Decorah Formation, Churchtown. Such bryozoans are common from the Ordovician to the Permian. There is a wide variety of types ranging from small forms resembling pencil lead to forms much larger than this specimen. The largest types seem to occur in the Pennsylvanian.

6. *Prasopora insularis.* (a) Bottom view, (b) side view. Width: 2.5 cm. Ion Member, Decorah Formation, Churchtown. A mound-shaped bryozoan apparently restricted to the Decorah.

7. Encrusting bryozoan on a crinoid column. Length: 2.5 cm. Ste. Genevieve Formation, Oskaloosa. Encrusting bryozoans can be found on a wide variety of organisms, including other bryozoans ranging in age from the Ordovician to the Permian.

8. Unidentified lacy bryozoan. Width: 2 cm. Cherryvale Formation, Winterset. A wide variety of lacy bryozoans range from the Silurian to the Permian. The best preserved specimens were found in the Pennsylvanian.

1

2

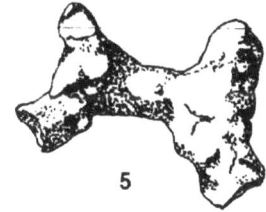
3

4

5

6b

6a

7

8

18

PLATE 19. Miscellaneous Fossils

1. *Diplograptus (Orthograptus) peosta.* Graptolite. Length: 2 cm. Maquoketa Formation, Granger, Minnesota. Graptolites are common in the Elgin Member of the Maquoketa and also occur in a few other deposits.

2. *Chondrites* sp. A burrow probably created by an animal in search of food. Length: 4 cm. Dunleith Member, Galena Formation, near Spook Cave, near McGregor. Such burrows come in a wide variety of sizes and are common in parts of the Ordovician. Similar burrows were found from the Cambrian to the Permian (see 6).

3. *Receptaculites oweni.* Fragment of a large green algae specimen. Width: 3 cm. Wise Lake Member, Galena Formation, Millville. Large specimens are common in the Wise Lake, but their extraction is very difficult.

4. *Ischadites iowensis.* A green algae relative of *Receptaculites* but smaller. Diameter: 3.5 cm. Dunleith Member, Galena Formation, near Spook Cave, near McGregor. Restricted to the Dunleith. A nearly complete, average sized specimen.

5. *Conularia trentonensis.* Conularid (primitive jellyfish). Length: 2 cm. Maquoketa Formation, Granger, Minnesota. A large specimen. Most common in the Elgin Member.

6. Part of a burrow from the Gilmore City Formation, Gilmore City. These and other burrows are common in parts of the Gilmore City. Specimens similar to this were also found in the Hampton Formation at Le Grand in the Coralville Member of the Cedar Valley Formation at the Coralville Reservoir. The Gilmore City offers the most abundant and varied burrow fauna found for this study.

7. Vertebrate fragment. Part of a fish tooth. Length: 2 mm. Burlington Formation, New London. Such fish remains (basically teeth and spines) are fairly common in several formations from the Devonian to the Pennsylvanian. The most noteworthy of these are the Solon Member of the Cedar Valley Formation, Juniper Hill Member of the Lime Creek Formation, Burlington Formation, Keokuk Formation, thin black limestones of the lower Cherokee Group, and several of the black shales of the Pennsylvanian. Sketched from a photo.

8. *Orbiculoidea missouriensis.* Inarticulate brachiopod. Width: 1.3 cm. Stark Member, Dennis Formation, Winterset. Common in some Pennsylvanian deposits. Very similar specimens were found in the Devonian and Permian.

9. Fusulinids. Length: 1 cm. Small fossils common in many shales and limestones of the Pennsylvanian and Permian. These come from the Beil Member of the Lecompton Formation at Weeping Water, Nebraska. larger than average specimens.

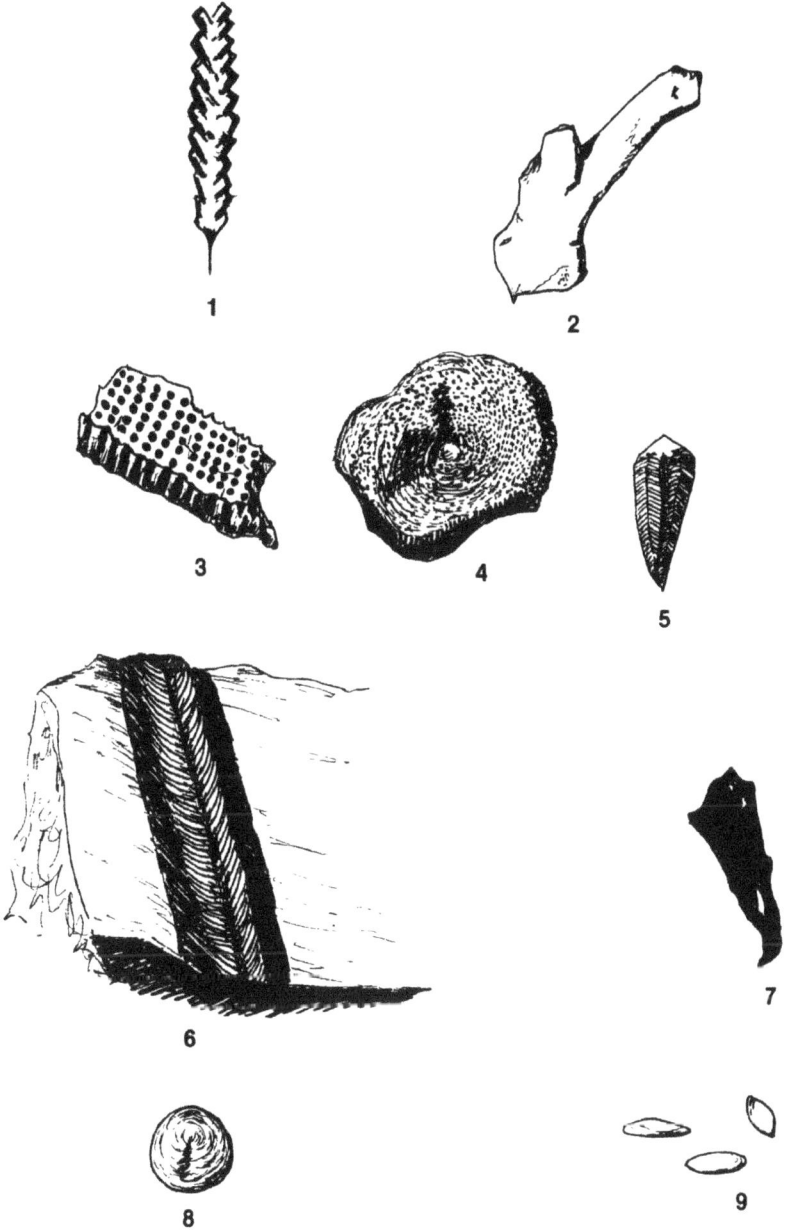

PLATE 20. Gastropods

1. *Hormotoma* sp. A large, weathered fragment. Width: 3 cm. Dunleith Member, Galena Formation, near Spook Cave, near McGregor. Smaller species are common in several Ordovician deposits.

2. *Hormotoma* sp. Width: 6 mm. Elgin Member, Maquoketa Formation, Graf. Fairly common in the Ordovician.

3. An unidentified low-spiraled gastropod. Width: 1 cm. Elgin Member, Maquoketa Formation, Graf. Fairly common in the Ordovician.

4. *Sinuites rectangularis.* Anterior view. Width: 1.8 cm. Elgin Member, Maquoketa Formation, Clermont. Also found in a few other Ordovician deposits, but most common in the upper Elgin.

5. *Ophiletina sublaxa.* Width: 1.8 cm. Maquoketa Formation, Granger, Minnesota. Not very common.

6. *Bellerophon* sp. Anterior view. Width: 1.5 cm. Dunleith Member, Galena Formation, near Spook Cave, near McGregor. Uncommon in the Ordovician. A similar species was also found in the Pennsylvanian.

7. *Holopea iowensis.* Width: 3 cm. Cerro Gordo Member, Lime Creek Formation, Rockford. Fairly common in the Cerro Gordo, but was not found in other deposits.

8. *Bucanella* sp. Apertural view. Width: 1 cm. Cerro Gordo Member, Lime Creek Formation, Rockford. Fairly common in the Cerro Gordo, but was not found in other deposits.

9. *Floydia concentrica.* Width: 3 cm. Cerro Gordo Member, Lime Creek Formation, Bird Hill. Usually fragmented. An uncommon gastropod.

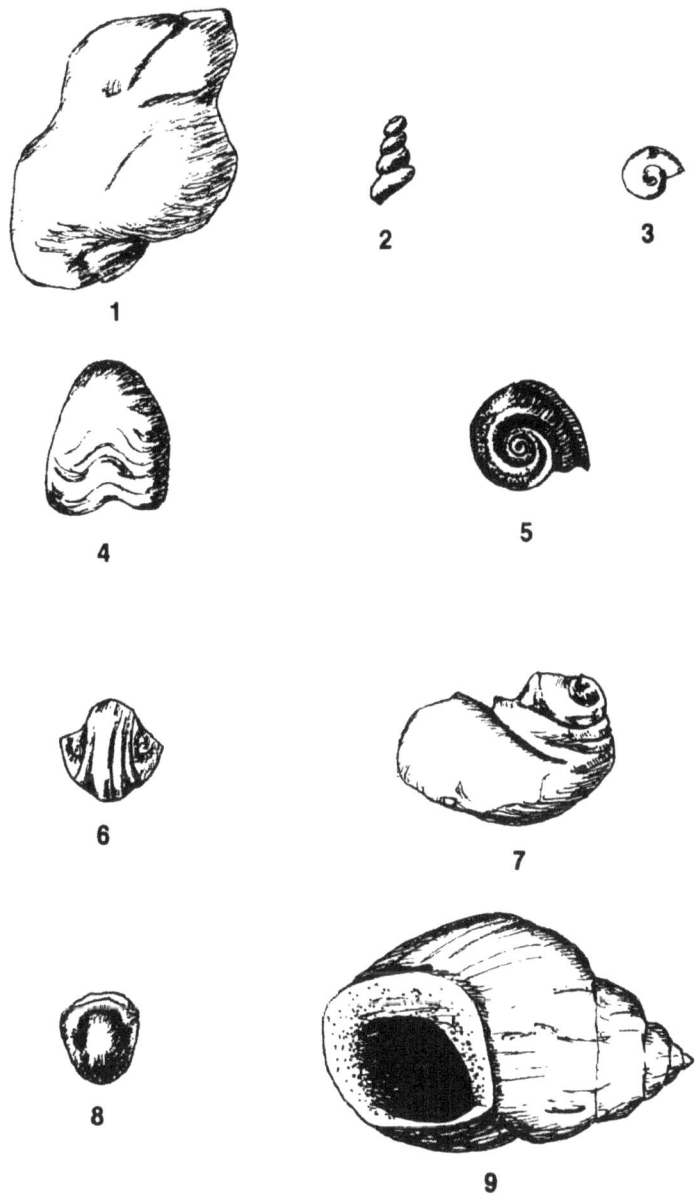

20

PLATE 21. Gastropods and Nautiloids

Gastropods

1. *Straparollus* sp. Diameter: 2 cm. Humboldt Formation, Humboldt. A common genus of the Paleozoic. A small species.

2. *Bellerophon crassus.* Anterior view. Width: 2 cm. Cherryvale Formation, Winterset. Common in parts of the Pennsylvanian.

3. *Anematina* sp. Width: 3.5 cm. Cherryvale Formation, Winterset. Not a common genus in the Pennsylvanian.

4. *Donaldina stevensana.* Width: 7 mm. Cherokee Group, Fort Dodge.

5. *Donaldina robusta.* Width: 1.5 cm. Cherokee Group, Fort Dodge. A fairly common genus of the Pennsylvanian.

Nautiloids

6. *Isorthoceras sociale.* Length: 5 cm. Elgin Member, Maquoketa Formation, Graf. Common in the Ordovician.

7. Unidentified nautiloid. Length: 3.5 cm. Wassonville Member, Hampton Formation, Wellman. Common in the Wassonville chert.

8. *Dolorothoceras circulare.* Length: 4 cm. Cherokee Group, Fort Dodge. Fairly common in the Pennsylvanian.

9. *Metacoceras* sp. Width: 3 cm. Cherryvale Formation, Winterset. Such fragments are fairly common in the Pennsylvanian and Permian.

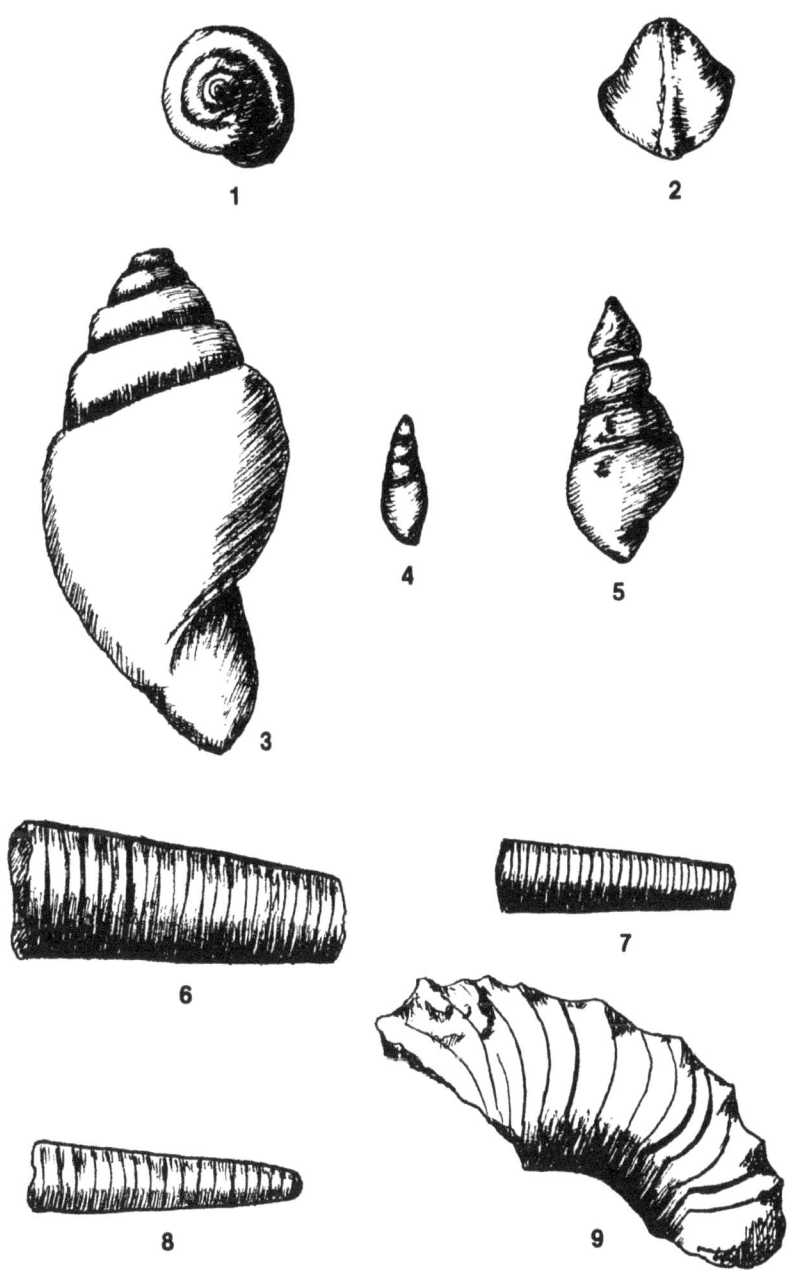

21

PLATE 22. Nautiloid

Endoceras ?fulgar. Width: 7 cm, length: 19 cm. Elgin Member, Maquoketa Formation, Clermont. Reconstruction of a poorly preserved and damaged individual. Although reaching larger sizes, the genus is generally not common and is found from the Ordovician to the Devonian.

PLATE 23. Echinoderms

1. *Dichocrinus campto.* Crinoid crown. Length: 1 cm. Gilmore City Formation, Gilmore City.

2. Unidentified crinoid calyx. Width: 1 cm. Gilmore City Formation, Gilmore City. Sketched from a photograph.

3. *Abatocrinus subaequalis.* Crinoid calyx (cup). Width: 2.5 cm. Burlington Formation, Burlington. The arms were attached at the small holes located around the middle of the calyx.

4. *Rhodocrinites wortheni.* Crinoid crown. Length: 4 cm. Gilmore City Formation, Gilmore City.

5. *Azygocrinus rotundus.* Crinoid calyx (cup). Width: 3 cm. Burlington Formation, Burlington.

6. *Rhodocrinites douglassi.* Crinoid crown. Length: 2 cm. Gilmore City Formation, Gilmore City. Differs from *R. wortheni* in having calyx plates with stellate ornamentation. The former has smooth plates.

7. *Catocrinus imperator.* Crinoid crown. Length: 7 cm. Gilmore City Formation, Gilmore City. This genus, as with the other genera on this page, occurs in the Burlington and Hampton formations in addition to the Gilmore City.

8. An unidentified echinoid complete with spines. Diameter: 3 cm. Gilmore City Formation, Gilmore City. Entire specimens such as this are uncommon.

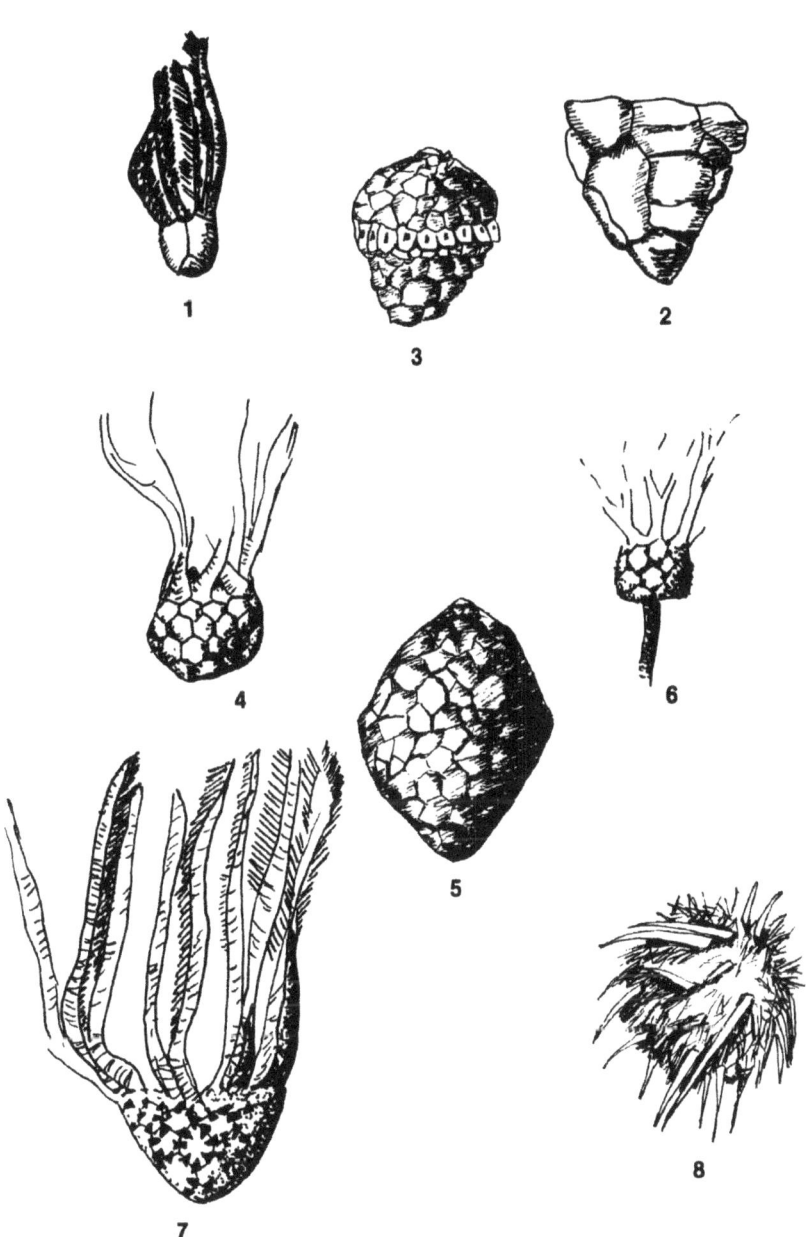

PLATE 24. Echinoderms

1. *Eucalyptocrinites crassus.* Crinoid crown. Length: 5 cm. Palisades-Kepler Facies, Scotch Grove Formation, Hunt Quarry, north of Cedar Bluff. Fairly common in the Hunt Quarry but rarely well preserved.

2. Both (a) and (b) are unidentified echinoderm plates. Width: around 5 mm. Ion Member, Decorah Formation, Churchtown. Found in a few Ordovician and Silurian formations but uncommon.

3. *Pentremites conoidea.* Blastoid. Length: 1 cm. Ste. Genevieve Formation, Oskaloosa. A large individual.

4. Crinoid column. Length: 2.5 cm. Hertha Formation, East Peru. This type of column was found only in the Hertha.

5. *Polusocrinus* sp. Crinoid calyx. Diameter: 3 cm. Cherryvale Formation, Winterset. Basal view.

6. Typical crinoid column and columnal (individual plate). Width: 8 mm. Wakarusa Formation, Unadilla, Nebraska. Crinoid columns and columnals were found from the Ordovician to the Permian, with a wide variety of types.

7. *Archeocidaris* sp. Echinoid spine fragment. Length: 2 cm. Kiewitz Member, Stanton Formation, Gretna, Nebraska. Echinoid spines and plates were found from the Devonian to the Permian. Some types are smooth.

8. Echinoid plate. Diameter: 1 cm. Grant Member, Winfield Formation, Odell, Nebraska.

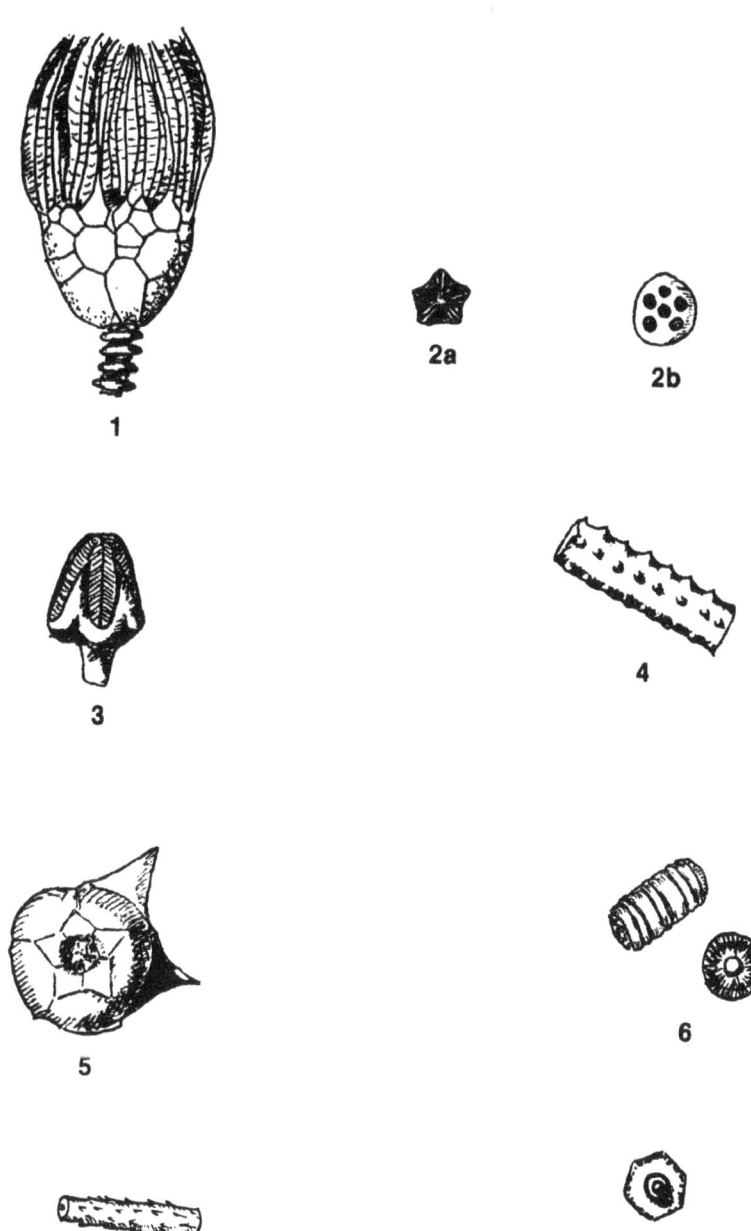

PLATE 25. Pelecypods

1. *Ctenodonta* sp. Width: 1.5 cm. Maquoketa Formation, Granger, Minnesota. Fairly common genus of the Paleozoic.

2. *Orthodesma subnasutum.* Width: 4 cm. Maquoketa Formation, Granger, Minnesota. Fairly common genus of the Paleozoic. A large individual.

3. *Vanuxemia hayniana.* Width: 2.5 cm. Maquoketa Formation, Granger, Minnesota. Not very common in the Ordovician. Specimen partially covered by rock.

4. *Allorisma* sp. Width: 4 cm. English River Formation, Burlington. A fairly common genus found from the Devonian to the Pennsylvanian.

5. *Paracyclas sabini.* Width: 2 cm. Cerro Gordo Member, Lime Creek Formation, Bird Hill. Fairly common in the Cerro Gordo. A similar pelecypod occurs in the Cedar Valley Formation.

6. *Aviculopecten* sp. Width: 3 cm. McCraney Formation, Burlington. A fairly common genus of the Mississippian and Pennsylvanian. A similar Devonian genus is *Pecten.*

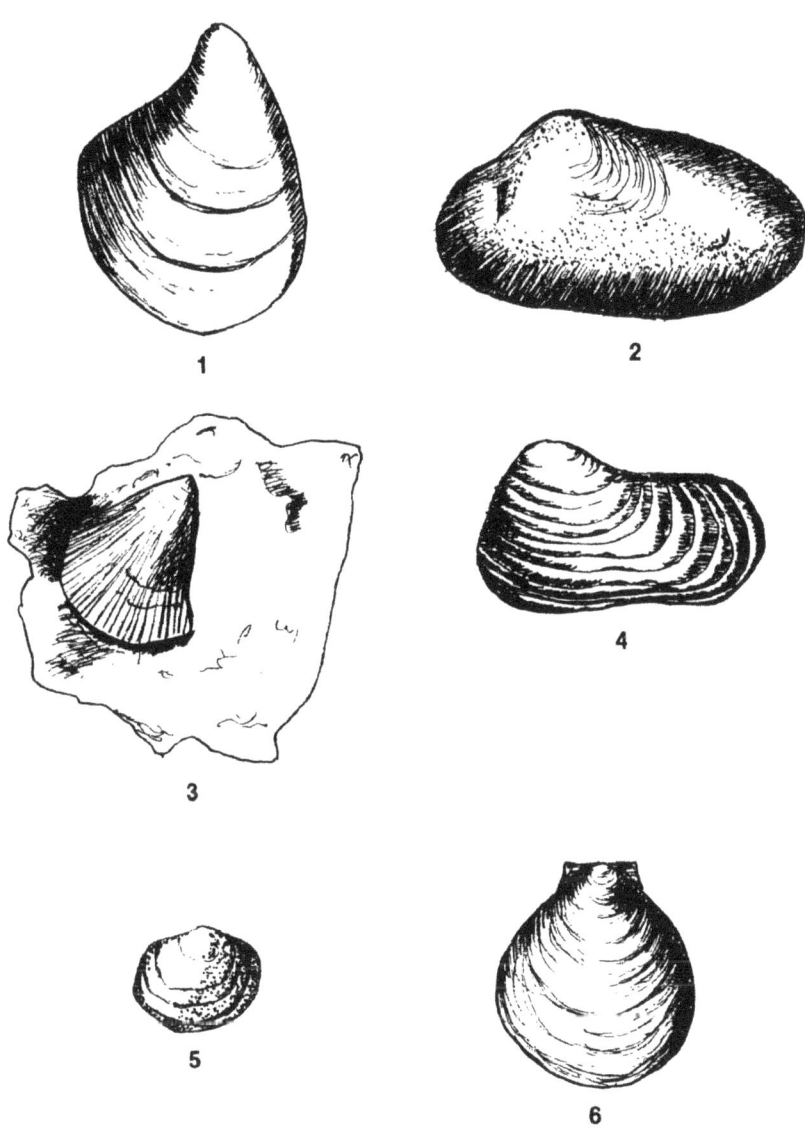

PLATE 26. Pelecypods

1. *Parallelodon tenuistriatus.* Width: 2.5 cm. Cherryvale Formation, Winterset. Not very common in the Pennsylvanian.

2. *Wilkingia* sp. Width: 3 cm. Cherryvale Formation, Winterset. A common genus in the Pennsylvanian, with some very large species.

3. *Aviculopecten providencesis.* Width: 2.5 cm. Cherryvale Formation, Winterset. Fairly common in the Pennsylvanian.

4. *Yoldia* sp. Width: 3 cm. Cherryvale Formation, Winterset. Fairly common in the Pennsylvanian.

5. *Myalina copei.* Interior of right valve. Width: 2.5 cm. Krider Member, Nolans Formation, Odell, Nebraska. Common in the Permian, with some very large individuals. Less common in the Pennsylvanian. A small specimen.

6. *Aviculopinna peracuta.* Width: around 10 cm. Krider Member, Nolans Formation, Odell, Nebraska. Fairly common in the Permian; also found in the Pennsylvanian. A large species was found in the Bethany Falls Member of the Swope Formation near Winterset.

7. *Acanthopecten coloradoensis.* Width: 4 cm. Krider Member, Nolans Formation, Odell, Nebraska. Not very common and usually poorly preserved. A similar species, *carboniferus,* occurs in the Cherryvale Formation at Winterset.

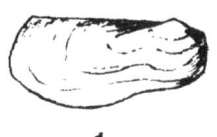

1

2

3

4

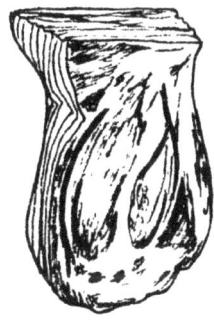

5

6

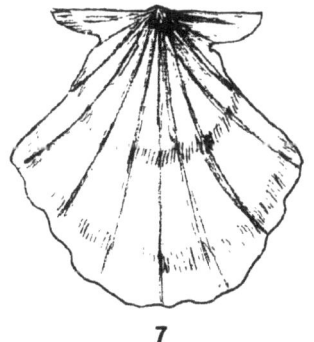

7

PLATE 27. Plant Fossils (all from the Cherokee Group, Fort Dodge)

1. *Sigillaria elegans.* "Bark" of a lycopod tree. A small fragment showing the scars arranged one above the other. Width: 2.5 cm. There are several similar species of this genus in the Cherokee but they do not appear to be as common as *Lepidodendron*.

2. *Lepidodendron* sp. "Bark" of a lycopod tree. Width: 12.5 cm. A common genus in the Cherokee.

3. *Aspidiaria* sp. The subsurface "bark" of a *Lepidodendron* tree. Width: 4 cm. Fairly common in the Cherokee.

4. *Lepidodendron aculeatum.* "Bark" of a lycopod tree. Width: 11 cm. Common in the Cherokee.

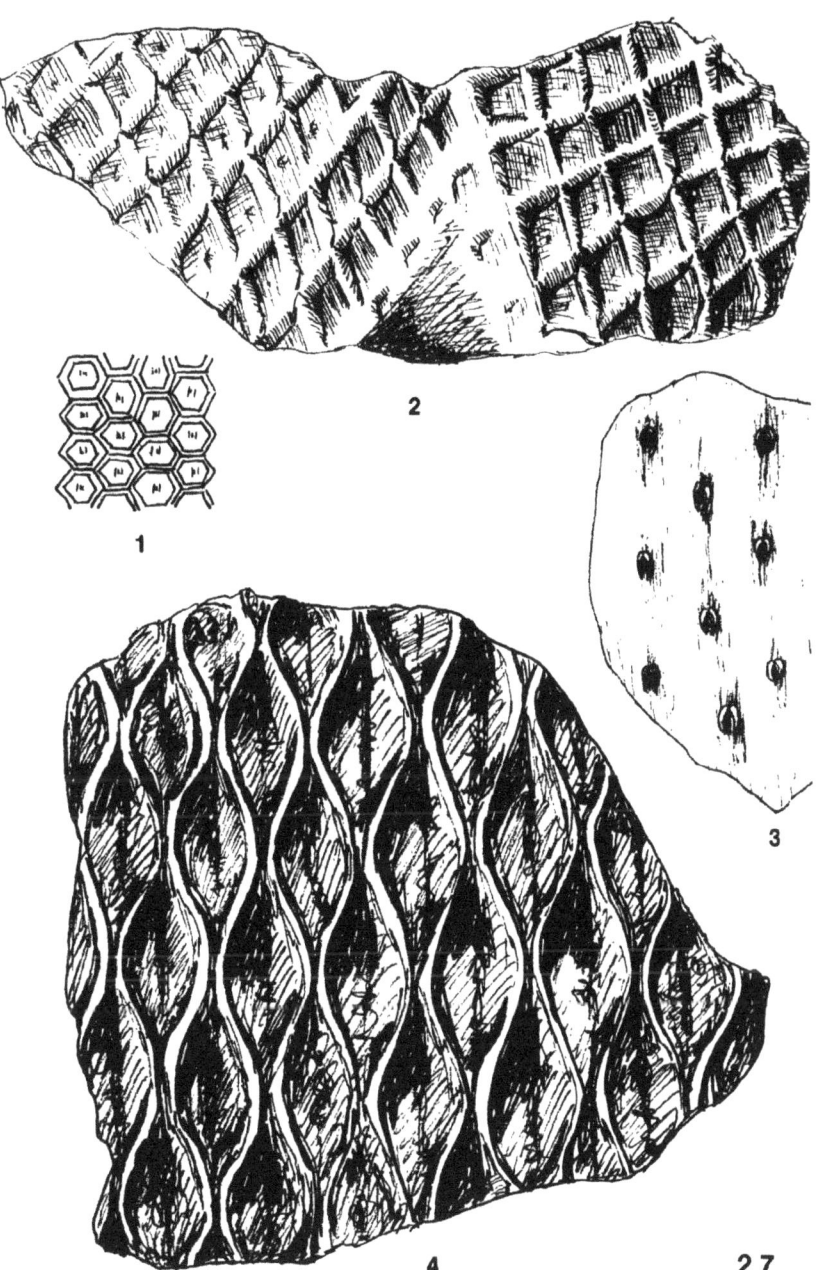

PLATE 28. Plant Fossils (all from the Cherokee Group, Fort Dodge)

1. *Neuropteris scheuchzeri.* Seed fern. An average sized leaf. Length: 14 cm. Usually fragmented but fairly common in the Cherokee. (Note: The midrib is not generally as distinct as the illustration indicates and does not continue to the apex. The same applies to illustrations 2 and 3 of Plate 29.)

2. *Macrostachya infundibuliformis.* Cone from a calamite. A nearly complete specimen. Length: 7.5 cm. Not very common in the Cherokee.

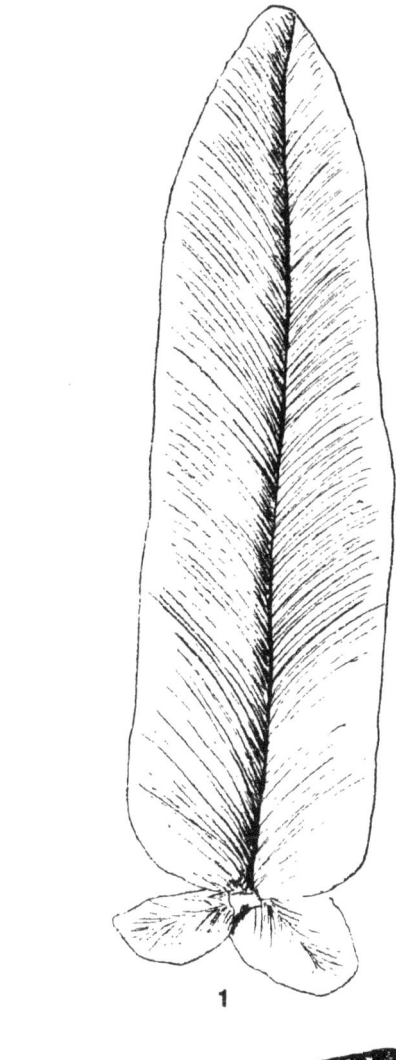
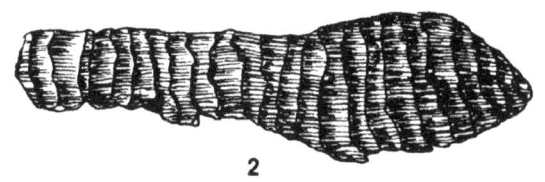

28

PLATE 29. Plant Fossils (all from the Cherokee Group, Fort Dodge)

1. ?*Neuropteris* sp. Seed fern. Part of a single pinnule. Length: 4 cm. Common in parts of the Cherokee.

2. *Neuropteris flexuosa*. A single pinnule from a seed fern. Length: 2 cm. Fairly common in the Cherokee.

3. *Neuropteris clarksoni*. Length: 4 cm. Similar to *N. flexuosa* but with longer pinnules. Common in parts of the Cherokee.

4. *Alethopteris serli*. Length: 4 cm. Another common seed fern of the Cherokee.

5. *Sphenopteris artemisaefolioides*. Length: 3 cm. A fairly common seed fern of the Cherokee.

6. *Lepidophyllum* sp. "Leaves" of a *Lepidodendron* tree. Length: 6 cm. There are two leaves lying side by side shown in the illustration. Common in parts of the Cherokee.

7. *Lepidostrobus* sp. Cone of a *Lepidodendron* tree. (a) Half a fragment, (b) fragment of a poorly preserved specimen. Length: 4.5 cm. Common in parts of the Cherokee.

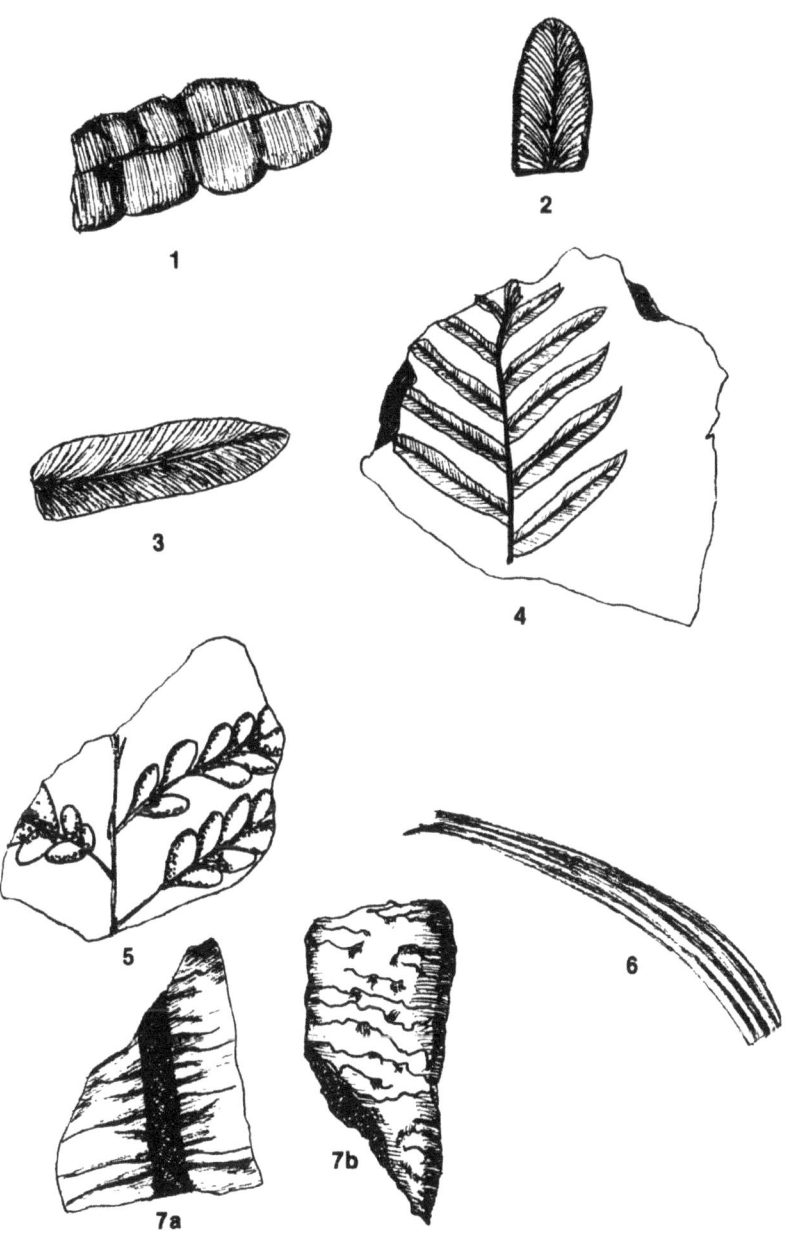

PLATE 30. Plant Fossils (all from the Cherokee Group, Fort Dodge)

1. *Cordaites* sp. A small piece of petrified wood from a *Cordaites* tree. Width: 7 cm. Common in the Cherokee but not well preserved at some localities. Some pieces are quite large.

2. *Calamites* sp. A piece of a broken stem from a sphenopsid (scouring rush). Length: 5.5 cm. Common in the Cherokee. Some specimens can be quite large.

3. *Aristia* sp. Cast of a limb of a *Cordaites* tree. Length: 9 cm. Common in the Cherokee.

4. *Cordaicarpus* sp. A seed in rock. Diameter: 1 cm. Common in parts of the Cherokee.

5. *Trigonocarpus* sp. A seed in rock. Width: 1.5 cm. Not very common in the Cherokee.

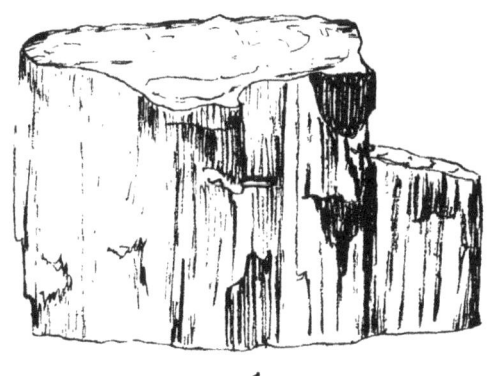

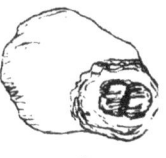
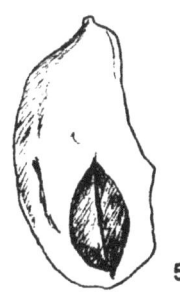

GLOSSARY

ARENACEOUS: Having a sandy texture.
ARGILLACEOUS: Composed of or containing considerable amounts of clay.
BIOHERM: A reef or mound-shaped structure built by or composed of organisms, particularly corals or stromatoporoids or both. Generally not bedded.
BIOSTROME: Similar to a bioherm but bedded and lacking the mound shape.
BRECCIATED: Rock containing sharp fragments that have not been eroded, as opposed to conglomerate, which is composed of rounded fragments.
BURROWS: Trails dug by creatures moving about on or in the sea floor.
CALYX: (1) The upper part or crown of a crinoid excluding the arms. (2) The cup of a single coral, or corallite.
CAST: In this book, an uncrystallized filling of a fossil mold.
CHERT: A dense siliceous rock found in limestones and dolomites. Generally white or black, but other colors are known.
COMMENSALS: Organisms that use the shell of other organisms for habitation but do not harm the host.
CONE-IN-CONE CALCITE: Calcite concretions arranged in cones, one inside the other.
CORALLITE: An individual coral, which grouped with others to form a colony.
COSTAE: Ribbing on a shell.
COSTELLAE: Very fine costae.
CRANIDIUM: The head part of a trilobite.
CRINOIDAL: Containing an abundance of crinoid plates.
DIMINUTIVE (DEPAUPERATE): Describes a fauna composed of exceptionally small fossils.
DISARTICULATED: No longer joined as in the bivalves whose shells are arranged in two parts or valves that, upon death, can separate from each other.
DOLOMITIC: Containing the mineral dolomite.
ENROLLED SPECIMENS: Pertaining to trilobites, some of which could curl up in a ball when threatened.
EPIFAUNA: Pertains to all the commensals in a fauna.
EQUIVALENT, LATERAL: A deposit at one locality occurring at the same level as a deposit at another locality.

EQUIVALENT, TIME: A deposit at one locality formed at the same time as a deposit at another locality.
FAUNA: The entire assemblage of animals in an environment.
FISSILE: Arranged in very thin layers.
GLABELLA: The central part of a cranidium on a trilobite, excluding the cheeks, which lie on the outer edge of the glabella.
GLAUCONITIC: Containing the green mineral glauconite.
INDEX FOSSIL: A fossil restricted to a certain stratigraphic level; therefore, it can be used as a guide in dating exposures.
INARTICULATE: In this book, pertains to primitive brachiopods whose shells are joined by muscles only, not a hinge.
LITHOLOGY: The physical characteristics of a particular rock.
MOLD, EXTERNAL: Impression in rock of the exterior side of a shell.
MOLD, INTERNAL: Impression in rock of the interior side of a shell.
OOLITE: A small circular grain, usually calcareous. Most common in limestones.
OOLITIC: Comprised of oolites.
PARTING: In this book, a very thin layer. Usually refers to a single shale layer in rock.
PYGIDIUM: The tail part of a trilobite.
REGRESSIVE LIMESTONE: Limestone deposited while the sea was subsiding.
SLUMPED: Rock that has slid down overlying deposits.
TALUS: Eroded material lying loose at the base of a slope.
TRANSGRESSIVE LIMESTONE: Limestone deposited while the sea was advancing.
TYPE SECTION (LOCALITY): Site or area where a particular deposit was first examined or is best exposed.
UNIT: In this book, pertaining to a particular unnamed deposit or a lithologically distinct layer in a deposit.
ZONE: In this book, a layer marked by a single characteristic such as an abundance of a certain fossil or mineral.

REFERENCES

READERS should be aware of the county geology reports in volumes 1–38, 1893–1941, of the Annual Reports of the Iowa Geological Survey. These are available in larger public libraries, and a few are still sold by the survey. Although quite old, they are helpful in locating collecting sites. State geological surveys may be obtained from the following: Illinois State Geological Survey, Urbana, IL 61801; Iowa Geological Survey, 123 North Capitol Street, Iowa City, IA 52242; Kansas Geological Survey, 1930 Ave. "A," Campus West, University of Kansas, Lawrence, KS 66044; Minnesota Geological Survey, 1633 Eustis St., St. Paul, MN 55108; Missouri Department of Natural Resources, Geology and Land Survey, PO Box 250, Rolla, MO 65401; Conservation and Survey Division, University of Nebraska, 113 Nebraska Hall, Lincoln, NB 68588; Wisconsin Geological and Natural History Survey, 1815 University Ave., Madison, WI 53706.

AGER, D. V. 1963. *Principles of Paleoecology.* New York: McGraw-Hill.
ANDERSON, R., ed., 1978. *42nd Annual Tri-State Geological Field Conference Guidebook on Geology of East-Central Iowa.* Iowa City: Iowa Geol. Surv.
ANDERSON, R., R. M. MCKAY, and B. J. WITZKE. 1979. *Field Trip Guidebook to the Cambrian Stratigraphy of Allamakee County.* Iowa City: Geol. Soc. Iowa and Iowa Geol. Surv.
BURCHETT, R. R. 1970. *Guidebook to the Geology along the Missouri River Bluffs of Southeastern Nebraska and Adjacent Areas.* Lincoln: Cons. Surv. Div., Univ. Nebraska.
———. 1971. *Directory of Nebraska Quarries, Pits, and Mines.* Lincoln: Cons. Surv. Div., Univ. Nebraska.
———. 1971. *Guidebook to the Geology along Portions of the Lower Platte River Valley and Weeping Water Valley of Eastern Nebraska.* Lincoln: Cons. Sur. Div., Univ. Nebraska.
BURCHETT, R. R., and D. A. EVERSOLL. 1974, rev. ed. *Inventory of Mining Operations in Nebraska.* Lincoln: Cons. Surv. Div., Univ. Nebraska.
BURCHETT, R. R., and E. C. REED. 1967. *Centennial Guidebook to the Geology of Southeastern Nebraska.* Lincoln: Cons. Surv. Div., Univ. Nebraska.

REFERENCES

BURR, J. H., Jr., and F. M. SWAIN. 1965. *Ostracoda of the Dubuque and Maquoketa Formations of Minnesota and Northern Iowa.* Minneapolis: Minn. Geol. Surv., Univ. Minnesota.

CARLSON, M. P., and A. J. BOUCOT. 1967. *Early Silurian Brachiopods from the Subsurface of Southeastern Nebraska* (repr. *J. Paleontol.* vol. 41, no. 5, Sept. 1967). Lincoln: Cons. Surv. Div., Univ. Nebraska.

CASANOVA, R. L. 1970, rev. *An Illustrated Guide to Fossil Collecting.* Healdsburg, Calif.: Naturegraph.

CASE, Gerard R. 1967. *Fossil Shark and Fish Remains of North America.* New York: Grafco Press.

CONDRA, G. E. 1927. *The Stratigraphy of the Pennsylvanian System in Nebraska.* Lincoln: Cons. Surv. Div., Univ. Nebraska.

———. 1933. *The Missouri River Traverse in Iowa, North of the Jones Point Deformation.* Lincoln: Cons. Surv. Div., Univ. Nebraska.

CONDRA, G. E., and C. E. BUSBY. 1933. *The Grenola Formation.* Lincoln: Cons. Surv. Div., Univ. Nebraska.

CONDRA, G. E., and E. C. REED. 1959, *The Geological Section of Nebraska.* Lincoln: Cons. Surv. Div., Univ. Nebraska.

CONDRA, G. E., and J. E. UPP. 1933. *The Red Oak–Stennett–Lewis Traverse of Iowa.* Cons. Surv. Div., Univ. Nebraska.

———. 1933. *The Middle River Traverse of Iowa.* Lincoln: Cons. Surv. Div., Univ. Nebraska.

Conservation and Survey Division Field Guides. 1969. Lincoln: Univ. Nebraska (around eight pages each).

Cass County—Weeping Water
Gage County—Odell-Krider Area
Otoe County—Unadilla
Pawnee County—Table Rock Area
Sharpy County—Gretna State Fish Hatchery Area

Dictionary of Geological Terms. 1962. Garden City, N.Y.: (Dolphin Books) Doubleday.

DORHEIM, F. H., D. L. KOCK, and M. C. PARKER. 1969. *The Yellow Spring Group of the Upper Devonian in Iowa.* Iowa City: Iowa Geol. Surv.

DUNBAR, C. O., and G. E. CONDRA. 1932. *Brachiopoda of the Pennsylvanian System in Nebraska.* Lincoln: Cons. Surv. Div., Univ. Nebraska.

Education Materials. Iowa City: Iowa Geol. Surv.

EM1 *Maquoketa Caves*
EM2 *Physiography of Iowa*
EM3 *Geodes*
EM4 *Fossil Collecting Areas of Iowa*
EM5 *Rocks and Minerals of Iowa*
EM6 *Rock and Mineral Collecting Areas in Iowa*
EM7 *Stratigraphical Column of Iowa*

FAGERSTROM, J. A., and R. R. BURCHETT. 1972. *Upper Pennsylvanian Shoreline Deposits from Iowa and Nebraska: Their Recognition, Variation, and Significance* (repr. Geological Society of America Bulletin,

REFERENCES

vol. 83, Feb. 1972). Lincoln: Cons. Surv. Div., Univ. Nebraska.
FENTON, C. L., and M. A. FENTON. 1958. *The Fossil Book.* Garden City, N.Y.: Doubleday.
GLENISTER, B. F. and S. C. SIXT. 1982. *Mississippian Biofacies-Lithofacies Trends, North Central Iowa.* Iowa City: Geol. Soc. Iowa.
HALE, W. E. 1955. *Geology and Ground-Water Resources of Webster County, Iowa.* Iowa City: Iowa Geol. Surv.
HANSEN, R. E. 1970. *Geology and Ground-Water Resources of Linn County, Iowa.* Iowa City: Iowa Geol. Surv.
HARRIS, S. E., JR., and M. C. PARKER. 1964. *Stratigraphy of the Osage Series in Southeastern Iowa.* Iowa City: Iowa Geol. Surv.
HECKEL, PAUL H. 1980. *Field Guide to the Upper Pennsylvanian Cyclothems in South Central Iowa. A Field Trip along the Middle River Traverse, Madison County, Iowa.* Iowa City: Geol. Soc. Iowa.
HEDGEPETH, J. W. 1971, rev. *Treatise on Marine Ecology and Paleoecology.* Vol. 1: *Ecology.* Boulder, Col.: Geol. Soc. America.
HERSHEY, H. G., K. D. WAHL, and W. L. STEINHILBER. 1970. *Geology and Ground-Water Resources of Cerro Gordo County, Iowa.* Iowa City: Iowa Geol. Surv.
HOGBERG, R. K., R. E. SLOAN, and S. TUFFORD. 1967, rev. *Guide to Fossil Collecting in Minnesota.* Minneapolis: Minn. Geol. Surv., Univ. Minnesota.
HORICK, P. J. 1974. *The Minerals of Iowa.* Iowa City: Iowa Geol. Surv.
JANSSEN, R. E. 1965. *Leaves and Stems from Fossil Forests.* Springfield, Ill.: Illinois State Museum.
JOHNSON, M. E. 1975. *Recurrent Community Patterns in Epeiric Seas: The Lower Silurian of Eastern Iowa.* Proc. Iowa Acad. Sci., vol. 82. Cedar Falls: Univ. Northern Iowa.
KARKLINS, O. L. 1969. *The Cryptostome Bryozoa from the Middle Ordovician Decorah Shale, Minnesota.* Minneapolis: Minn. Geol. Surv., Univ. Minnesota.
KELLY, KEPNER V. 1971. *Kelly's Guide to Fossil Sharks.* Ruskin, Fla.: M & M. Printing.
KOCH, D. L. 1970. *Stratigraphy of the Upper Devonian Shell Rock Formation of North Central Iowa.* Iowa City: Iowa Geol. Surv.
KOCH, D. L., and H. L. STRIMPLE. 1968. *A New Devonian Cystoid Attached to a Discontinuity Surface.* Iowa City: Iowa Geol. Surv.
KRUMBEIN, W. C., and L. L. SLOSS. 1963, 2nd ed. *Stratigraphy and Sedimentation.* San Francisco: W. H. Freeman.
LADD, H. S. 1971, rev. *Treatise on Marine Ecology and Paleoecology.* Vol. 2: *Paleoecology.* Boulder, Col.: Geol. Soc. America.
LANDIS, E. R., and ORVILLE J. VAN ECK. 1965. *Coal Resources of Iowa.* Iowa City: Iowa Geol. Surv.
LANGFORD, G. 1963. *The Wilmington Coal Fauna and Additions to the Wilmington Coal Flora.* ESCONI Associates, Illinois.
LEMISH, J., D. R. BURGGRAF, and H. J. WHITE, eds. 1981. *Cherokee Sandstones and Related Facies of Central Iowa.* Iowa City: Iowa Geol. Surv.

LEVORSON, C. D., and A. J. GERK. 1972. *A Preliminary Stratigraphic Study of the Galena Group of Winneshiek County, Iowa.* Proc. Iowa Acad. Sci., vol. 79. Cedar Falls: Univ. Northern Iowa.

LEVORSON, C. D., A. J. GERK, and T. W. BROADHEAD. 1979. *Stratigraphy of the Dubuque Formation (Upper Ordovician) in Iowa.* Proc. Iowa Acad. Sci., vol. 86. Cedar Falls: Univ. Northern Iowa.

MILLER, A. K., C. O. DUNBAR, and G. E. CONDRA. 1933. *The Nautiloid Cephalopods of the Pennsylvanian System in the Mid-Continent Region.* Lincoln: Cons. Surv. Div., Univ. Nebraska.

MOORE, R. C., ed. 1965. *Treatise on Invertebrate Paleontology.* Part H: *Brachiopods*, 2 vols. Boulder, Col.: Geol. Soc. America and Lawrence: Univ. Kansas Press.

PABIAN, R. K. 1970. *Record in Rock—A Handbook of the Invertebrate Fossils of Nebraska.* Lincoln: Cons. Surv. Div., Univ. Nebraska.

PABIAN, R. K., and J. A. FAGERSTROM. 1972. *Late Paleozoic Trilobites from Southeastern Nebraska* (repr. *J. Am. Paleontol.* vol. 46, no. 6, Nov. 1972). Lincoln: Cons. Surv. Div., Univ. Nebraska.

PABIAN, R. K., and H. L. STRIMPLE. 1974. *Fossil Crinoid Studies* (repr. "Paleontological Contributions" Univ. Kansas Paleontological Inst., Nov. 1974). Lincoln: Cons. Surv. Div., Univ. Nebraska.

———. 1974. *Crinoid Studies.* Part One: *Some Pennsylvanian Crinoids from Nebraska.* Part Two: *Some Permian Crinoids from Nebraska, Kansas, and Oklahoma* (repr. *Bull. Am. Paleontol.* vol. 64, no. 281, 1974). Lincoln: Cons. Surv. Div., Univ. Nebraska.

PARKER, M. C. 1967. *La Porte City Chert—A Devonian Subsurface Formation in Central Iowa.* Iowa City: Iowa Geol. Surv.

RAUP, D. M., and S. M. STANLEY. 1971. *Principles of Paleontology.* San Francisco: W. H. Freeman.

RHODES, F. H. T., H. S. ZIM, and P. R. SHAFFER. 1962. *Fossils: A Guide to Prehistoric Life.* New York: Golden Press.

ROLLINS, H. B. 1975. *Gastropods from the Lower Mississippian Wassonville Limestone in Southeastern Iowa.* New York: American Museum of Natural History.

ROSE, J. N. 1967. *Fossils and Rocks of Eastern Iowa.* Iowa City: Iowa Geol. Surv.

SCHAFER, W. 1972. *Ecology and Paleoecology of Marine Environments.* (English trans.) Chicago: Univ. Chicago Press.

SHIMER, H. W. 1945. *An Introduction to the Study of Fossils.* New York: Macmillan.

SHIMER, H. W., and R. R. SHROCK. 1972. *Index Fossils of North America.* Cambridge, Mass.: M.I.T. Press.

STARK, M. P. 1973. *The Geology of the Winterset and St. Charles Quadrangles, Madison County, Iowa.* M.S. thesis, Iowa State University Library, Ames.

STEINHILBER, W. L., O. J. VAN ECK, and A. J. FEULNER. 1961. *Geology and Ground-Water Resources of Clayton County, Iowa.* Iowa City: Iowa Geol. Surv.

THOMAS, M. C. 1968. *Fossil Vertebrates—Beach and Bank Collecting for Amateurs*. Published by M. C. Thomas, 519 Harbor Drive, Venice, FL 33595.

TIDWELL, W. D. 1975. *Common Fossil Plants of Western North America*. Provo, Utah: Brigham Young Univ. Press.

WITZKE, B. J. 1980. *Middle and Upper Ordovician Paleogeography of the Region Bordering the Transcontinental Arch*. West-Central United States Paleogeography Symposium 1, Denver, Col.

_____. *Silurian Stratigraphy of Eastern Linn and Western Jones Counties, Iowa*. Iowa City: Geol. Soc. Iowa and Iowa Geol. Surv.

INDEX

Adair County, 101, 113, 114
Allamakee County, 8, 9, 10, 11, 12, 14, 19
Altamont, 80, 81
Anamosa (Gower), 35, 36
Anna (Pawnee), 80
Aplington, 37, 51, 52
Appanoose County, 78
Argentine (Wyandotte), 99, 100
Auburn, 116, 117
Avoca (Lecompton), 111, 112, 113

Bandera, 80
Beil (Lecompton), 111, 112, 113
Benton County, 39, 42
Bertram, 38
Bethany Falls (Swope), 82, 85, 87, 89, 96
Big Springs (Lecompton), 111
Black Earth (St. Lawrence), 11
Blackjack Creek (Fort Scott), 79
Blanding, 21, 22, 29, 30
Block (Cherryvale), 88, 92, 93
Bonner Springs, 100
Boone County, 78
Brady (Gower), 36
Brainard (Maquoketa), 24, 27, 28, 30
Bremer County, 42
Buchanan County, 39, 41
Buck Creek (Scotch Grove), 33
Burlington, 4, 53, 55, 56, 57, 64, 65, 66, 67, 68
Butler County, 51

Calhoun, 113, 115
Canville (Dennis), 88, 92
Captain Creek (Stanton), 101, 103

Caseyville, 4, 72, 73
Cass, 103, 109
Cass County, 111
Cedar County, 34, 36
Cedar Fork Creek (Burlington), 64, 65, 66
Cedar Valley, 37, 39, 40, 41, 42, 43, 44
Cerro Gordo (Lime Creek), 48, 49, 50
Cerro Gordo County, 48, 50
Chanute, 89, 97, 98, 99
Chapin (Hampton), 7, 54, 59, 60
Cherokee, 4, 69, 71, 72, 73, 74, 75, 76, 77, 78, 79
Cherryvale, 88, 90, 92, 93, 94, 95, 97, 98
"Chert Beds" (Blanding), 29, 30
Clayton County, 9, 12, 16, 17, 18, 20, 21
Clermont (Maquoketa), 24, 27
Coal City (Pawnee), 80
Coggon (Wapsipinicon), 38
Coon Valley (Jordan), 11, 12, 14, 15
Cooper Creek (Lenapah), 81, 82, 85, 86
Coralville (Cedar Valley), 42, 43, 44
Cresswell (Winfield), 122, 123

Dallas County, 78, 80
Davenport (Wapsipinicon), 38, 40
Decorah, 14, 15, 16, 17, 18, 19, 20, 22
Deer Creek, 113, 114, 115
Delaware County, 30, 32
Dennis, 87, 88, 89, 90, 91, 92, 95, 96, 97
Des Moines County, 52, 53, 55, 57, 64, 65, 67, 68

Dolbee Creek (Burlington), 55, 56, 57, 64, 65
Doniphan (Lecompton), 111
Drum, 89, 91, 97, 98
Dubuque, 22, 23, 24, 30
Dubuque County, 23, 27, 28, 30
Dunleith (Galena), 8, 14, 15, 17, 18, 20, 21, 22, 30
"Dyson Hollow" (Stanton), 103, 104, 105

Eagle City (Hampton), 7, 55, 59, 61, 62
Elgin (Maquoketa), 22, 23, 24, 25, 26, 27
English River, 37, 52, 53, 55, 56, 57, 59
Ervine Creek (Deer Creek), 114, 115
Eudora (Stanton), 101, 103

Farley (Wyandotte), 100
Fawn Creek (Scotch Grove), 33, 35
Fayette County, 26, 27
Fillmore County, 23
Floyd County, 44, 46, 48
Fontana (Cherryvale), 88, 90, 92, 93
Fort Atkinson (Maquoketa), 24, 27
Fort Scott, 79
Franconia, 10
Franklin County, 51, 60, 61
Fremont County, 114
Frisbie (Wyandotte), 99

Gage County, 122
Galena, 8, 12, 14, 17, 18, 20, 21, 22, 23, 30
Galesburg, 88, 92, 96
Gilmore City, 4, 7, 63, 64
Glenwood, 14, 15, 16, 17
Gower, 34, 35, 36, 38, 39
Grant (Winfield), 122, 123
Guttenberg (Decorah), 14, 15, 16, 17, 22

Haight Creek (Burlington), 56, 57, 64, 65, 66
Hamilton County, 74
Hampton, 4, 7, 53, 55, 56, 57, 58, 59, 60, 61, 62

Hardin County, 8, 62, 64
Harmony Hill (Glenwood), 14, 17
Hartford (Topeka), 113
Harveyville, 117, 118
Haskell (Cass), 103
Henry County, 68, 69
Herington (Nolans), 122
Hertha, 81, 85, 86
Hopkinton, 21, 22, 29, 30, 31, 32, 33
Houston County, 10, 13
Howard, 115
Humboldt County, 7, 63
Humboldt Oolite, 7, 8
Hushpuckney (Swope), 86, 87, 96

Iola, 97, 98, 99
Ion (Decorah), 14, 15, 16, 22
Iowa Falls (Hampton), 7, 55, 62
Iowa Point (Topeka), 113
Ironton (Wonewoc), 10
Island Creek (Wyandotte), 100

Jackson County, 31
Johnson County, 42, 43, 44
Jones County, 33, 35
Jordan, 11, 12, 14, 15
Juniper Hill (Lime Creek), 48

Kanwaka, 111
Kenosha (Tecumseh), 112, 113
Kenwood (Wapsipinicon), 38
Keokuk, 65, 66, 67, 68
Kereford (Oread), 111
"Kiewitz" (Stanton), 103, 104, 105
King Hill (Lecompton), 111, 112
Krider (Nolans), 122, 123, 124

Labette, 80
Ladore, 86, 96
Lake Neosho (Altamont), 80
Lane, 100
La Porte City (Hopkinton), 32, 33
Leavenworth (Oread), 111
Le Claire (Gower), 34, 38
Lecompton, 111, 112, 113
Lee County, 65, 66
Lenapah, 81, 82, 85, 86
Lime Creek, 37, 48, 49, 50
Linn County, 38

Little Pawnee (Cass), 103
Lodi (St. Lawrence), 8, 10, 11, 12
Lone Rock, 10, 11
"Lower Quarry Beds" (Blanding), 29, 30
Lyon County, 9

McCraney, 53, 54, 55, 56, 57
McGregor (Platteville), 14, 16, 17, 18, 19, 22
Madison County, 79, 80, 81, 85, 87, 88, 91, 95, 96, 97, 98, 99, 100, 101
Mahaska County, 69, 78
Maple Hill, 37, 52, 53, 55
Maquoketa, 22, 23, 24, 25, 26, 27, 28, 30
Marion County, 78
Marshall County, 59
Mason City (Shell Rock), 44, 45, 47
Maynes Creek (Hampton), 58, 59, 60, 61, 62
Middle Creek (Swope), 86, 96
Mine Creek (Pawnee), 80
Mitchell County, 44
Monroe County, 78
Montgomery County, 110, 111
Mosalem, 22, 27, 30
Muncie Creek (Iola), 97, 98, 99
Muscatine County, 39, 72, 73
Myrick Station (Pawnee), 80
Mystic Coal (Labette), 80

Neda, 24
New Richmond (Shakopee), 14
Nolans, 122, 123, 124
Nora (Shell Rock), 44, 46, 47
Norwalk (Jordan), 11, 12
Nowata, 81

Odell, 122
Olmsted County, 19
Oneota, 12, 13, 14, 15
Oread, 110, 111
Ost (Tecumseh), 12, 113
Otis (Wapsipinicon), 38
Otoe County, 116
Owen (Lime Creek), 48, 49, 50

Paddock (Nolans), 122
Palisades-Kepler (Scotch Grove), 33, 34, 35, 38
Paola (Iola), 97, 99
Pawnee, 80
Pawnee County, 117
Pecatonica (Platteville), 14, 16, 17, 19, 22
Platteville, 14, 15, 16, 17, 18, 19, 22
Plattford, 103, 109
Plattsburg, 100, 103
Plattsmouth (Oread), 110, 111
Pleasanton, 81, 82, 85, 86
Pocahontas County, 63
Prospect Hill, 54, 55, 56, 57

Queen Hill (Lecompton), 111
Quindaro (Wyandotte), 99
Quivera, 91

Rakes Creek (Tecumseh), 112, 113
Rapid (Cedar Valley), 39, 40, 42, 43
Raytown (Iola), 97, 98, 99
Reading, 117, 118
Reno (Lone Rock), 10, 11
Rock Bluff (Deer Creek), 113
Rock Grove (Shell Rock), 44, 45, 46, 47
Rock Lake (Stanton), 103, 104

Ste. Genevieve, 69, 70, 71, 74
St. Lawrence, 8, 10, 11
St. Louis, 67, 68, 69, 71, 74
St. Peter, 14, 15, 16, 17
Scotch Grove, 31, 32, 33, 34, 35, 36, 38
Scott County, 34, 72
Severy, 114
Shakopee, 14, 15, 17
Sharpy County, 102, 109
Sheffield, 37, 50, 51
Shell Rock, 44, 45, 46, 47
Shoemaker (Cass), 103
Sioux Quartzite, 9
Solon (Cedar Valley), 39, 40, 41, 42
South Bend (Stanton), 103, 104
Spechts Ferry (Decorah), 14, 15, 16, 17, 20, 22
Spergen, 67, 69, 71
Spring Branch (Lecompton), 111

Spring Grove (Wapsipinicon), 38, 39
Spring Hill (Plattsburg), 103
Stanton, 100, 101, 102, 103, 104, 105, 109
Stark (Dennis), 88, 89, 90, 92, 96
Starrs Cave, 7, 53, 54, 55, 56, 57, 59, 60
State Quarry, 44
Stoner (Stanton), 100, 101, 102, 103, 104, 105
Swope, 82, 85, 86, 87, 89, 96

Tecumseh, 112, 113
Tête des Morts, 21, 22, 29, 30
Tonti (St. Peter), 14, 17
Topeka, 113, 115

Van Buren County, 66
Van Oser (Jordan), 11, 12, 14, 15
Vilas, 100, 101, 103

Wakarusa, 116

Wapello County, 78
Wapsipinicon, 38, 39, 40
Warsaw, 67
Washington County, 57, 58
Wassonville (Hampton), 55, 56, 57, 58, 59, 61
Waubeek (Scotch Grove), 33, 35, 36
Waukon (Jordan), 11
Wea (Cherryvale), 88, 91, 92, 93, 94
Webster County, 69, 71, 74, 75, 76, 77
Westerville, 92
Willow River (Shakopee), 14, 17
Winfield, 122, 123
Winona County, 13
Winterset (Dennis), 87, 88, 89, 91, 92, 95, 96, 97
Wise Lake (Galena), 5, 8, 21, 22, 23, 30
Wonewoc, 4, 10
Worland (Altamont), 80, 81
Wyandotte, 99, 100

About the Author

ROBERT CHARLES WOLF is a dedicated amateur fossil collector specializing in Paleozoic fossils from Iowa and parts of Minnesota and Nebraska, including invertebrates, trace fossils, plant fossils, and vertebrates. A self-taught student, he has been collecting for sixteen years, including six years of intense field work, and has written for *Earth Science* magazine. He is an affiliate member of the Geological Society of Iowa.

www.ingramcontent.com/pod-product-compliance
Ingram Content Group UK Ltd.
Pitfield, Milton Keynes, MK11 3LW, UK
UKHW041441020226
10460UKWH00024B/175